Acclaim for *The M*

"We shouldn't be too surprised to discover that a singer-songwriter as gifted and sensitive as Rebecca St. James has produced an amazingly moving novel—one that young women will find both relevant and deeply satisfying. Beautifully crafted with coauthor Nancy Rue, *The Merciful Scar* will not only touch your heart, it might just help heal it."

—KARI JOBE, DOVE AWARD–WINNING
ARTIST AND SPEAKER ON THE REVOLVE TOUR

"My brother Joel and I speak after shows to teens and young adults across the country. Because of this, we know that the message of this book is relevant and timely! The mix of humor, insight, and drama in *The Merciful Scar* helps to powerfully convey needed truth. Congrats to our sister Rebecca and Nancy on a great book!"

—LUKE SMALLBONE,
FOR KING AND COUNTRY

"*The Merciful Scar* is a tender, beautiful, and insightful book about a difficult subject. Nancy Rue and Rebecca St. James have crafted a heart-touching story that feels more real than imaginary. While reading, you might need to remind yourself that these characters are fictional. The plotlines, twists, turns, and heart-wrenching situations will wrap around your heart in such a way that you can't help but be affected."

—LORI TWICHELL,
FICTIONADDICT

"Welcome to Sarah's world! And right now, it's not an easy place to be. With poignant insight and passion, Rebecca St. James and Nancy Rue have birthed a story that immediately draws you in, and, before letting you go, will touch the deepest levels of your heart."

—ROBERT WHITLOW,
BEST-SELLING AUTHOR OF *THE CHOICE*

"Rebecca St. James and Nancy Rue have crafted a beautiful and moving story about how an unexpected difficulty can truly be a blessing in disguise. Anyone reading will not only be entertained, but also inspired as *Sarah's Choice* reveals that no matter the circumstances, God does work everything for our good. Having traveled the country to speak to thousands of young people, I think this book is especially timely for the challenges many of us are facing. I am sure this book will touch many hearts!"

—Lila Rose, president of Live Action, a media-based nonprofit dedicated to building a culture of life

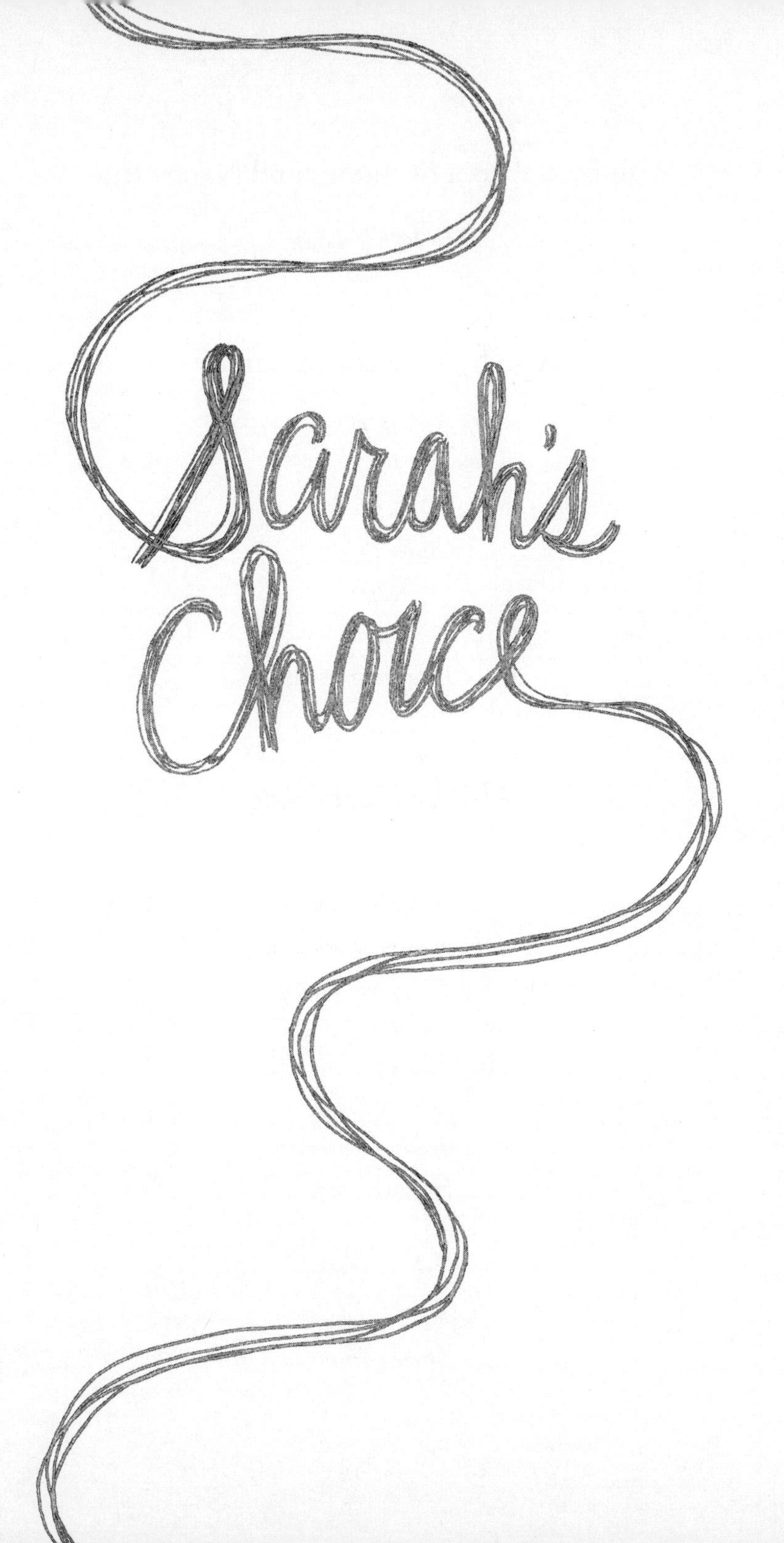
Sarah's Choice

Also by Rebecca St. James and Nancy Rue

The Merciful Scar

Also by Rebecca St. James

What Is He Thinking??

Pure

Wait for Me

Sister Freaks

She

Loved

40 Days with God

Also by Nancy Rue

The Reluctant Prophet series

The Reluctant Prophet

Unexpected Dismounts

Too Far to Say Enough

The Sullivan Crisp series

Healing Stones

Healing Waters

Healing Sands

Tristan's Gap

Antonia's Choice

Pascal's Wager

Sarah's Choice

A Novel

Rebecca St. James and Nancy Rue

THOMAS NELSON
Since 1798

NASHVILLE MEXICO CITY RIO DE JANEIRO

Published in Nashville, Tennessee, by Thomas Nelson. Thomas Nelson is a registered trademark of HarperCollins Christian Publishing, Inc.

Authors are represented by the literary agency of Alive Communications, Inc., 7680 Goddard Street, Suite 200, Colorado Springs, CO 80920, www.alivecommunications.com.

Thomas Nelson, Inc., titles may be purchased in bulk for educational, business, fund-raising, or sales promotional use. For information, please email SpecialMarkets@ThomasNelson.com.

Library of Congress Cataloging-in-Publication Data

Rue, Nancy N.
Sarah's choice : a novel / Rebecca St. James and Nancy Rue.
pages cm
ISBN 978-1-4016-8924-7
1. Christian fiction. I. St. James, Rebecca. II. Title.
PS3568.U3595S37 2014
813'.6—dc23

2013047472

Printed in the United States of America

14 15 16 17 18 19 RRD 6 5 4 3 2 1

This book is dedicated to the incredible people whose belief in the sanctity of all life spurs them to share hope and help with those in Sarah's situation every day. You protect the lives of both mother and baby, and you are our heroes.

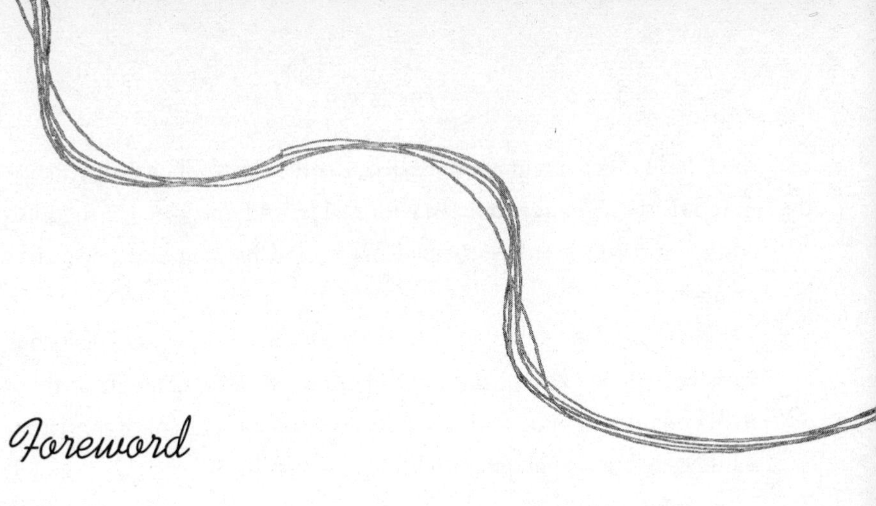

Foreword

Everyone enjoys singing along when you know the singer means the lyrics she sings. Everyone likes to listen to a speaker you know is passionate about the topic he or she addresses. Everyone relishes reading a book when you know the author writes from the heart and draws from a wealth of experience.

With these thoughts in mind, can I let you in on a secret?

You're gonna love *Sarah's Choice*! In this novel, my good friend Rebecca St. James along with best-selling author Nancy Rue, share a story that will reach you on so many levels. Their writing is just like her singing . . . fresh, creative, and from the heart . . . bold yet compassionate, knowledgeable but gracious, and funny yet honest.

In America, it's easy to become numb to the numbers: Over fifty million abortions in the past four decades. But thankfully, people like Rebecca and Nancy boldly keep the issue before us. Being a family friend of Rebecca's for years, I know that she has used her music platform to encourage countless women to make wise decisions with their unplanned pregnancy. Rebecca truly cares. She's helped support crisis pregnancy centers nationwide and mentored struggling young women. She's also helped many find healing and hope after an abortion.

Rebecca and Nancy are both mothers, and one can't help but wonder if their love for the unborn comes shining through in these pages because of this. Perhaps especially since this book was written while Rebecca was pregnant with her first child.

God is good.

May *Sarah's Choice* remind you of that truth.

Dave Stone
Pastor, Southeast
Christian Church

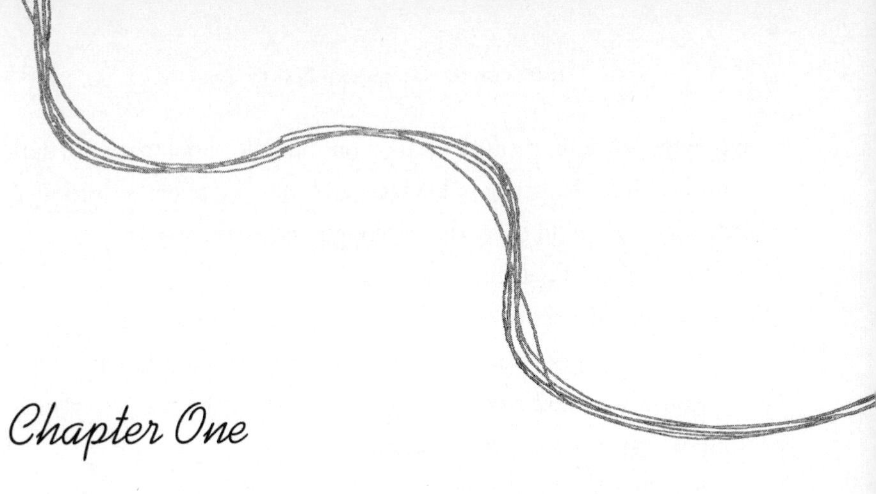

Chapter One

Last night's dinner was up before Sarah that morning. Between tripping over two pairs of boots and stomping on her briefcase, she barely made it from the daybed to the bathroom before the jalapeños put in their second appearance.

The tiny black-and-white floor tiles blurred to a fuzz as she pressed her forehead to them. For once she was grateful the radiator wasn't working. Again.

Ohmygosh, she hated to throw up. Hated. It.

She doused her face with cold water—because it would take at least five minutes for any *hot* water to come through the faucet—and muttered a few threats against Matt. He was the one who ordered the jalapeños on the nachos, knowing full well his parents would be watching every choke and spew.

The boy was cute, but shameless.

She managed to avoid an encore now by skipping the coffee—in fact, the entire kitchenette—and taking enough deep breaths to hyperventilate a hippo as she leaned on the sink, shook back the dark tendrils of hair that stuck to her face, and squinted at her reflection. A little makeup would cover that asparagus-green tinge, right?

Okay, a lot of makeup.

You should stay home, the sunken brown eyes told her.

And miss work with the promotion being decided? Uh, no. Thad Nussbaum wouldn't risk a sick day right now if he had the plague. Sarah wasn't sure she *didn't,* actually.

Another dive for the toilet. She definitely hated to throw up.

Avocado-skinned or not, she needed to get a move on. After that round she chugged a half bottle of Pepto-Bismol and stepped over a stack of how-to-succeed books on loan from Megan to get to the desk crammed between the daybed and the bathroom door. Fortunately she only had to paw through one layer of unpaid bills to find Megan's list.

1. Dress professionally. You're not in grad school any more. Go monochromatic if you can, but with a splash of color. Advertising IS a creative field—at least that's what they tell me. And do NOT wear that ratty scarf.

Sarah groaned, not a difficult sound to manage at that point. She hoped the money she'd spent on wardrobe improvements at T.J. Maxx, under Megan's step-away-from-the-jeans-skirt tutelage, would be worth it if—when—she got the promotion. Between that and the new briefcase, no wonder AT&T was threatening to turn off her phone.

The other bills were tucked into their compartments in the organizer, although they still glared at her no matter how tightly she closed their little plastic drawers. As for her personal bills . . . she looked for something to cover them up so they, too, wouldn't give her the stink eye when she got home from work.

The only thing she could come up with to conceal them without doing a complete renovation of the entire studio apartment was the framed picture her mom gave her on Thanksgiving, which she hadn't hung up yet because . . . she just hadn't.

In spite of the queasies, Sarah had to grin at the photo. Megan would have a complete meltdown over Sarah at twelve: hair straightened in an attempt to look like a dark-haired Christina Aguilera and a too-big royal-blue choir robe with a large and admittedly tacky cross for a zipper pull. The identical robe looked so much better on her father. But then, anything he wore was handsome because he was in it. The photographer had caught Sarah looking up at her father, eyes whispering "I'm gonna make you proud, Daddy" . . .

A lump in the throat paired with nausea: not a good choice.

Sarah pressed the photo facedown on the stack and headed for the closet to attempt monochromatic with a splash of color.

Ten minutes later she was as close as she was going to get. The shopping spree notwithstanding, it wasn't like there was a whole lot to choose from in there. Black pencil skirt with boots, tailored white blouse, charcoal fitted sweater trimmed in apricot, subtle jewelry. Then the wool camel coat—a cast-off of Megan's—and the paid-too-much-for-it-even-on-sale leather briefcase.

She paused, the multi-brown scarf between her hands. With so many pulled strands it was starting to resemble a very sad boa, but it still smelled like Dad—all British Sterling and strong coffee and some musky undefinable thing that was just him. One whiff at the right moment and she could almost hear him saying, *You've got this, SJ.*

Yeah, she was wearing the scarf. Sorry, Megan.

Okay—a final look in the full-length mirror and she was out of there.

Almost out of there. Hand on the knob, she saw something had been slipped under the door. Looked like a Christmas card without an envelope. Before she even picked it up, Sarah knew it was from Catfish.

Merry Christmas, Ms. Collins he'd written under a drawing of what was probably supposed to be the Grinch. *But Santa won't be visiting you if you don't pay the rent. Sincerely, Your Building Manager.*

Sarah tossed the thing toward the desk, but not before she smelled him on it: that whole hipster, unbathed, let's-see-how-long-I-can-wear-these-jeans-before-the-rips-get-too-big-to-be-legal aroma. If she met him face-to-face this morning she would probably puke on his shoes.

The chances were good he'd made the delivery in the wee hours and was still asleep. Catfish was a wannabe musician who stayed up half the night pretending he was making a living playing the sitar and then slept half the day. Sarah could probably make it to the car without running into him.

The studios all opened onto open walkways, not the best scenario for brutal subzero Chicago winters. But the Sandburg Arms had once been a Motel Four and the renovators obviously hadn't wanted to spend the money on closing it in. Or on much of anything else for that matter.

Like a super who would at least throw some cat litter on the cement steps when the ice set in.

Sarah picked her way down them and then checked to be sure the proverbial coast was clear of all things Catfish before she hopped between the icy patches to the parking lot. As she passed his first-floor apartment, holding her breath so she wouldn't take in any fumes wafting under the door, she made him a silent promise that once she got this promotion, she'd pay the back rent and bid him a cheery good-bye as she moved out.

After she paid off the ones in the plastic compartments.

No wonder she was queasy, Sarah decided as she stitched her faded red Toyota through the early morning traffic. "Rush" hour was a complete misnomer. Cars crawled off the Ike onto West Congress and huffed around the Loop with maddening slowness. Exhaust coughed from every vehicle as hot vapors met frigid air and created a mist so heavy you could cut it into cubes.

She'd lived here all her life, except for the six years she spent in New York at college, and she'd spent more hours sitting on the Eisenhower Expressway than she had on her own couch. When had this smell become so nauseating?

The train probably wouldn't be much better when it came to fumes, but it was definitely faster. Too bad she needed a car during the day to deliver projects outside the city proper. And too bad Carson Creative didn't give her a company car for that. Although right now, any vehicle would call up the heaves. Ugh.

A distraction—that's what she needed. Sarah pushed the motivational CD Megan had given her into the ancient player and waited for the way-too-enthusiastic-for-8:00-a.m. voice to tell her that success was 90 percent attitude.

Or as Megan put it under number 2 on the list:

> From the time you arrive at Carson Creative Services in the morning until you pull out of the parking garage at night, you have to keep your game face on. You can't let down. You never know when a potential client will walk in, so you have to wear a constant expression that says, "I can sell anything for you."

Sarah glanced in the rearview mirror. She could only hope any client she saw today wanted an ad campaign for acid reflux medication.

She turned off Mr. Positive Attitude. She needed to focus on the road anyway. Snow was now plastering the windshield with wet, heavy clumps the size of bear paws, and her wipers weren't in optimal shape.

Neither, apparently, was her engine. Just as she inched the Toyota into the State/Jackson intersection, it died. At least five horns blared and more than one window opened so a driver could spew out angry, frosty breaths and a multicolored string of expletives.

It was Chicago, after all.

Sarah turned the key with a vengeance and stomped repeatedly on the gas pedal, just the way Matt had told her not to do. What he *had* told her to do currently eluded her.

"Come on, Buzz," she said, although that definitely hadn't been included in Matt's instructions. "Don't do this to me. Not today."

She could feel the trail of traffic behind her virtually seething as she continued pumping and pleading. The engine struggled to turn over, while the cars with the green light on either side of her struggled to avoid sliding into her like bumper cars. Any minute this was going to turn into a scene from *The Blues Brothers.*

Most were successful in screeching to an icy halt. One had to veer around her while its driver hollered—as only a native of Chicago could—"Get that $%##@!!! hunk of junk off the road, lady!"

"I'm working on it," Sarah muttered. Her teeth were clenched so hard she could feel the enamel eroding.

One more foot jam and Buzz wheezed himself back to life. Together they limped the remaining few blocks to Michigan Avenue and managed to climb to her space in the parking garage, where she pulled in beside Megan's white BMW SUV. Before Sarah had really gotten to know Megan—what was it, five months ago now?—she'd always had her for a sports model: something black and fast-looking even when it was standing still. Ten minutes into their friendship and Sarah knew a Boxster wouldn't fit the image Megan was going for. Megan slid from the front seat of that SUV now with more grace than Sarah could manage on her best day, especially while simultaneously holding two Starbucks cups.

She eyed the Toyota as it shuddered itself into a coma. "Don't worry," she said. "You'll be buying a brand-new one soon."

Sarah closed the car door with a gentle hand and waited. Nothing fell off. There was at least that.

"Don't jinx it," she said.

Megan handed her a cup. "Are you talking about the car or the promotion?"

"Both." Sarah pretended to take a sip, but the very steam of the latte beckoned to what was left of the nachos. Matt was so dead. She stuck him back in *his* little plastic compartment and tried to focus.

"I can't vouch for your vehicle." Megan gave Buzz the look she usually reserved for the backs of high-maintenance clients she'd charmed out the door. "But the promotion is practically a done deal."

Sarah should have such confidence. Actually, anyone should. Megan oozed the stuff. Her hair was always sleek enough and blonde enough, as if roots were terrified to even show up. Her makeup was magazine flawless, down to the eyeliner that lifted in perfect tilts at the corners of her blue eyes. Eyes that said, *I have this handled so why are we even talking?*

But it was Megan's *mouth* Sarah could never hope to emulate. Full. Strong. Slightly ironic. If you could make it smile, you might as well call the day as good as it was going to get. Sarah usually could, which she figured was the reason Megan had taken her on.

But Megan was miles from a smile now as she assessed Sarah.

"What?" Sarah said.

"You look terrible."

"I'm just a little nauseous."

"Nerves?"

"Jalapeños. And Matt's parents."

Megan's eyebrows lifted in velvety arches.

"I like them, but they don't like me."

"The jalapeños or the parents?"

"Both." Megan continued to survey Sarah until a male figure dashed past them, calling, "You shouldn't be carrying that stuff, Audrey! Let me give you a hand!"

Sarah tried not to roll her eyes. That was on the list too. Something about avoiding obvious reactions to the juveniles you have to work with. But she couldn't help muttering to Megan: "Look at him. He just . . . schmoozes."

"Thad Nussbaum's picture is next to the word *schlemiel* in the dictionary."

Sarah made a mental note to look it up and watched the wiry, almost-panting Thad help a very pregnant Audrey Goetze wriggle out from behind the wheel of her Suburban. He piled her briefcase, her lunch tote, and a bag of what appeared to be knitting onto his person like a Sherpa, leaving Audrey empty-handed to waddle her way to the lobby door.

She was *so* pregnant.

"He's wasting his time anyway." Megan nodded Sarah toward the same door. "We're talking '*Arrivederci,* Audrey.'"

"What makes you say that?"

"I know she's not coming back after she has that kid. Seriously, you haven't seen the way she glows when you bring up the whole baby thing? She turns into Rudolph the Red-Nosed Reindeer."

Sarah let out a guffaw. Not a wise choice, what with the nausea threatening again. She took in a long breath as Megan pushed open the glass doors and let her through.

"Even if Audrey does come back, she won't be working the ConEx account. Too much travel." Megan shook her head as they watched Thad lug Audrey's belongings up the stairs to the second floor, grinning and assuring Audrey that she still looked great.

She didn't look great. She looked like the Pillsbury Doughboy.

Audrey had never been the glamorous account executive, not like Jennifer Nolte or, come to think of it, Megan, who was a peg below in the echelon. Audrey wore business suits from Macy's and was always the consummate professional at meetings, but she was Eleanor Roosevelt to Jennifer's Jackie Kennedy. Now when her maternity sweaters strained across her belly like plastic wrap, it was hard for her to even pull that much off.

Megan nudged Sarah with her elbow. "You're right. Thad does schmooze."

"He's like a little puppy dog." Sarah followed Megan up the steps. "He does everything but lick her face and say, 'Like me! Like me!' "

Megan waited for Sarah to fall into step beside her in the hall and lowered her voice as if she were about to impart the details of the Area 51 conspiracy.

"Thad's not smart enough to know that's not going to get him anywhere."

"What should he be doing? Chasing after Henry and Nick and—"

"No. He should be chasing after *me*."

"He did chase after you and you practically freeze-dried him with your eyes."

Megan stopped and narrowed those eyes at Sarah. "I mean he should be getting the same kind of advice I've been giving you."

Sarah felt her brow pucker. "Don't give him any ideas."

Megan produced one of her almost-smiles as they entered the maze of cubicles bordered by glass-walled offices. "Not to worry. You're my only protégée."

"And how am I doing?"

"Fabulous. But no more jalapeños." Megan lifted only one of the velvet eyebrows. "And how many times have I told you to lose that scarf?"

Megan eased into her fishbowl of a space with its on-trend black leather and metal décor. Sarah leaned against the sign on the door that read: **Megan Hollister, Assistant Director of International Accounts** and tried to suppress a sigh that would broadcast envy up and down the hall.

"In a couple of months, you'll have an office like this," Megan said.

"What do you do, read my face?"

"I just remember what it was like working in a prairie-dog cell. And I didn't have as much going for me then as you do now."

Sarah resisted the urge to snort. "I can't imagine that. What is it that I have—"

"You know exactly what you want." The blue eyes dug in. "And you won't give up until you get it."

That brooked no argument. Except Sarah didn't just want it. She needed it. But since *Never, ever look desperate* was somewhere around number 6 on the list, Sarah just gave Megan a firm nod and headed straight-shouldered down the hall. Behind her Megan called: "But get rid of that scarf."

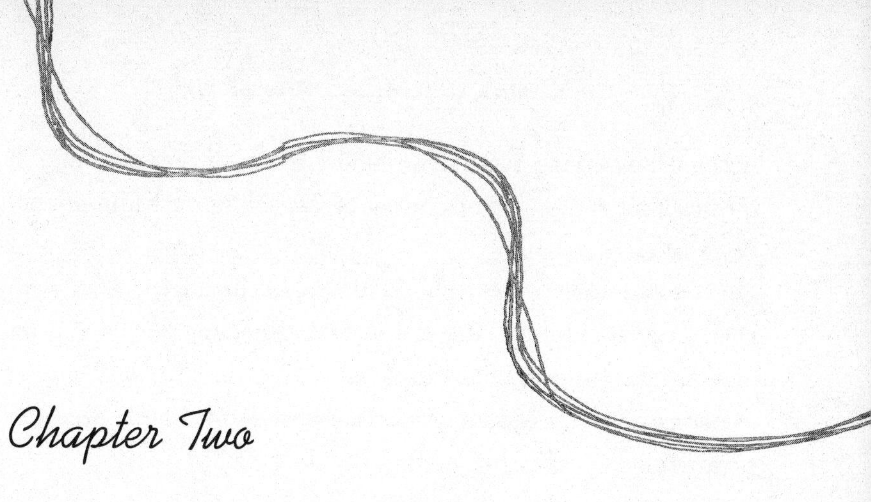

Chapter Two

Sarah was actually hanging *up* the scarf in her several-pegs-below-executive cubicle when she saw the Post-it note on her computer screen.

SEE CARSON IN WATERMARK CONF ASAP

Carson.

Henry Carson. Of Carson Creative Services.

This. Was. It.

Or close enough. Sarah smoothed her hands over the sweater. She'd already been through more interviews for this promotion than it took to be approved for the Supreme Court bench, and that didn't even include the surveillance. By Nick Kellog, V.P. of Campaign Development, all but looking over her shoulder while she wrote the copy for the ConEx account proposal and going over it like it was the Louisiana Purchase. And by Jennifer Nolte, Director of Domestic

Accounts, observing Sarah's every move in production meetings, in the break room . . . as she came out of the stall in the bathroom, for Pete's sake.

But this was the first time Sarah would come face-to-face with Henry Carson himself. Megan had been grooming her for this for months. She was ready. She had to be.

So go down the Megan List. *Dress professionally.* Check. *Keep your game face on.* Check. *Show no fear.*

Good luck with that one.

Sarah felt her shoulders start to sag, but she soldiered them back into place. *Go with your strengths* was somewhere on the list, and Megan had nailed what at least one of them was: she knew exactly what she wanted. And this was it. It had to be.

The only remaining question was, should she throw up now, or after the meeting?

Sarah seldom had a reason to go into the Watermark Conference Room, named for the large account that had basically launched Carson Creative in the early 1990s. Its gleaming African mahogany was usually reserved for people in a higher tax bracket. That definitely applied to the three people who greeted her when she walked in. Nick sported a cashmere jacket and practically had Bulls season tickets sticking out of his pocket. Jennifer, of course, dressed several-zeroes-on-a-paycheck better than Megan, which was saying something, and easily paid more for her precise bob haircuts and chestnut dye jobs than Sarah made per pay period. As for the manicure—

"Please sit down, Sarah," Henry Carson said.

Sarah realized she was standing there like the new girl in middle school, hands sweating onto the back of a leather chair, boot heels leaving divots in the three-inch carpet.

"Please," Carson said again.

His voice was warm, warmer than Sarah expected, and he was far less tidy-looking than the other two. Maybe when you were the owner and CEO you didn't have to be polished like the heirloom silver. His short gray hair was boyishly mussed, and his glasses hung precariously at the end of his nose, and he wasn't wearing a jacket at all, cashmere or otherwise. Although the striped shirt was clearly Brooks Brothers or better, the sleeves were rolled to his forearms as if he were ready to talk football over a beer. Or maybe that was just to show off the conspicuously understated Rolex watch.

"My colleagues speak very highly of you," he said as Sarah tucked herself into the chair she'd lathered up. "I just wanted an opportunity to meet you in person before we make our final decision."

It *did* sound like they were about to discuss the Bears' quarterback. Looked like it too. Mr. Carson's small brown eyes, set happily amid a spray of well-earned facial lines, all but coaxed, *Come on. I want you to do well.*

Sarah unclenched her hands in her lap. "If I'm given this opportunity, I can assure you, sir, that you will not be disappointed."

Henry Carson leaned back in his more massive version of the leather chair, removed his glasses, and smiled at her. It was almost fatherly.

"Please. You're practically middle management, Sarah. You don't have to call me sir."

"Thank you—"

"Mr. Carson will do just fine."

Sarah caught the edge of Nick's snicker before she realized it was supposed to be a joke. She smiled and nodded even though, seriously, it wasn't that funny.

"Sarah," Jennifer said. "We just have one more question for you."

Sarah nodded yet again. Megan had drilled her enough times. She was ready for anything short of the Spanish Inquisition.

"Are you sure you'll be comfortable with all the travel back and forth to Baltimore?"

That was it? Sarah almost giggled.

"Absolutely. I'm actually looking forward to it."

Jennifer sniffed. "You'd think we didn't have Skype and e-mail."

Before Sarah could decide just exactly what Jennifer expected her to say, Henry Carson once again smiled paternally at Sarah.

"We really called you in here to see if *you* have any questions."

She did. And she'd told Megan she was afraid to ask them. And Megan had told her she was crazy not to and if she didn't, she could forget getting any more coaching from her.

Sarah forced herself to look steadily at Father Carson. "Yes. I was wondering if . . . um." Not good. *Avoid voice padding* was somewhere on the list. "I mean, I'd like to know what kind of raise I can expect with this position."

Nick leaned sideways toward Mr. Carson. "You *had* to open that door, huh?" He turned to Sarah, eyes sardonic. "When I got my first real promotion up at Y&R, I asked the boss for a raise too. You know what he said? 'Nick, I'd love to pay you what you're worth. But we have a minimum wage law in this state.'" Nick cocked his head. Not a strand of gelled hair moved.

And she was supposed to do what with that? Henry Carson saved her with a chuckle. Only men his age and in his position could pull off chuckling without sounding like they were the entertainment at a children's birthday party.

"We'll bring you up to fifty-five, Sarah."

She knew the game face was slipping but she couldn't help it. Megan had assured her it would be more. She *needed* it to be more.

Jennifer shuffled through some papers in a folder in front of her. Nick smothered a smirk with his hand. Henry Carson just leveled his Father of the Year gaze over his glasses and waited.

Sarah readjusted her face. "That's very generous, sir . . . Mr. Carson. I just thought it would be a little closer to sixty."

"Fifty-five is pretty close to sixty."

"Not as close as fifty-nine," Jennifer said.

Both men glared at her.

"We can discuss this further after we've made our decision," Mr. Carson said. "Sarah, any more questions?"

Sarah shook her head and he stood up, hands parked in his pockets. "Thank you. This company is indeed lucky to have bright young people like you."

"I'm the lucky one, Mr. Carson."

Nicely done. At least she'd come up with a graceful exit line.

"You know, of course," Nick said, "this position is temporary until we see whether Audrey is really coming back."

"Hello-o," Jennifer said out of a small hole in the side of her mouth.

"Oh, right. Sorry. We have to maintain the politically correct illusion that she'll be on the job again after maternity leave."

Megan was right again.

"Despite the fact," Nick went on, "that she spent the last two years driving up our health insurance costs using every means possible to *get* pregnant. It must have cost a hundred dollars a sperm—"

"Hello-o again." This time Jennifer used her whole mouth. Sarah was beginning to like this woman.

"I'm sorry," Nick said, "but those are the facts."

Jennifer looked at Sarah. "And you didn't hear them here."

Henry Carson was by now at Sarah's elbow. "Naturally we are

obligated to keep Ms. Goetze's job open for her." He nudged her gently toward the door. "But the world can't grind to a stop while she makes her decision. The work goes on."

"I couldn't agree more." Sarah's voice sounded bright, even to her. As long as she had the man's attention—"I was wondering when you were going to make *your* decision."

"Smart question." He pushed the glasses back up the nose as he consulted a schedule projected on the wall. "The next phase of the ConEx planning starts in two weeks." His eyes twinkled at her. "We'll need to make our decision by then, won't we?"

December 23.

Sarah typed a series of exclamation points on her computer calendar and let the hope amp up. She'd kept it in check ever since she'd started the application process, but it was hard to do now. Now that Jennifer Nolte was clearly on her side. And Mr. Carson was giving her fatherly looks. And Nick was . . .

All right, so Nick was just Nick. He probably wouldn't trust any woman who still had her ovaries. Even at that, maybe it was finally okay to dream.

Of giving Catfish a check and her final notice. Maybe even holding her breath and hugging his scrawny neck and wishing him a Grammy for Best Album by a Sitar Player. Of kissing Buzz Lightyear's faded hood and saying good-bye before she cruised off the lot in a car that didn't lapse into a coma at every traffic light. Straight to American Medical Credit and Midwestern Regional Medical Center and everyone else who was waiting for money. With each check she handed them she would grow closer to freedom.

And to pleasing the faint voice in her head that whispered louder than Megan could bark. *Be sure to count the cost, SJ.*

Sarah nodded as if her father were there squeezing her shoulder and went to the calculator on her cell phone. "Fifty-nine," Jennifer had said. Could she do it for that? Of course she *could*, but how long would it take?

She had the figures in her head and she entered them for the hundred and third time at least. That total, plus her basic living expenses—and actually paying the rent on time and getting a better used car . . .

Sarah leaned back in the chair and blew air out slowly between her lips. A year—eighteen months at the most—and she could have it all paid off. A year and a half and she might actually start living again.

I can take care of Mom, her mind whispered back.

"I saw you go into a meeting with the Big Three."

Sarah whirled in her chair to face Thad, who was hanging in her doorway. Literally. Like a gibbon.

"You're not in trouble, are you?" he asked. Hopefully.

Sarah wasn't sure if the sudden recurrence of the nausea was jalapeño-and-Matt's-parents or Thad-related. She fought it down with a look she hoped would frost the cubicle.

"No, Thad. But thanks for asking. I appreciate your concern."

He let his very long arms fall and crept inside, wrists poking out of his jacket sleeves.

"Can I *help* you?" Sarah said.

Thad fingered the murky-blond soul patch on his chin. "Have you heard when they're making their decision?"

"Have *you*?"

"I figure it's any day now."

"Probably."

He thrust his hand forward. Sarah stared at his oversized college ring for a full five seconds before she realized he wanted a handshake.

"Listen, whichever one of us gets that job," he said as he pumped her arm, "no hard feelings, okay?"

"Sure," Sarah said.

She really did kind of owe Thad, actually. If it weren't for him being such a brownnoser, Megan probably wouldn't have adopted her as a project.

As Sarah looked at him now, leering at her with actual drool forming at the corners of his mouth, Sarah could see him in the break room that day in June, talking about how he was going to nail Audrey's position. She had *just* announced she was three months pregnant. Everyone else was so happy for her because she and her husband had tried for so long to get that way—according to the office gossip—and there he was, ready to snatch her position out from under her the minute she had the first labor pain.

When he left the break room, Megan had turned to Sarah with those searing eyes and said, "You should go for it too."

Sarah remembered looking behind her to make sure Megan was talking to her. They'd never done more than commiserate over the disgusting things people left in the refrigerator for months at a time. But from that moment on, even before the position was actually announced, they were inseparable at work as Megan groomed and shaped and all but cut Sarah's toenails.

Sarah didn't kid herself. At first it had more to do with Thad *not* getting the job than Sarah having it. But it had become more than that, and Sarah was grateful. She'd worked with Audrey briefly on another account, and Jennifer oversaw her application process, but it was Megan who showed her how to play the game.

"I'm serious—if you get it—no sweat."

Sarah blinked at Thad. He still had her hand between his, and speaking of sweating . . . he was.

"If you'll excuse me," she said.

I have to go throw up. For more reasons than one.

She left Thad rehanging himself in the doorway as she charged to the restroom.

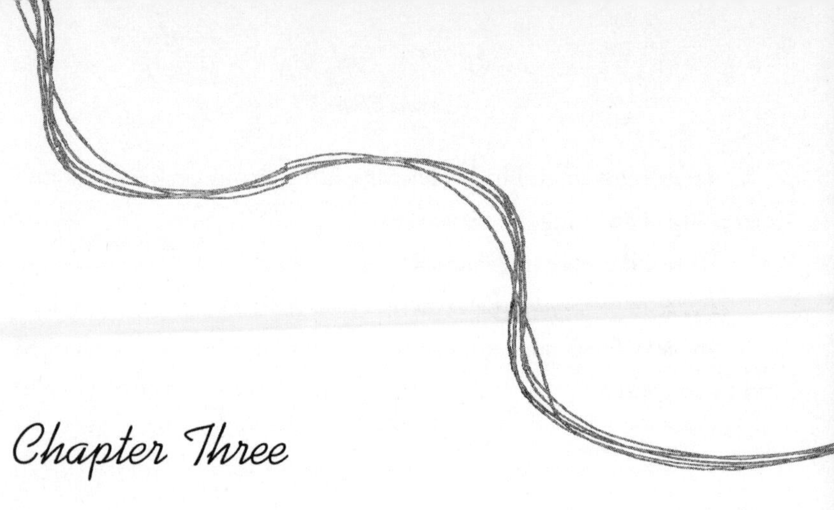

Chapter Three

"If you will take your places at the starting line, the United Financial 500 is about to begin." Matt Evans held up a fan of ten-dollar bills. "Any more bets?"

A cigarette-alto rasped from inside the cubicle behind him. "There are laws against that in this state, Evans."

Matt grinned. "You'll get your cut, Cherie. You on lookout?"

"Don't bet on it."

"That's my girl." Matt poised the money-laden hand in the air. "Gentlemen, start your engines . . . wait for it . . ." He lengthened the pause until the veins bulged in the drivers' necks before he said, "Go!"

Amid a burst of cheers from the white-shirted, neck-tied crowd standing on desks to see over the tops of their cubicles, Caleb Clark and Michael D'Amato shot from the end of the hall, pushing their wheeled desk chairs at a speed that rivaled the L train. When they reached the edge of the first doorway, Wes Oliver yanked away a yellow legal pad repurposed as a caution flag, and Caleb and Michael leapt into the chairs with their knees in the seats and leaned toward the finish line.

This was the part that made the whole thing. Matt was already grabbing his sides as Caleb's chair sideswiped Michael's and sent it careening against Cherie's cubicle. He barely heard the expected, "You guys are dead to me," over the money-mad cries of the fans. Michael recovered and knocked Caleb into a three-hundred-sixty–degree twirl, crossing the finish line a chair-length ahead of his competitor.

"Yes!" Matt shouted over the deafening din. Caleb had been the clear favorite, which meant after everyone got their cuts, including Cherie, he'd be forty bucks richer.

The noise spilled into the hallway as Matt's fellow would-be financiers made their way toward him, hands out.

"That was so rigged!"

"C'mon, man—it was a clear win."

"I wanna see a replay."

"I should have thought of that," Matt said. "I'll take video next time."

"If you're still here next time," a voice croaked. "Red flag. Red flag."

Bodies escaped into offices with the skill of Houdini. The two who had no chance of getting back to theirs without being apprehended dove into Matt's, Wes under the desk, Caleb flattened against the inside of the partition. Matt had hardly stuffed the winnings into his pocket and slid his chair into place to conceal Wes when Clay Nelson appeared in the doorway, stroking his rusty goatee.

"Hey, Uncle Clay," Matt said. "Something I can do for you?"

Clay didn't answer. He merely beckoned with one hand, left eyebrow cocked. Matt sighed. The man missed nothing.

Matt slid his chair back and nodded Wes out. While Wes extricated himself, Caleb peeled his back from the partition wall. Clay stood aside to let them both pass. Matt had to suck up a grin as they raised their thumbs over Clay's head and disappeared. They knew as well as he did Matt wasn't going to catch any heat. Although . . . Uncle Clay's eyes didn't have their usual gleam this morning.

He folded his arms across his tweed jacket front and leaned in the doorway.

"What next, Matt? Betting on elevators?"

Matt picked up his cell phone and checked for text messages. "Dude, that was this morning."

"No surprise there. You know, if Novak gets wind of any of this, I'll be forced to make an example of you."

No message from Sarah. Matt set the phone down and picked up the tennis-sized ball of colored rubber bands he'd constructed himself. "Why me?"

"How 'bout because you're the ringleader."

"No. More like . . ." Matt pretended to gaze out a nonexistent window. "The circus master."

He looked back at Clay. No laugh. Time for another approach.

"Hey," Matt said, "saw my mother last night. She says hello."

Matt could almost feel his own eyes sparkling as he waited for Clay to deliver the perfect one-liner about his sister. There was nothing like the reassurance that Clay thought she was as bordering-on-ridiculous as Matt did.

But he didn't get so much as a lip twitch.

Matt tossed the ball onto the desk. "What's wrong, Uncle Clay?"

"Wrong? What could be wrong?" Clay grunted. "Unless you count the good news your Aunt Jerri gave me this morning."

"She's cutting up her credit cards again."

"No. She's pregnant. Again."

Matt sat straight up in the chair. "No way! Come on, that's

amazing. Congratulations, Uncle Clay." He let his grin go wide. "Any idea who the father is?"

Clay squinted at him. "You're funny. Like a colonoscopy."

"What's funny is you with a little baby. I mean, you're so . . . old."

"Come to think of it, you have something else in common with a colonoscopy."

"Man." Matt pressed a hand to his chest. "That was needlessly harsh."

"Do you realize I managed to get through three children without changing a single diaper? Now I'm forced to defend my record." He glared at Matt. "And don't even think about starting a pool."

Matt raised both hands. "What? You think I'm insensitive?"

No reply.

"But seriously, Uncle Clay—haven't you two ever heard of birth control?"

"You mean that thing that works *100 percent of the time*? *That* birth control?"

Matt waved him off and picked up the gripper a guy at the gym had talked him into buying. Something about a crushing grip being essential to your overall fitness. "It'll be okay. You guys are great parents." He bit off: *Better than mine.* His mother was Clay's sister after all, and the poor guy didn't need to go there today.

"Do you know how much it's going to cost to send this kid to college?" Clay said. "We're looking at a hundred grand minimum. Maybe a hundred and fifty. And that's a state college. If he commutes."

Matt's desk phone rang. Clay nodded at it.

"Take your call. I need more coffee. A *lot* more coffee."

Matt leaned back and grabbed the phone, eyes still on Clay's retreating form. Poor dude.

"Your girlfriend's on the line," Cherie croaked in his ear.

"Sarah?"

"I'll tell her you asked that."

"Just making sure. Last time you told me it was my girlfriend it turned out to be my mother."

"Yeah, well, you hadn't talked to your mother in a month."

And it had been a good month until then.

"Put her through," he said.

He still held his breath until he heard Sarah's voice. Sarah's *excited* voice.

"I think I got it!"

"Nice!" Matt gave the chair a celebratory twirl. "What did I tell you, Sar? Didn't I tell you you had that thing? Didn't I call that?"

He waited and pictured Sarah shaking all that fudge-colored hair over her shoulders and wrinkling the exactly five freckles on her cute nose.

"So tell me where you're taking me to celebrate."

Just the right touch of flirty with a hint of edgy. He loved it.

"And *not* where we took your parents last night. What were you thinking with that Mexican hole in the wall? I thought your mother was going to pull a surgical mask out of her purse."

"I warned you she was like that."

"So you took them right to a spot where I could see it in action."

"Are you mad at me? You're mad at me."

"No."

Matt grinned. "Yeah, you're mad."

"No I'm not. I think she would have complained if we'd gone to a White House dinner."

That was his girl.

"Don't think you're getting out of talking about last night," she said, "but where are you taking me *tonight*?"

"How 'bout that's for me to know and you to find out?" he said.

"Who *says* that anymore?"

"I'm reviving it."

"What time am I going to 'find out'?"

"I'm picking your sweet self up at your place at seven and I'm gonna take you for a *ride.* Wait 'til you check out the new suspension system I put in the 'Maro."

"That's what I live for," she said.

Her voice was syrupy with sarcasm. Yeah. He loved that too.

Sarah wanted to leave work on the stroke of five that day, just in case Buzz completely died and she had to take a tow truck all the way to Oak Park. But she had to put together the anticipated website costs for the ConEx account and she wanted the report on Nick's desk before tomorrow's deadline. Before Thad got his part turned in. That's what Megan had advised over lunch since, as she put it, "This job is not a *fait accompli* yet, so keep showin' 'em what you're workin' with."

So it was closer to five thirty when Sarah hurried through the parking garage. Not enough time for a bubble bath, but still enough for a total hair redo. A whole morning of trips to the ladies' room to heave had landed it in a messy bun for the rest of the day. At least she didn't feel like losing her lunch any more.

Her steps slowed, though, when she saw Audrey standing next to her big-enough-for-quintuplets Suburban with an arm full of bulging "It's a Boy!" gift bags. Sarah hadn't made it to the lunchtime shower; Megan had insisted they go out so Sarah could give her every detail of her meeting with the Big Three and they could plan her continuing strategy.

The red-faced Audrey was clearly losing the battle with the bags and the briefcase and the lunch and the knitting. Where was Thad now? Sarah reached her just as a tiny sweater impaled on steel needles threatened to take a dive to the garage floor.

"Thank you!" Audrey said as Sarah relieved her of the three biggest bags.

Sarah nodded—into the face of a neon-blue teddy bear.

"Isn't that the cutest thing?" Audrey's blunt-cut dark hair splashed against a round cheek. "Everybody was just too generous. We won't have to buy another thing." She gave Sarah a smile with a slight endearing overbite. "Thank you for the gift card. If we do need to get anything else, that should do it."

"That was from Megan *and* me," Sarah said, and didn't add that Megan had footed the bill for the whole thing. "Do you want these in the back or . . . ?"

"You can just put them on the other side of the car seat."

Sarah leaned into the car and almost collided with what looked like the bucket seat out of a limousine. The thing had so many straps on it, she was sure a master's degree was required to operate it.

She deposited the bags and backed out of the car. "You already have the baby seat in there?"

"Well . . ." Audrey patted the belly protruding from the coat she could no longer button. "I already have the baby."

"I guess there's that."

"So did they give you the job?"

Sarah felt her eyes widen. Audrey had gone from Ultimate Mama to Account Manager with the merest shift in tone.

"Um, they called me in but they didn't say anything definite."

Audrey shrugged. "You'll get it. Just between you and me, I don't think Thad is quite ready yet."

It took every amount of willpower Sarah had not to grab Audrey by both arms and shout, *What do you know? You know something, don't you? You can tell me!*

And then Megan would stop speaking to her.

But another tactic showed itself, one so easy Sarah almost felt guilty as she said, "Thanks, but the job's only temporary anyway."

"I wouldn't be so sure about that." Audrey shifted back to Mama Mode, hands on her belly again. "I'm getting quite attached to this little guy. Oh! He's kicking. Do you want to feel?"

Gee, Audrey, we were never that close—

"Here." Audrey grabbed Sarah's hand and pressed it against her stomach. The "little guy" did not seem pleased and pressed back. There was no doubt a tiny foot was staging the protest.

"Did you feel him?"

Once again Megan was right: Audrey glowed, although Rudolph wasn't the image she brought to mind. Audrey might have had trouble *getting* pregnant, but *being* pregnant was obviously what she was made for. "He's just so wonderful," Audrey said. "I can't imagine myself leaving him to fly to Baltimore five times a month. What could be worse?"

Sarah couldn't even begin to relate, which made her feel somehow small at the moment. She groped for humor and found a piece.

"Actually *living* in Baltimore," she said. "That would be worse."

Audrey laughed and opened the driver's side door. "Okay, time to squeeze myself in here. I better have him soon or I'm not going to be able to fit behind the wheel."

Sarah didn't stay to help her with that.

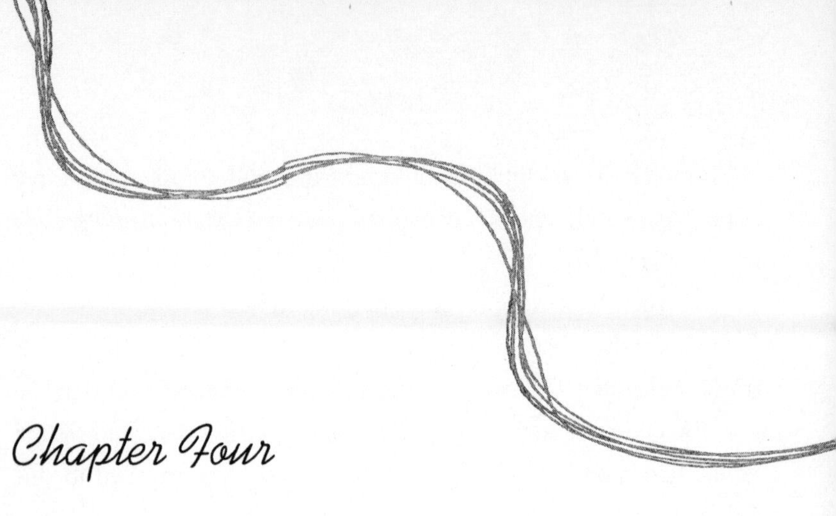

Chapter Four

Matt kept where they were eating a secret until he pulled "the 'Maro"—his red-velvet-cake–colored 1969 Camaro—up to valet parking at Lola, where he practically made the valet sign a sworn statement not to scratch, dent, or ding it. They hadn't been there since their one-year-of-dating anniversary six months before. Only a step down from the highest-end restaurants downtown, Lola featured classy, low-lit ambience, a menu full of served-with-a-(insert something unpronounceable)-sauce entrées, and a wine list Sarah had never been able to get all the way through before the server came for the order. She was sure this was more what Matt's father had had in mind the night before when he told Matt to pick a restaurant.

"We're not splitting the tab tonight," Matt whispered to her as they passed through the bar to the maître d's stand. "I've got this."

"I won't argue with you," Sarah whispered back, although she usually did. She wanted this to be a good night and she wouldn't mess it up by arm-wrestling him for a check she couldn't afford.

"Isn't that Nick what's-his-nose?"

Sarah looked where Matt was nodding and almost groaned. Nick Kellog was ensconced at the bar, sipping a Manhattan and watching ESPN. Even with his tie loosened, he looked exactly the same as he did in the office. Same gelled-in-place hair. Same sardonic expression.

And probably the same attitude toward women of childbearing age.

"Just keep going," Sarah murmured to Matt. "It's you and me tonight."

The maître d' led them to a cozy booth tucked into the back of the dining room. Matt took Sarah's hand and kissed her fingers. One of about five hundred reasons why she couldn't resist being with him.

She'd sworn off relationships after college, after the one she'd thought was serious had turned out to be one-sided. Hers. Since at that point she couldn't imagine one turning out any other way, she'd focused on grad school. She dated some but purposely kept it casual because she was so close to getting a good job and being more likely to meet guys who were interested in building a life.

And then life had become about her dad.

After that, she'd gone for a social life for sure. It hadn't been hard to find guys to date for fun. She was in a profession full of young, ambitious, educated people with bright personalities, and most of them were visibly and shamelessly relieved to hear that she wasn't in the market for a husband. It didn't matter to them why and she never bothered to tell them.

But then there was Matt.

It was hard to ignore his red-tinged dark curls and his this-side-of-puppy brown eyes and his runner's build. Or, more than that, the personality package: part goofy wit, part still-innocent, part just plain decent. The decent had grabbed her first and kept her as close as she intended to get.

It was a good thing he had those three parts, because the fourth part drove her a little nuts.

At least he waited until the maître d' left the table before he gave the menu a low whistle and said, "Man, look at these prices."

"It's not like this is the first time you've been here."

"Thirty-eight bucks for a pork chop?"

"You picked the place!"

"Maybe I'll just have an appetizer. Aw, c'mon—three shrimp on a skewer for nineteen-ninety-five?"

"Matt!"

The brown eyes sparkled at her over the top of the menu. "Gotcha."

"You are made of slime." She wrinkled her nose. "I'll have the bread and water, please. The bread is complimentary, isn't it?"

"Sar, I'm sorry. I shouldn't tease you tonight. Come on. Tell me what you're dreaming of with this promotion."

"Paying my bills."

"And after that?"

Sarah had no resistance to the coaxing.

"*After* everything's paid off, I'm thinking of a loft apartment at Water View. Megan showed me her place and it's in a great neighborhood. Well, better than the one I'm in right now."

"Sar, the 'hood is a better neighborhood than the one you're in right now."

"And when you call the building manager with a problem, he actually comes and fixes it."

"You dissin' Catfish again?"

"When did I ever stop?"

"You're going to let me help you pick out a newer car, right?"

"Pick one out, yes," Sarah said. "Build me one, no."

"What? What is that?" He touched the tip of her nose. "Have I told you that I love it when you wrinkle that thing?"

"One hundred and three times. But don't stop now."

"Not planning on it. And listen, don't get too comfortable."

"With what?"

"You may be ahead in the wage race for now—"

"There's a race?"

"But soon, I'm going to be pulling in multiple streams of income from every which direction."

Sarah's shoulders tightened. Until then it had been a good night. She could keep it that way if she didn't say what she couldn't keep herself from saying. She at least tried not to sound like his father.

"You're not trying to sell gym memberships on the side again, are you?"

"Hey, that's not fair. That would've worked if they'd had free weights. How was I supposed to sell memberships without free weights? They were just too limited in what they had to offer."

Sarah leaned forward. "Like a realistic commission. You lost, what, eight hundred dollars on that, uh, business venture?"

"Listen, here's what's gonna happen." Matt set up the scene with both hands. "I'm gonna pass my Series Sixty-Five exam, and then it's good-bye to the boiler room and hello big time. Okay?"

Sarah took a deep breath. She'd promised herself . . . But she'd heard it before, this plan to pass the exam that would qualify him to operate as an investment advisor representative. She had in fact heard it the very *night* before when Matt told his father the same thing. She would probably hear again—and again—how advising disgustingly wealthy people on portfolio management strategies would set him up for life. Just for tonight, though, maybe she could pretend this was the time it would really happen. Especially after *last* night.

"Okay," she said. "I know you can do it."

Matt grinned, the way no one else could grin. There was always that.

"So let's do what we came here to do and celebrate," he said. "C'mon, you want to start with a drink? Glass of wine?"

Sarah checked in with her stomach. It was better but why chance it? "I'll have a ginger ale."

"Ginger ale?" Matt looked like he was trying to figure out a quadratic equation. "What's up? You don't want a real drink? It's Friday night."

"I'm cutting back."

"Because . . ."

"I threw up this morning. And I have you to thank. That was the last time I'll ever let you talk me into jalapeños—especially with your parents. Which brings me to . . ."

Matt groaned. "I thought this was supposed to be a celebration—not a wake."

"You want to hear this," Sarah said. "Trust me."

He pulled out his cell phone and glanced at it. "I'm timing you. You get five minutes. Then we're moving on."

Sarah waited until the server took their drink orders and Matt told him to bring calamari too. Then she grabbed both of his hands.

"I know why you wanted me to meet your parents—even though they were only in town for, what, two hours?"

"No, see—"

"Let me finish."

Sarah pulled out the mental drawer she'd parked all of this in the night before as she lay in bed seething. It was all there, ready for the telling. She'd discarded the part about Matt's mother and father being the coldest, most unfeeling people she'd ever met, even in her line of work. Judging from the fact that even though they hadn't seen him in three months, they greeted him like he'd been underfoot all day, he already knew that.

"Your mother spent the whole time inspecting me," she said, "and your father basically acted like I wasn't there. So I figured out that you didn't invite me so they could meet me and love me. You invited me so I could see why you don't ever call them or go see them, and then I'll stop telling you all the time that you should."

A slow version of the grin started its way across Matt's face.

"The whole evening was about your father grilling you about your future, and your mom grilling me about my past. And the really creepy thing was, they did it all under the guise of impeccable manners and witty repartee."

"You mean the jokes about the advertising business."

"And the cuts about your investment firm and your car and the color of my lipstick."

"Your *lipstick*?"

Sarah leaned into the table. "When your mother informed me we were going to the ladies' room, I knew it was so she could check out whether I get my cosmetics at the Estée Lauder counter or the grocery store. I thought about offering to strip down to my underwear so she could see the tags."

Matt's smile faded. "I'm sorry, Sar. And you're wrong. I invited you so my father wouldn't be in my face the entire evening."

"How'd that work out for you?"

He reached for his cell phone. "Has it been five minutes yet?"

"Okay, so here's the deal." Sarah squeezed the hand that was halfway to the phone. "From now on I'm not going to get all up in your business about the Series Sixty-Five. I don't care what your father says, you can do this. Okay?"

The grin reappeared, big and sloppy. "Wait, let me write this down. And I want you to sign it and date it."

He pushed a napkin toward her, but the server appeared with the drinks and set her ginger ale on it. When he was gone, Matt nodded at her glass.

"Let's get back to you throwing up this morning. Where did this happen?"

"At home, and then—"

"That was a serious waste of vomit. You should have saved it for work. Then you could have used it as an excuse to take the day off."

"And Thad could have used it as an excuse to snag the promotion. And besides—Matt—that is disgusting."

His eyes shone. "No, it's smart, is what it is. So can you eat?"

"Yes, I can eat. And I want everything." She wrinkled her nose at him. "Including dessert."

Matt decided to lay off the teasing for the rest of the evening.

In the first place, she was being cool about his parents. They hadn't been at the table at Los Compadres for two minutes last night before he knew it was a mistake. It was obvious his mother thought Sarah was a prospective wife for him—and that she wasn't having it. Of course, Sarah had played up to him like she was, just to set his mother off. Yeah, he loved her for that.

Besides, Sar was happier tonight than he'd seen her since—maybe ever. She'd worked her tail off for this promotion and she deserved some straight-up support. Not hard to do for a woman who was beautiful, smart, and as funny as he was, if not more so. What she saw in him he wasn't sure, but he didn't let himself toy with that question too often.

When the server brought a dessert to share—a volcanic chocolate thing compliments of the house because Matt told him the lady was celebrating and deserved as much—Sarah gave him her biggest dazzler of a smile of the evening and said, "I love that we're sharing this whole thing, Matt. You know it means a lot to me."

"I know."

Her brows knit together. "Which is why I don't get Audrey."

Whoa. Sometimes talking to her was like watching a soccer game. You never knew where the ball was.

"You mean the woman you're replacing? The one that's about to give birth in the parking garage?"

"Yeah. I mean, she goes to college, then graduate school. She spends years working her way up through the ranks. She and her husband are obviously financially comfortable. And then she just gives it all up to stay home with a baby."

Matt scooped up a spoonful of molten chocolate. "You want kids someday."

"I do. But I want to be able to provide for them without constantly worrying about where I'm going to get the money to pay the bills." She tilted her head, spoon suspended between her and the diminishing volcano. "Does that sound mercenary? Because it isn't just about the money."

"No, but it's a lot about the money." Matt pushed the plate toward her. She'd picked through the whole meal. She probably had more room left than he did. "At least according to Uncle Clay it's about the money."

"I don't follow."

"He and Aunt Jerri are having another baby. A surprise."

Sarah's jaw dropped. "They didn't say anything about it Saturday when we were over there."

"She just told him this morning."

"That's four kids, Matt."

"Yep."

"I really like Clay and Jerri's family, but . . . that's a lot of children."

"He thinks so. He's completely freaking out."

"That part surprises me. He's such a family guy. He was out there messing around on the snowmobiles with them longer than you were."

"I guess he thought they were done having kids. He's forty-two. She's, like, thirty-nine. Like I said, it's the money thing. He's already worried about how he's gonna send the kid to Harvard."

"I get that." Sarah pressed her mouth into a straight line.

Matt leaned back in the booth. "In a way it's his own fault."

"How so?"

"He should've never stayed at United after he got his financial advisor license. He'd be making way more money as a midlevel broker anywhere else than as a manager there."

"Why'd he stay?"

Matt felt a laugh bubble up. "Aunt Jerri was pregnant. Seemed like she was *always* pregnant. I guess the management job offered more security."

"Exactly my point. I want to have choices."

Matt nodded. "Yeah. It seems like you always lose when you let circumstances dictate your future."

She nodded back.

"Sarah?"

Matt looked up to see that Nick person approaching from a table away. He glanced at Sarah to see if he should shake the guy's hand or pretend he had the wrong couple. Sarah gave Nick the professional version of her smile.

"Hi, Nick. This *is* your kind of place, isn't it?"

Sarah, you little minx.

Nick turned to Matt. "It's Mike, isn't it?"

"Matt," Sarah said, before Matt could accept Mike and let it go at that.

Nick gave him what Matt considered a frozen fish handshake. "Sorry about that. I think we worked together . . . ?"

"You did an ad campaign for United Financial," Matt said.

Matt was a gofer then, the only job Uncle Clay could get him at the time, and he'd poured many a cup of coffee for Nick Kellog during planning sessions. The best thing that came out of that was discovering Sarah.

Nick switched Matt off and focused on her. "Good meeting today. You handled yourself like a pro with Henry. And just so you know, he tries that joke on everybody who calls him sir. You're the first person I ever saw who pulled it off without looking like an idiot."

"It was . . . amusing," Sarah said.

How she did that was beyond Matt. He himself could usually finagle his way out of any situation somehow, but Sarah had a way of saying the right thing the right way to the right person and somehow meaning it.

He had zero hope of ever pulling that off. Or of achieving the polish Nick Kellog had shined onto himself. It was nine o'clock at night and the guy looked like he'd just shaved and put on that pricey jacket he'd probably been wearing since 7:00 a.m. Even with what was no doubt his third drink in his hand, his small talk with Sarah was as smooth as the bourbon in that glass.

Matt rubbed at his cheek. This wasn't the first time he'd wondered if somebody like Nick Kellog was what Sarah hoped Matt would become. He could hear his father delivering the line: *If you can't support it, don't chase it.* Probably the wisdom of experience from paying for all his mother's Botox.

When Nick was gone, Sarah narrowed her eyes.

"How is it that every time I'm around him I want to launch into a diatribe on women's rights?"

"Forget him," Matt said. "What next?"

He shouldn't have asked. Sarah broke into another smile not meant for him, and Matt twisted to look over his shoulder. He barely choked off a groan.

It was Constricta.

Actually her name was Megan, but Matt could never see her without thinking of a boa ready to squeeze the life out of any situation that included him. Even before she reached their table, her eyes were so tightly narrowed on him they were practically crossed. Any minute now they'd switch sockets.

"Nick said you were here," she said to Sarah.

"You didn't tell me you were dating him!"

Megan's eyebrows shot up. Matt always wondered if they were tattooed on. "I'm not," she said. "I'd rather eat glass."

Huh. He thought they would've made a great couple. Two reptiles. It would just be a matter of who ate whom first.

"We're having a management dinner." Megan tapped the table with a manufactured fingernail. "Next quarter you'll be there with us."

Then she darted her snake-eyed gaze at Matt. Without even a flick of the tongue, she managed to get the message across: he wouldn't be attending . . . it was way above his pay grade.

When Constricta had slithered away, Sarah slid her hand across the table and touched his.

"I'm sorry. I know Megan isn't your favorite person."

"What I don't get is why she's yours."

"She's not. She's just helping me with this promotion and I appreciate it." Sarah shrugged. "She's about the only person I can halfway relate to at work, and besides . . ."

She tilted her head at him, letting a curl or two whisper against her cheek. She could pretty much have anything she wanted when she did that.

"Besides what?" he said.

"I don't have that much time for girlfriends. I spend all my free time with you."

"So-o-o-o, like I said, what's next?"

She didn't miss a beat. "I could go for a kiss. Maybe two."

"Waiter, check please."

Sarah wrinkled her nose at him.

It was all right again.

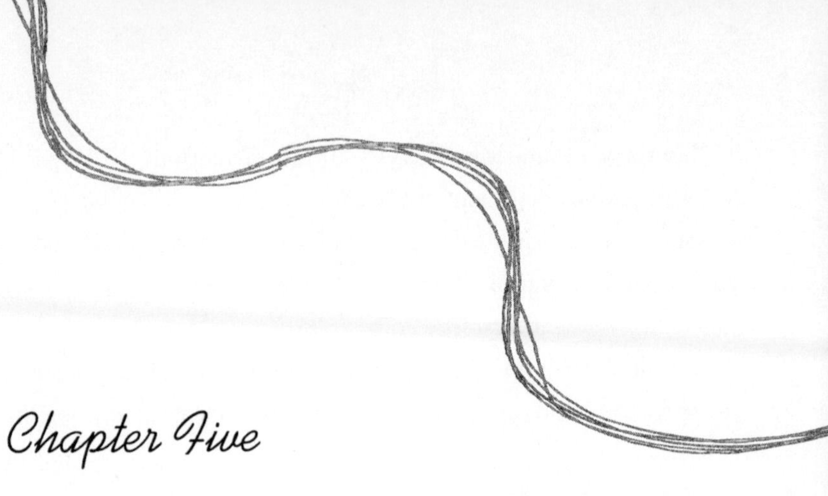

Chapter Five

"Catfish, you seriously need to get a real job."

Sarah leaned over to pick up what looked like a kindergarten art project slid under the door. Bad move. Last night's filet mignon teased at her throat. She took a minute to sag against the wall before she opened the latest *PAY THE RENT!* notice, written on an origami spider.

She tossed it on the desk with the others and returned to the day-bed and her peppermint tea. Hopefully that would go down and stay down. Enough with the stomach thing, already.

Actually, it probably wouldn't go away until this mess was taken care of—the mess in question being the bills in the plastic compartments, the ones she always paid first. The ones she was manning up and facing this morning. A few hundred dollars here, a little heart-burn there. It was a chronic pain in the financial stomach.

Especially when new surprises kept showing up. She picked up the one that had come yesterday and simultaneously fought off another urge to toss her cookies. The ringing of her landline saved the day. Until she saw that it was her mother. She was in a compartment by herself.

Okay, do not answer with, *Mom, do you realize it's only 8:00 a.m. on a Saturday?* Do. Not.

"Hi, Mom," she said.

"Hi, honey. I didn't wake you and Matt up, did I?"

Sarah's jaw tightened. "Matt. Why would you wake up Matt?"

"I know he stays over now and then."

Fifteen seconds into the conversation and Sarah was already throttling her tea mug. She'd never defended her stance on sex with her mother and she wasn't going to start now. She couldn't imagine herself saying, "Mom, I no longer care that the church tells me it's wrong to have sex outside of marriage or that God will be disappointed in me if I do—so what difference does it make?" She might as well set her mother on fire. It wouldn't even help if she told her she would never sleep with any guy she didn't have feelings for, which had eliminated everybody before—

"Sarah, all I'm saying is that this is not God's plan for your life. You have all the benefits of marriage with none of the responsibilities."

Sarah glared at the Sea of Accounts Payable she was drowning in. "Mom, there is no way you can say I'm not responsible."

"In many ways you are, but—"

"Is this why you called?"

In the long-suffering pause that ensued, Sarah closed her eyes. She hadn't meant to be so abrupt, but if she didn't cut her mother off she was in for the Sermon on the Mount.

She went for a sunnier tone. "What time's your party tomorrow?"

"That *is* why I called. I wanted to tell you what I want for my birthday."

Good. Safe territory.

"Too late," Sarah said. "I already got you something."

"I'll take that, too, but I want to see you at church tomorrow for my birthday."

So much for safe.

"Mom, I don't know. I'm not feeling well." Which wasn't a lie. Sarah set the mug on the bedside table and hauled in a deep breath. She'd be lucky to get through this call, much less a sermon.

"Funny how you're always sick on Sunday morning."

Another silence, which Sarah made no attempt to fill.

"Can't I have my two daughters sitting by my side in church at least once a year?"

That Sarah *could* imagine because she'd done it for months after her father died—sat beside her mother on Sundays because she was so fragile a refusal to go would have shattered her. Sat there and shut down week after week after week while the praise songs told her God loved her more and more and she believed it less and less. Church had only given her something to bang her angry head against. She'd stopped going the week she'd moved in here and didn't have to see her mother looking the way she probably did at this exact moment: white-knuckling the phone, blinking rapidly, rubbing her other hand up and down her thigh. It wasn't worth it to leave her that way. Given her emotional fragility, this could go south fast.

"Okay," Sarah said.

"Thank you, honey." Mom's voice shook. "You know how much this means to me. More than the party."

"We'll be there for that too—"

"I'm thinking a nice ham with scalloped potatoes—or maybe that sweet potato casserole with the little marshmallows the boys like. Which sounds good to you?"

Sarah got out, "Whatever you want, Mom," before she plastered her hand over her mouth.

"All right, I'll see you tomorrow. The service is at ten—"

"Oh, Mom, wait." Sarah swallowed hard and picked up the paper she'd been contemplating when the phone rang. "I thought I had all the bills for MRMC on a payment plan, but I just got another one for three hundred and forty dollars."

Her mother's voice fell. "I'm sorry. I got that too and I forgot to talk to you about it. Apparently an old invoice for one of your dad's MRIs has been bouncing around the system."

"Mom, it's been three years. How can they do that?"

"I don't know. I'll call and set up separate payments—"

"No. Don't."

Agnes's voice was practically inaudible at that point. One more ounce of stress and Sarah would be paying off *her* hospital bills too.

"My holiday bonus is coming up," Sarah said. "I'll just pay it off with that and keep on with the other payments. Okay?"

"Sweetie . . . thank you."

"I thought we agreed you'd already given me a blanket thank-you."

"I know but—"

"We're all doing our part."

Sarah was tempted to insert a hint about the promotion, but that could wait until she had it in writing. Besides, it was time to end this call. There was no denying the nausea now.

"A mom couldn't ask for a better pair of daughters."

"She could, but she wouldn't find them. Love you, Mom."

"I love you too!" Matt called from the kitchen.

Sarah checked for a dial tone. If Mom had heard that, she'd be in for a commentary tomorrow on the woman caught in adultery. Agnes always had an entire pile of stones at the ready for her.

Matt appeared around the corner. "I made you some toast."

Sarah sniffed and gagged. "You *burned* me some toast. Baby, please get that out of here before I puke."

"You sick again?"

"I'm serious!"

Matt retreated, plate of blackened bread in hand. Sarah curled into a fetal position and breathed.

"You can't blame it on jalapeños this time, Sar," Matt called from the kitchen. "Or my parents. What did your mom want?"

My soul.

"She wants me to go to church tomorrow."

Matt reappeared, pulling on a T-shirt. Too bad. Even in her pitiful state, the fact that bare-chested was a good look for him didn't escape her.

"That doesn't sound so bad. I can do that."

Sarah lifted her head. "You don't have to go."

"Will you still speak to me tomorrow night if I don't?"

"Probably not."

"Then there you go. And I'm not missing one of your mom's dinners."

"She sure isn't going to feed you if you show up for the party and not the church service."

Matt pulled her to a sitting position and kissed the top of her head. "I'm looking at it this way: while we're hanging out at church, I might find some candidates for my new business opportunity."

Sarah moaned. "We already went through this at 1:00 a.m. It's not a business; it's a cell phone pyramid scheme."

"And I told you, there is absolutely no risk involved. It's a liberal payout with minimal effort."

"Since when does life work that way?"

Matt blinked down at her, and with good reason. The words had come out pointier than she intended. In fact, just last night she'd promised not to say them at all. A homily-heavy conversation with her mother always left her feeling like a porcupine.

"Sorry," she said. "This is about me, not you. I have to live in the real world."

"This real world?" Matt motioned to her personal bills still piled on the desk.

"That's the one."

"Here's what we're going to do with the real world today." He pried the drawer open and with the side of his hand, swept the whole pile into it and shimmied it shut. "What are we having for dinner at your mom's?"

"Marshmallows."

Matt sank down next to her and pulled her into his lap. The daybed creaked. "I like Agnes."

"I like her too . . . when she isn't doing her Billy Graham imitation. Are you sure you want to go with me?"

"How else are you going to get there? Last I heard Buzz Lightyear was on his last wheels. Why did you name the thing that anyway?

"It's a TOYota. He was my favorite character in *Toy Story*. I was in high school when my dad bought it for me—why did you bring that up?"

"Why won't you let me work on it?"

"Because you should be studying. And because I'm about to buy a new one."

"You deserve it, Sar." Matt tilted her chin up and kissed her nose. "Just so you know, your mother can't hold a candle to mine when it comes to running your life."

"I saw that."

"You didn't see all of it. While you were getting your coat, she cornered me with the same stuff she keeps calling me about. She says my father wants me to come home for a 'family' Christmas."

"Oh. He didn't say anything about that at dinner."

"That's because it's not his idea. It's hers."

"Then I don't understand—"

Sarah stopped herself. The last time Matt went back to Philadelphia for the holidays he regressed so far he installed two sub woofers in his Camaro. Now she knew why.

"Have you told her no?" Sarah said.

"Like you tell your mother no? What if your dad were still around, though—would he do something like that?"

"Okay. I get it," Sarah said quickly. "Now don't talk anymore."

"Why?"

"Because if I just sit here perfectly still, I won't throw up. I hate to throw up."

He tightened his arms around her. She was probably going to throw up anyway, but she just wanted a minute to sink into his cuteness and his niceness and not think about the fact that he wasn't as good at keeping things in their compartments as she was. Come to think of it, he didn't seem to have any. His life was more like a succession of jungle gyms and swing sets.

"Matt," she said.

"Yeah."

"Let go—"

He did. Just in time for her to careen into the bathroom and give up the filet mignon.

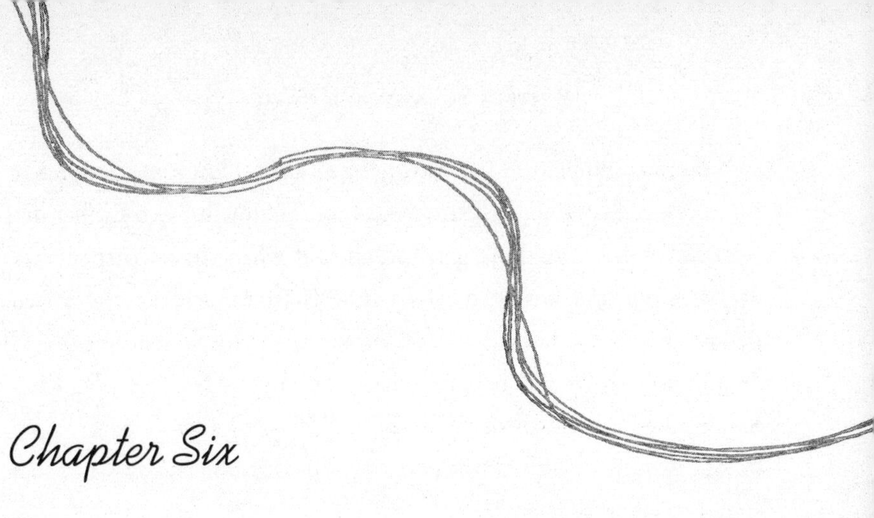

Chapter Six

Matt spent the rest of the morning with his head under Buzz Lightyear's hood. Sarah had hers under the toilet seat lid until she sent him out for ginger ale. Between that and the fast-emptying bottle of Pepto, she managed to make it past lunch without another bout. She was just about to fall into afternoon unconsciousness when her cell rang.

"Hey!" Sarah said. She covered the phone with her hand and said to Matt, "It's your Aunt Jerri."

Matt broke into an annoying rendition of an infant crying until Sarah shooed him back outside to the cold and the greasy rags.

"I hear congratulations are in order," Sarah said.

Jerri gave what Sarah always thought of as a juicy laugh. She was that kind of person. You squeezed her and realness came out of her pores.

"Yeah, surprise, right?" Jerri said. "But that's not why I called. I want to hear about your dinner with the Evans Estate Thursday night."

Sarah could picture Jerri sitting in an almost lotus position, ready for Sarah to dish the dirt. Sarah was more than willing to fill her in.

"What I totally don't get," Sarah said when they'd turned over every clump and analyzed it, "is how Matt came from those two people. I felt like I was in a bad movie with this stereotypical rich couple nobody would believe existed. And yet Matt is . . . good." Sarah raked a hand through her hair. "Okay, I know he covers up a lot of insecurities with all the crazy stuff he does, but really—he's just so decent. And they are so . . . not."

"I hear you. Jolene's had so much work done she hardly bears any resemblance to her*self* anymore."

"She's definitely got the Joan Rivers thing going on."

"Oh yeah. And if it's not that, it's some physical ailment. She actually talked a doctor into removing her healthy gallbladder the week of Matt's graduation from college. Just so she could show up and be the martyr. On pain meds."

This was making Agnes look better by the second.

"Matt was just born good," Jerri went on. "I didn't know Jolene before she married Matthew Senior—Esquire, as he calls himself—but Clay said she was a lot like Matt is now and her husband just ruined her. Turned her into a society . . . she-wolf."

"He did a thorough job."

"I know, right? It was Clay who brought the good out in Mattie. He was more like a big brother than an uncle." Jerri's voice went soft. "Jolene has always been more about Matthew Senior's daughters from his previous marriage than she is about her own kid. She didn't know what to do with a boy. Clay did everything for him, and Matt was heartbroken when Clay and I moved from Philadelphia to here when Matt was in high school. I know we're the reason he came to Illinois to go to college. Clay has just always felt like he needed to look after him."

"Thank heaven," Sarah said.

A silence fell, something unusual in a conversation with Jerri.

"Look, Sarah," she said finally, "I really wanted to make sure Jolene and Esquire didn't run you off. You're good for Matt."

Sarah felt herself tighten. "We have a lot of fun together."

"Fun." Jerri gave a grunt that was as succulent as her laugh. "I was afraid of that."

"I don't follow," Sarah said.

"Matt has a hard time showing who he really is. He's never gotten past what his parents tell him he is, no matter what Clay tries to do for him. He doesn't even try to get their approval—he gave up on that a long time ago. But he doesn't see how he can be anything, really, if he can't be what they want him to be."

Sarah knew where Jerri was taking her. And she didn't want to go there.

"You, on the other hand, obviously have it all together, and Matt respects you. Am I making any sense at all?"

Too much sense. About the wrong thing.

"We definitely balance each other out, if that's what you mean." Sarah knew her voice sounded as high and strained as a middle schooler lying to her mother. "He shows me how to loosen up, and I show him that there's actually a serious side to life."

Jerri grunted again, with less juice this time.

"I sense we've gotten into none-of-my-business territory," she said. "So—what I'm hearing is that Jolene and his majesty didn't turn you off to the clan completely?"

"Not at all," Sarah said. "And listen, thanks for the insights."

"For what they're worth," Jerri said.

The disappointment leaked through as she hung up, and Sarah felt a pang. That would have been a great conversation if she thought there was any future in understanding where Matt came from. Maybe there would be someday. But for now, and for a while to come, Matt and marriage couldn't be in the same sentence. She just hoped she hadn't sounded too snarky with Jerri. She liked her. She liked Clay.

She liked Matt.

They were late getting to the service Sunday morning. Matt couldn't leave Catfish in the apartment parking lot with a dead battery. He gave him a jump while Sarah hid in the bathroom.

"Hey, thanks dude," Catfish said when Matt had his aluminum can of a '93 Buick running. If you could call it that. The engine was only banging on four cylinders, and the thing was a V-8. "I owe ya."

Matt considered asking him to take it out of Sarah's rent, but he didn't want to bring it up. She had already downed what was left of a bottle of Pepto just to get out of bed with that bug she had. She didn't need this kid in her doorway smelling like last week's laundry.

"It's all good," Matt said. "Just don't shut it off until you get where you're going."

He made sure the land yacht had rounded the corner before he texted Sarah that it was safe to come out. She looked amazing—some kind of flowy dress thing with her hair all shiny and her legs taut in a pair of heels. If she hadn't still looked a little green around the gills, he would have stopped her for a kiss. Besides, she informed him they were late enough already.

"Like you care about us getting there on time," Matt said.

"I don't. My mother does."

Yeah, better not to give Agnes a reason to pour on any more guilt. Must be a mother thing.

Matt made good time getting from Oak Park to Elmhurst where the church was, but there wasn't a space left in its acres of parking lot even though the thing was big enough to hold the crowd at a U2 concert.

"Is it always this crowded?"

"Just at Christmastime when the people who only come one season a year show up." Sarah gave a grunt. "Like us."

Matt finally located a spot on the street two blocks up and let Sarah haul him down the icy sidewalk. He liked the back view of her. When they slipped inside the vestibule, amid a forest of poinsettias that looked like someone had robbed a florist shop, she was the one who stopped him and gave him a pillowy kiss.

"Thanks for coming with me," she whispered. "I don't know if I could have done this alone."

He pulled her closer. "It's not like I'm gonna miss football or anything."

"No games today?"

"Only the last of the regular season." He gave her a martyred look.

She gave *him* the nose wrinkle and glared past the Christmas tree at the door between them and the sanctuary. "At least you didn't have to put up with this every week like I did growing up."

Before he could correct that, she sighed and pushed open the door.

Okay, so it wasn't *every* week, but he'd done his share of squirming in a pew when he was a kid, because his father made them go: *Belonging to a church and a country club is good for business,* was the rationale.

And the experience wasn't all bad. As he and Sarah stood in the back, craning their necks for sight of the Collins clan, Matt couldn't help remembering the Christmas pageants he was in until they barred him from participation because he always stole the scene from the Holy Family in his self-styled roles as a rapping shepherd or a break-dancing camel. It used to tie his father's jaw muscles into square knots.

"There they are," Sarah whispered and padded off down the side aisle.

Agnes had saved them a place in, of course, the front and on the other side of her, which meant they had to climb over Justin, Sarah's brother-in-law, and Denise, her sister, and their two munchkin boys, not to mention Agnes herself. The shaking of hands and kissing of cheeks and pinching of kid noses were enough to stop the entire service until they got settled, but the pastor continued to preach . . .

"'How will this be,' Mary asked the angel, 'since I am a virgin?'"

Now *there* was a line to come in on.

Matt finally got himself squeezed in between Sarah and an eighty-ish woman who also insisted on shaking Matt's hand with her knotty one. By then he became aware that the pastor was way into his sermon. Somewhere around point 2.

"'The Holy Spirit will come on you, and the power of the Most High will overshadow you. So the holy one to be born will be called the Son of God. Even Elizabeth your relative is going to have a child in her old age.'"

Matt suppressed a grin. Impossible not to think of Aunt Jerri.

"'Nothing is impossible with God.'"

Dude. Was this guy reading his mind? Matt gave him a closer look and almost blurted out, *Hey, I know him!* Where had he seen him before?

Next to him Sarah's body felt like a steel rod, but she was almost smiling at the pastor.

"What's this guy's name?" Matt whispered to her.

"Reverend Al Smith."

Didn't ring any bells.

"'I am the Lord's servant,' Mary answered. 'May it be to me as you have said.' Then the angel left her."

The reverend closed his Bible. Matt moved his lips closer to Sarah's ear.

"I know him from someplace."

"I've known him since I was five."

Sarah let the smile glimmer for a minute. Reverend Al obviously wasn't the reason she'd given up church. Matt had never asked her why she had. That topic was as off-limits as talking about her father. She'd cut off that subject just yesterday morning.

"Today I want you to look at this story beyond the familiar words to the reality. Put yourself in the place of that little Judean girl, who couldn't have been more than sixteen or seventeen."

Sorry, Rev. I'm gonna have a little trouble pulling that off.

"She was young and innocent, but not so naive as to be unaware of the implications of her decision."

Ya think? Matt leaned forward on his knees. This guy had a way of making you feel like you were in a one-on-one conversation with him. Where the Sam Hill had he seen him before? A little on the chubby side, balding, quirky mouth—

"She had more to worry about than disappointed parents and an angry fiancé."

Matt nodded. From the time he was a teenager and finally got this part of the story, he always felt like you had to hand it to Joseph for hanging in there with Mary.

"Her life literally hung in the balance. There was an excellent chance that she would be stoned to death when she began to show."

Tough crowd back then.

Matt glanced at Sarah. Man, she was beautiful when she was

intent like that. Made him want to get this cell phone thing going, make some decent money.

Take care of her.

Whoa.

He pulled himself back to the good rev.

"What could she tell that angry mob? That she had a vision? That an angel had appeared to her?"

Yeah, not so much.

"Do you think they would have believed that? Would that have stopped the stones?"

As if on cue, a scuffle ensued in the pew. Justin and Denise's boys were going at it on the floor like Junior WWE.

Without taking their eyes off the pulpit, Denise grabbed the little one by the seat of his pants and Justin got the other one by the collar. They were plunked down on either side of their parents before Reverend Al could even move on to point 3. Slick.

The two blue-haired women in the pew in front of them obviously didn't share his take on it. They turned and looked at Justin and Denise with their lips drawstrung in. Beside him Sarah's body got so tight he thought rigor mortis was setting in. Talk about your domino effect.

"Mary said, 'I am the Lord's servant. May it be to me as you have said.' What courage. What faith. She was going to obey the vision the Lord gave her regardless of the cost, because she knew God would keep his promise."

"Right," Sarah whispered.

Matt looked at her in time to see the smile evaporate.

He sure wasn't going to ask her why.

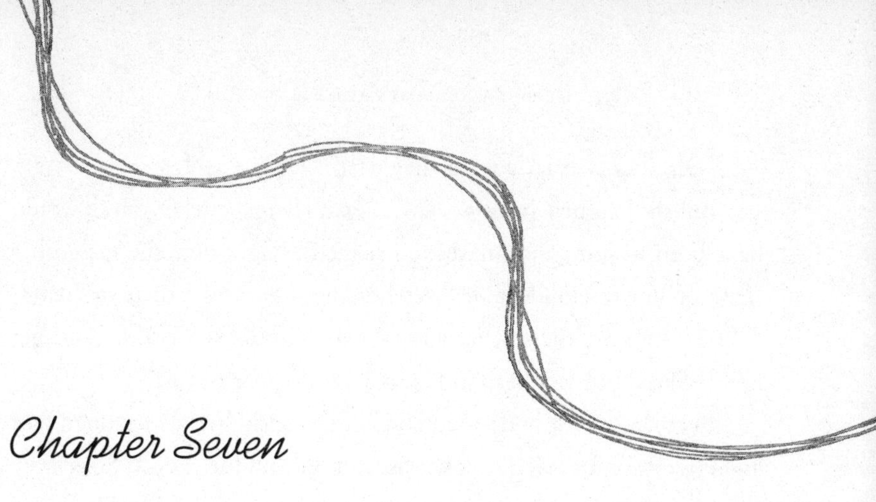

Chapter Seven

Sarah and Matt arrived at her mom's house in Elmhurst just minutes after Denise and Justin pulled up in a van Matt said needed a tune-up, but Sean and Tim, who had ridden with "Nana," were already into the party hats and noise makers. As if they *needed* noise makers.

Sarah gladly slammed the door on the church compartment and opened the family one. This was where her mother was at her best—as long as she could keep those two drawers from opening at the same time.

Sarah's mother smiled beatifically at her grandsons and slid a clove-dotted ham into the oven, then rearranged one of the six nativity scenes the boys had apparently already been into. Somehow Oscar the Grouch had shoved the angel off the top and Cookie Monster was in the hay with the Baby Jesus, but Agnes just kept beaming with not a wisp of salt-and-pepper hair out of place.

"You weren't this patient when *we* were kids," Sarah said to her.

"I wasn't a grandmother then." Her voice rose, songlike. "The ham just has to heat through. You boys want a cookie to hold you over?"

"Oh, that is exactly what they need," Denise said.

But she laughed. Sunny Denise always laughed when Sarah would have been wailing and gnashing her teeth. Right now she tossed her mass of butter-blonde hair over her shoulder and called to Justin, "Whose kids are these? Can you take over until their real parents get here?" She shook her head at Sarah. "Those poor people."

Justin, a stocky, honey-haired Chicago native with a deadpan face and effervescent eyes, put down his camera and lifted both boys away from the heaping plate of sugar cookies on the coffee table. He tossed Sean to Matt, who proceeded to fly the kid around the living room and turn him into a machine gun—all accompanied by Tim jumping on the antique loveseat wailing, "*My* turn! *My turn!*"

"Did you girls see the table?" Mom called from the kitchen.

Sarah peered into the dining room, although she knew what she'd see: every Christmas plate and felt-holly–covered napkin ring and angel candlestick holder that had been on the Collins' table in this very room from December 1 until New Year's Day since before Sarah was born. Denise, four years older, could attest to that. Until three years ago, Sarah had craved the sight of it. Since then, it had just seemed . . . forced, as if her mother were trying not to notice that something was so achingly missing.

"Come taste this sauce," Agnes sang out.

Sarah pushed through the swinging door into the kitchen, where Denise was gazing into a bubbling casserole of cheesy potatoes. Sarah's stomach announced it was not pleased at the prospect of eating *those*. At least her mom hadn't gone with the marshmallow thing.

"Here." Agnes held out a spoon brimming with hollandaise, but Sarah shook her head.

"I'll wait until it's on the asparagus."

"Pilot to bombardier—pilot to bombardier!"

The other door swung open and Matt swooped into the kitchen. Tim shrieked, "Get Aunt Sarah!"—a command Matt followed without hesitation, vibrating the "machine gun" close to her face with green stuff dripping from its nose like melted birthday candles. "Got her!" Tim cried, and Matt whooshed them out the other door where Justin was poised to catch it on his Minolta.

"Matt's so good with kids." Denise wiggled her eyebrows at Sarah.

"Don't go there."

"Where are we not going?"

Sarah kissed her mother's cheek. "Nowhere. Not with all this amazing food about to go on the table."

Her mother beamed even brighter, and Sarah felt a pang of guilt. It took so little to make her light up like that. Sarah would do it more often, if she didn't always have to pick through a minefield to get there.

"That ham should be done. Denise, would you check it?"

Denise opened the oven and Sarah tried not to gag. If she got through this meal without at least one trip to the bathroom, it would be a bigger miracle than the loaves and the fishes.

Ugh. Why had she thought of fish?

Actually, she shouldn't have worried. So much was going on at the table no one seemed to notice that she took half portions and basically just pushed everything around. Sean stole all the ham off Tim's plate, which led to a reenactment of the Battle of the Bulge, and Matt got both of them going by showing them how to blow bubbles in their milk with a straw. Denise was still laughing when the froth spilled over onto the tablecloth, and Nana continued to smile like the Virgin Mary herself.

"Welcome to my world," Justin said to Sarah—and then joined in the competition. Give it two minutes and Matt would be laying bets.

Sarah was grateful for the chaos so she could head for the kitchen and scrape her plate into the trash can. How she'd get through the birthday cake part she wasn't sure.

Justin brought out more party hats and horns that unfolded when you blew into them and made the obnoxious noises the boys obviously thought were as hilarious as burping. Denise produced the oversized sheet cake she'd baked, complete with fifty candles. Sarah's father had always insisted on the correct number of candles.

His last cake had had forty-seven.

Sarah joined in the cacophonous singing of "Happy Birthday" with more zest than she felt, but it was too late. The vision of Dad was already there and it wasn't going away. Him enthroned at the head of this very table, scalp hairless, face ashen, flesh sagging on his cheekbones, but his small, happy brown eyes shining with the hope they'd been given that once chemo was over, there was a chance he'd go into remission—that there would be more candles on birthday cakes to come.

"Let me count," he'd said that day. And made them wait while the wax spilled onto the frosting and he numbered every single one to make sure Agnes hadn't cheated. Then with a rattled breath he attempted to blow out the tiny flames . . . and dissolved into bone-wracking coughs. Sarah leaned over his shoulder and puffed out the remaining forty. And wished from her very gut that she could breathe that air into him.

"You okay, Sar?"

Sarah opened her eyes at Matt, crouched beside her with his party hat posed rakishly on his curls.

"As soon as the dishes are done," she whispered, "let's—"

"Got it," he said.

When the presents were opened and the fifty candles were licked by little tongues and the ice cream was stowed back in the freezer before Matt could plop yet another scoop onto the boys' plates, Denise and Sarah insisted their mother retire to the living room while they took care of the dishes. The quiet of running water and her sister's unflappable voice settled both Sarah's nerves and her stomach.

"How do you stay so calm with all of that going on all the time?"

Denise giggled like a tiny bell. "Getting worked up only escalates things. And I have Justin. He's like a rock."

"Still . . ." Sarah stuffed the towel into a snowflake-etched glass and gave it a twist. "Do you ever wish you'd waited until you were a little better off financially before you had kids?"

Another giggle. "Are you serious? Our civilization would have died off centuries ago if everybody waited until they could *afford* to have kids."

Sarah set the glass on its matching tray. "Well, *I'm* waiting."

"How does Matt feel about that? He looks like he could handle about four of them right now."

"Shut *up*!"

"Oh, come on. I see how you two are with each other. You're not talking marriage yet?"

"Uh, no."

"Why not? He's adorable."

"Because it takes more than 'adorable' to pay the bills. And besides, I'm not going to saddle him with all of mine."

Denise's smile faded, and she kept her eyes on the dishwater. "You wouldn't have bills if you hadn't taken on—"

"That was my choice, and I'm not backing out on it."

"We're not as financially bad off as you think we are, Justin and I. We could help more."

"You're making sure Mom gets her personal bills paid."

"But it's her money."

"Look, you coming over here every single day to check her mail is huge."

Sarah didn't add that doing that herself would qualify her for psychiatric treatment. It was hard to be snarky around Denise.

It was also hard to bring up tough subjects. She focused on the next snowflake glass.

"I hate to bring this up," she said, "but somehow Mom saw an old bill for Dad that came through here. I don't know why we both got it, but she was about to call them on her own."

Denise's eyes widened. "I am so sorry. It must have gotten stuck in with some catalogs or something. I'm going to have to start going through everything page by page."

"Don't even think about doing that. I'm just giving you a heads-up."

"I feel bad—"

"Oh. My. Gosh. What is that?"

"This?" Denise held up one of the small plates with the reindeer in the center, its face currently smeared with a gelatinous glob of everything that had been on the table. "It's Sean's version of a train wreck. Matt taught him how to do that at Thanksgiving."

"Excuse me," Sarah said, and took off for the bathroom at a dead run.

After that it was definitely time to go home. She pried Matt away from his sales pitch to Justin—who wouldn't want to make money while talking on his cell phone?—and asked him to get the coats.

"Sarah, you're not leaving, honey?" Mom said.

Sarah was sure her mother would have gotten up and dragged

her bodily away from the door, but Tim was asleep in her lap in the kid-rocking chair, drooling on her embroidered Christmas sweater. Grandchildren apparently trumped everything. But that didn't stop her from taking Sarah where she didn't want to go.

"Did you enjoy the service?"

"It was fine, Mom."

"Then you should come to our Wednesday night Bible study." She spoke as if Sarah had just gushed that the whole experience had been life-changing. "So many prayers have been answered."

"I don't think so, Mom." Sarah brushed her mother's hair with her lips and took her coat from Matt.

"But you've always loved Reverend Smith." Agnes looked at Matt. "He was so good to us when Sarah's father was sick—"

"Bye, Mom." Sarah took Matt's arm. "Happy Birthday."

"You're coming to decorate the tree, aren't you? We can't do it without you."

"We'll see."

"Friday," Mom said, looking at Matt again. "I'm making a pot of vegetable soup. We always have that on tree-trimming night."

"Sounds awesome," Matt said.

Sarah nearly whimpered. To her mother, that was as good as an affirmative RSVP. In writing.

"I'll expect you then!"

"Mom, if you wake that kid up I'm taking back your present," Denise said.

Sarah was grateful for the attempt on Denise's part, but her mother was like a homing pigeon.

"We'll start at about six. Does that give you enough time after work?"

Matt planted a smooch in the exact middle of Agnes's forehead. "Now I know where Sarah gets her gift of persuasion. You're irresistible."

Her mother was actually blushing as Sarah tugged Matt through the front hall and out the door.

"*You're* shameless," she said as they hurried through the just-starting snow to the Camaro. "But thank you. Thank you for the whole day."

"Hey, when have I ever turned down ice cream and cake?"

She tucked her hand into his. "I made you miss your football game."

"I've been following it." Matt held up his cell. "Thank God for smart phones and a four-point spread."

"Could we not talk about God any more today? Please?"

Matt grinned. "Then how about: thank the Steelers for the hundred bucks I just won."

"That'll work," Sarah said.

Matt turned on the radio in the car so he wouldn't miss the next game. Sarah didn't ask if he had any money riding on this one. She was actually glad not to have to talk. It was going to take all the mental energy she had to get things back into their respective compartments.

As usual, her mom had managed to bring up church again. But at least with Matt there she'd been able to avoid the usual dialogue, the one that went something like:

AGNES: I don't understand why you stopped going to church when you moved out.

SARAH: Because I need some space, Mom.

AGNES: You don't need space from God, Sarah!

(**SARAH** bites down on the inside of her cheek so she won't say, "No, I need space from you!")

That wasn't entirely true, though. It was space from her mother's religion that Sarah wanted. Space from those people with the clichés they'd delivered with the casseroles when her father died.

Macaroni and cheese and *It was God's will.*

Broccoli and chicken and *Now Bill's with God.*

Three-cheese lasagna and *Aren't you just grateful he was saved?*

Every time her mother started to weep in front of them, someone was tacitly designated to say, *Agnes, be strong. Let your faith hold you up.*

Sarah recrossed her legs with a vengeance. Matt gave her an only slightly startled glance and went back to the Forty-Niners. Or was it the Raiders?

Mom *did* stop crying. And the minute she did—the food stopped coming. Couples she and Dad used to spend time with stopped including her. Only the single women called, all with the goal of "getting her mind off of her grief."

Sarah tried to shove the rest of it into its mental drawer but as usual, it wouldn't go. Every time it came out she had to wrestle with it. *Let me get this straight: you just lost the absolute love of your life—you're so vulnerable a cross-eyed look would knock you over—you've suffered from emotional instability in the past and you can't work, so you're living on disability, and the life insurance policy your husband left you has to be used to pay some of his medical bills, and you won't get Social Security for another twelve years if there's any left—and you're supposed to help raise money for a mission in* Haiti*?*

Were they serious?

Why weren't they raising money to help her pay off what Dad's insurance didn't cover? Why didn't anyone from the church ever come over and shovel the snow from her walkways? For that matter, why didn't anybody just let the poor woman grieve?

"What's going on with you?"

Sarah turned from the side window to look at Matt. They were at a stoplight and he had his head cocked at her. The lights from the sidewalk winked playfully across his face, but his eyes were serious.

"Why?" Sarah said.

"Because you look like you're about to take somebody out." His eyebrows came together. "It's not me, is it? You want me to turn this off?"

Sarah conjured up a nose wrinkle. "It's not always about you," she said, and pulled out a smile to go with it.

Behind them a horn blared.

"I'm drivin' already," Matt said into the rearview mirror. "Can't you see we're bonding here?"

He grinned at Sarah and turned up the radio.

He'd taken some of the fire out of her conversation with herself, but a few flames still flickered.

Like the one where that one woman—what was her name? the one with the endless supply of sweater sets—had the nerve to say to Sarah's mother the Sunday after her father's funeral that she hoped she could still count on Agnes to bake five dozen cupcakes for Vacation Bible School—that it would do her good to serve others. That from the woman who hadn't so much as sent a sympathy card.

The months of going to church with her mother so Agnes wouldn't shatter into small pieces was one thing Sarah was glad to leave behind when she realized her living at home was costing her mother money she couldn't afford and moved to the studio apartment. That was when she'd learned how to keep the angry things in little drawers so she could focus on moving forward.

She just wished her mother would stop opening them.

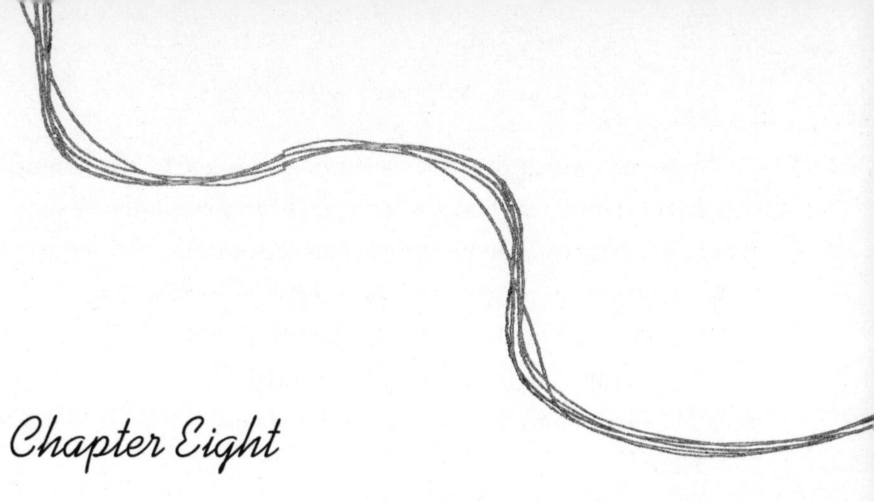

Chapter Eight

By the time Sarah pulled into the parking garage the next morning, she'd arrived at an undeniable conclusion: her mother had not sneaked jalapeños into the scalloped potatoes.

Yeah, well, duh. Two bouts of hanging over the toilet since she got up and one near miss when she wound up behind a delivery truck spewing out who knew what from its exhaust pipe? And on Day Four? That wasn't like any virus she'd ever had.

Through a tangled thread of thought, she had come to another conclusion. It had gone something like:

This is worse than when I used to get sick with my period those first couple of years.

And it's not even time for my period.

No, wait, maybe it is. I don't exactly mark it on my calendar.

So what's it been since I had one? Six weeks? Longer?

Before Halloween.

Longer.

She sat now with her head on the steering wheel and tried to snap off that thread. There was no way. Matt might be let's-live-in-the-moment about everything else, but he was religious about using condoms. And they'd only been sleeping together for a couple of months. And . . .

And oh, as her mother would say, holy bad word.

Megan tapped on the passenger window and Sarah unlocked the door. She slipped into the seat beside her and said, "More jalapeños?"

"Nope."

"That's what I thought. Come on."

"Where are we going?"

"Straight to the restroom. I picked up a little something for you on the way in."

"Not coffee," Sarah said.

"Uh, no, babe. A pregnancy test."

Sarah shook her head. "I can't be pregnant. We always use protection."

"Then if it's negative we're going straight to the nearest gastroenterologist. If you keep coming to work looking like death recycled, you can kiss that promotion good-bye."

"I didn't see that on the list," Sarah said.

The only person in the restroom was Audrey, hurrying out of a stall when they arrived.

"Are you still here, girl?" Megan said, and then pretended to inspect her makeup while Audrey washed her hands.

"I'll be here until I go into labor. My due date's the twenty-fifth." Audrey smiled her endearing overbite smile. "I'm not getting that much done, though. It seems like all I do is pee."

"Mmmm. Can't relate."

If Audrey sensed Megan's voice was devoid of sincerity, she didn't let on, but Sarah winced. She was suddenly cold all over.

"Speaking of peeing," Megan said when Audrey had waddled out, "have at it." She handed Sarah a thing that looked like a thermometer with a Q-tip at the end.

"I'm telling you," Sarah said, "I can't be—"

"So go in there and prove me wrong."

"It's probably just a waste of money."

"I hope so. Now pee on the part that looks like a sponge. You'll know in a matter of minutes."

Megan's eyes went through her. Sarah slipped into a stall.

It was just a little short of humiliating to have Megan standing out there waiting for her urine to splash into the toilet. All thoughts of embarrassment were chased out when she saw the word that came up and pointed its digital finger at her.

No.

Nonononono.

But what did *pregnant* mean besides yes? One flat, stone-hard yes.

"Well?" Megan said.

Sarah leaned her forehead against the metal door and let the cold shiver through her. Beyond that she felt nothing at all.

"I'm going to take that as an affirmative."

"Are these things ever wrong?" Sarah said.

She heard the door bang, followed by Megan slicing someone with "*Occupado*!"

That someone tried to say, "I just need to—" but Megan was obviously shoving the door closed. "I said, *occupied*!"

Sarah's first thought was, "I hope that wasn't poor Audrey." Her second was, "Now *I'm* poor Audrey."

"You can come out," Megan said.

Sarah forced herself to emerge, still holding the stick. "What's the accuracy of these things? They can't always be right."

Megan took it from her and shook her head. She suddenly seemed far more than just four years older than Sarah. And a whole lot smarter.

"Should I see a doctor or something?"

"Or something. You get to work. I'll set it up." Megan's eyes went through her again. "Don't make any lunch plans."

Sarah managed to get herself to her office with her game face on, but she tossed that mask the minute she could sit down with her back to the doorway—that same minute that she found herself face-to-face with the photo of her and Matt. Justin had snapped it at Thanksgiving when she and Matt had stolen five minutes in the hallway by the stairs at her mom's house. He'd caught them with their arms around each other, their faces bright with wonderful surprise.

I've got a real surprise for you now, Matt. But you're not going to think it's wonderful.

"Sarah?"

She jumped, knocking over the frame and a stack of folders. When she twirled her chair around, her foot caught on her briefcase, which she had unceremoniously dumped on the floor on her way in. Nice moves to make in front of Jennifer Nolte.

Jennifer's large hazel eyes were bemused. "You okay there?"

"Cramped quarters," Sarah said.

"You may not have to be saddled with this much longer."

Jennifer tucked one side of the chestnut bob behind her ear and whispered like she was passing on gossip in the girls' locker room. As she'd always done in middle-school days, Sarah leaned forward to take it in.

"I just came by to see if you have lunch plans. I'd like to take you out, discuss a few things with you." One eyebrow twitched. "Strictly off the record."

Really? *Really?*

Sarah dug up the wherewithal to pretend to look at her calendar on her phone. Then she frowned, which didn't take any pretending. "I hate that," she said. "I have an appointment at lunch. I could change it—"

"Don't do that. I know how long it can take to get in to see people." Jennifer squeezed Sarah's forearm. "I'll catch you another day."

Any day before now, Sarah would have pounced on that, suggested they set a date right then. But for the first time since she saw the word *pregnant* come into accusing view, it hit her.

This would change everything.

"You feeling okay?" Jennifer said.

"I haven't had any coffee yet," Sarah said.

"For heaven's sake. You better go fix that."

She gave Sarah a wry look and tapped away on three-inch heels. Sarah sagged in the chair. Yeah. She better go fix that.

Cherie didn't bother with calling Matt on the phone this time. She just croaked over the top of her cubicle: "Evans! Your father's on line one."

"I'm not here," Matt said.

"I'm running out of excuses, Evans."

"Tell him I'm trapped under something heavy. No, tell him I'm with an associate."

That was basically true. Wes was perched on the edge of Matt's desk, smirking.

"I'm keeping track of what you owe me," Cherie said.

"You know I'm good for it."

Her "Huh!" shook the cubicle wall.

Wes picked up Matt's rubber band ball and tossed it from hand to hand. "Man, I never turn down a call from my dad. We get to the end of the conversation and he always says, 'How's your cash flow, son? Do you need money?' "

The imitation of a doting father didn't work, not with Wes's spiky hair and his baby face. Matt shook his head.

"If my father ever said that to me, you'd have to call the paramedics because I'd go into cardiac arrest." It would be more like: *You decide to talk to me and I know you need money.* "All right, let's get serious. You got the thing I told you to get?"

"Borrowed it from my brother's garage."

"Then it is *on*." Matt lowered his voice to a rasp. "I'm snagging the keys right after lunch."

"You're a genius. So what time?"

"He usually leaves about six so—"

"Evans! It's your girlfriend. You want me to tell *her* you're trapped under something heavy?"

"No, Cherie. Put her on."

Matt nodded Wes toward the doorway and picked up the phone midway through the ring. Hand on the mouthpiece, he hissed, "See you at five."

"I can't see you at five, Matt. I don't get off until five."

Sarah's voice verged on testy. Matt sat up in the chair.

"I was talking to Wes. But I'd rather talk to you. What's up?"

"Breakfast."

"Again? Listen, you want me to take you to a doctor?"

She didn't answer.

"Sar?"

"I'm going to see one at lunch."

"I'll go with you."

"No!"

Matt felt stung.

"Sorry," she said, though she sounded less than contrite. "Megan's taking me."

Matt bit back his impulse to say, *Oh, then it must be a designer doctor you're seeing. Somebody with a foreign accent, no doubt. Dispensing snake oil.* Sarah obviously wasn't in the mood. And suddenly neither was he.

"Are you scared of what he'll say, Sar? Because you sound funky."

Actually she sounded like she wanted to pinch his head off.

"I don't know what I am, okay? I don't even know why I called."

"You called because you know I'm here for you. Okay, look, after work we'll go to the Fourth Street Grill. Whatever the doc says, that'll cheer you up."

"Cheer me up. Right." She let out a sigh so heavy Matt could feel it weighing down the phone.

"Are we on?" he said.

"I'll meet you there. Six thirty."

"Call me when you finish at the doctor, okay?"

Nothing. She'd hung up.

Matt sat there for a minute, the receiver pressed to his forehead. What just happened? That wasn't Sarah's witty edge he'd heard. That was something bordering on homicide. Except what had he done . . . besides watch the end of the game last night instead of studying for his Series Sixty-Five exam? That warranted a *Ma-att*, not an *I don't even know why I called.*

He replaced the phone and picked up the bag of sunflower seeds he was calling breakfast. She said she'd thrown up *her* breakfast. That had been going on since Friday. Matt dismissed that with his hand. He'd be cranky, too, if he puked everything he ate. This doctor of Megan's would probably tell Sarah she was just under too much stress.

Matt finally felt himself grin. He was the guru of avoiding stress. Which meant he was just what Designer Doctor was going to order.

Yeah. It was still okay.

Megan turned on the windshield wipers as the Beemer crawled from the parking garage into the snow. "We're going to a clinic in Lincolnwood," she said. "We shouldn't run into anybody we know there."

"I feel like a fugitive," Sarah said.

"We just don't want anybody knowing about this. It's none of their business."

Sarah tried not to squirm as Megan glanced at her.

"You didn't call Matt, did you?"

"Yeah."

"Did you tell him?"

The right answer to that was clearly no. Sarah was glad she could truthfully shake her head.

"I was going to, but he just wanted to cheer me up."

"You can't tell him." Megan's voice invited no argument. "At least not until you've decided what to do. It's your body, your choice. He'll only complicate things."

That last part was probably true.

"Anyway, if you decide not to have it, it's best he never even knows about it. Especially if you want to continue the relationship."

Sarah was having enough trouble believing this was happening herself. How could she expect sunny-side-up Matt to take it in? She flashed on an image of him staring at her from the latest swing set, slack-jawed and dumbfounded.

Too late. It was already complicated.

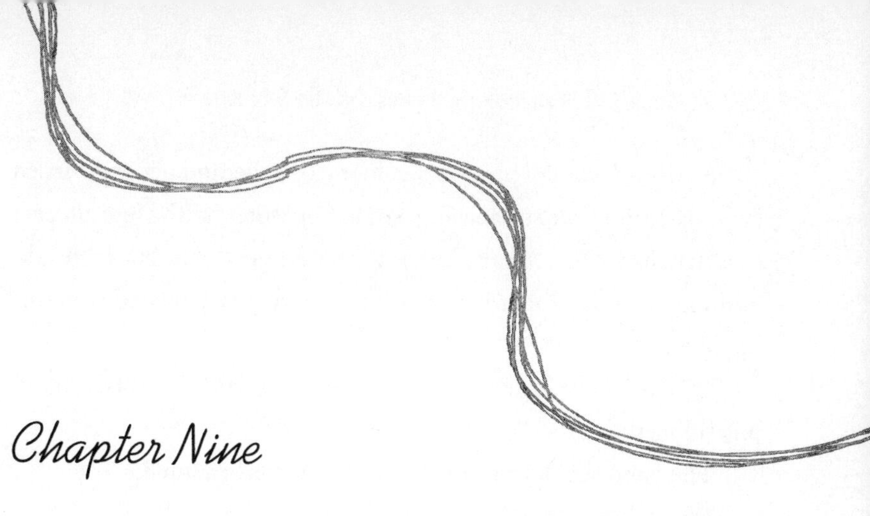

Chapter Nine

Sarah tried to uncomplicate it as she sat on the examining table in room 2 in a gown too flimsy for the cold room and her ragged nerves, waiting for someone to come in with the test results. Her legs dangled like a kid on a swing. She felt about that young and about that stupid. The poster above her head singing the praises of the morning-after pill didn't help.

If it was taking this long the results of their urine test must not match hers, right? And they were trying to figure out why she'd missed a period? That was why she'd come to the clinic anyway, to prove that state-of-the-art pregnancy test—and Megan—wrong, so she could get back to the life she'd had six hours ago.

Sarah folded her hands against her forehead. She was practically a visionary when it came to shaping the future in her mind, but whoever-it-was coming back to tell her she wasn't pregnant after all just wasn't coming into view. It got stuck somewhere between reality and the icy numbness.

"Hi, there."

A fiftyish woman pressed the door closed behind her and carried her clipboard to the stool facing Sarah. She wore a stiff white lab coat that matched a few streaks in her otherwise gray hair, but there was nothing else crisp about her. A warm, rounded face invited the sharing of angst.

"I'm Michelle," she said. Her name tag said she was a nurse practitioner.

The hand she put in Sarah's was as cozy as her smile.

"You a little tense?"

Sarah nodded.

"Well, you *are* seven weeks pregnant. I don't think that comes as a surprise." Her lips formed a pout. "And certainly not a happy one, I take it."

Sarah shook her head and willed herself not to curl into a ball.

Michelle hugged the clipboard. "Any idea what you're going to do?"

"I can't have an abortion."

Now—that *was* a surprise. How could she say it when she hadn't even thought it?

Michelle appeared unfazed. "No one is saying you should. Let's not get ahead of ourselves, okay? Have you told the father?"

The father. How much did that title not fit Matt?

"If you don't mind my asking, are you in a committed relationship?"

That depended on what she meant by committed.

"Have you discussed marriage and children?"

Sarah locked her hands at the back of her neck. All these questions with all the same answers. No. No. And no.

Michelle set the clipboard on the examining table and folded her own hands around her knees. Her voice went softer. "Okay, it's a lot to consider. Would you mind if I walked you through it?"

What Sarah wanted to walk through was the door, but she

shrugged. Shrugged. Who was this clueless Sarah who had somehow moved into her body?

Michelle nodded as if Sarah had wholeheartedly agreed. "You have the adoption option, of course, and we have literature on that if you're interested. A lot of women have trouble letting go of their babies once they see them, so I won't minimize the emotional trauma of that choice."

What was she even talking about?

"Or you can keep your baby and raise it on your own. I can give you some understanding of what you'll face there." She waited. When Sarah didn't—couldn't—respond she went on. "There's the financial aspect to consider. The average first-year cost of having a baby is sixteen thousand dollars. Now, that includes medical care, and I see that you have good health insurance."

"I do."

"So let's subtract the medical, which leaves you with about eight thousand dollars in expenses."

Sarah's head spun.

"Is your health insurance through your employer?"

"Yes."

"So you'll be able to keep that if you can maintain your job and take care of your child."

Your child—

"Do you think you can manage that?"

"I don't know, but I just know that I can't have an abortion."

Michelle had prodded the words from her this time, and now they hung in front of Sarah, clearer than before. But she still had no idea where they came from.

"May I ask why you're opposed to the procedure? Is it on religious grounds?"

"Yes," Sarah said.

Was someone else now speaking for her? Had she just agreed to *religious* grounds?

Michelle nodded, sage as a crone. "I understand. I was raised in a faith environment too . . ."

Sarah wasn't even on speaking terms with God—

" . . . but there's one thing you have to remember about the Bible: it's not a science textbook . . ."

Sarah hardened to plastic every time Agnes tried to push her back to those beliefs that had gotten her nowhere—

" . . . we know now that the fetus undergoes the entire evolutionary process, from single-cell organism to complex life form . . ."

She'd given up trying to stand on any religious grounds—

"Right now," Michelle said, pencil in hand, "the fetus is no larger than this eraser. It's just a little clump of cells." She tucked the pencil inside clasped hands and filled the air between herself and Sarah with a sympathetic sigh. "Is it alive? Of course it is. But no more alive than . . . a wart." She patted Sarah's knee. "Just something to consider as you make your decision."

Suddenly the warm, have-a-cookie smile left Sarah cold, and for the first time in the course of the conversation, she lied.

"You've been very helpful," she said.

Whatever else the woman said before Sarah got to the door morphed into empty noise. She said something about *your direction.* Sarah's only direction right now was out.

She passed the reception area where she'd checked in on a computer outside the thick glass that separated the staff from the patients. It had struck her as overkill on the way in. Now it was somehow horrifying. She got as far as the end of the hall when Megan caught up with her. She handed Sarah her coat and steered her to a corner near the elevator.

"You look like you're about to pass out," Megan said. "What—"

"A wart."

Megan searched her face. "Okay, listen to me. You've been cool ever since this morning. You don't have to lose it."

That ship had already sailed. Sarah groped for the shore. "She compared a baby to a *wart.*"

"I'm sure she compared a *fetus* to a wart."

"Are you *serious*?"

"Okay, it was a bad analogy on her part. But—"

"And she kept calling it a procedure—like it was a tummy tuck." Sarah pressed her hands to her face. "It's not a procedure, it's a . . . horrible operation."

"Sarah. *Sarah!*" Megan curled her fingers around Sarah's sleeve. "You can't let this get to you. Open heart surgery's horrible, too, but some people have to have it."

Have to? Was that what they thought: it was something she *had* to do? She always knew what she *had* to do, and she wasn't feeling that right now. What she was feeling was . . . far more than she was used to feeling. And she didn't know what to do with it.

"Let me just breathe for a minute," she said. "I need to get my head straight."

Megan bore her eyes into Sarah's. "We'll get you through this, okay? Let's go."

"Wait." Sarah felt her collar. "I left my scarf."

"Yeah, you did." Megan grimaced. "It's in the waiting room. I thought we were finally going to be rid of that thing."

"You go ahead. I'll meet you out front."

Even after the elevator doors sighed shut, Sarah stood there for a minute. Megan was right: she did have to pull it together. That was how she always confronted things—head-on, considering the facts, looking at the consequences, weighing the positives and negatives. But at the moment all she could see was the positive proclaimed with a single word on a stick.

When she was certain she could cross the hall without getting lost in her own bewilderment, she slipped into the waiting room and found Dad's scarf behind a chair. Five bucks said Megan had stuffed it there on purpose.

Sarah wrapped it automatically around her neck and paused, fingering a woebegone thread. The smell was there, but no whisper came—nothing saying, *SJ, try this—do this—*

And maybe that was a good thing. She already had enough words wrestling in her head, not the least of which was the yes she'd given to "Is this based on religious grounds?" And the "I can't have an abortion." And the "It's a horrible operation." None of that had come from any factual part of herself. And all of it threatened to get her in a half nelson and take her down right here in the hallway.

Which was probably why she didn't see the elderly woman until she almost plowed into her.

"I'm so sorry—"

Sarah steadied the old lady's arm, and with another muttered apology headed for the elevator.

"Sarah."

She stopped and turned. "I'm sorry," she said again. "Do I know you?"

She studied the woman's face as she moved toward Sarah as if it hurt to walk. This had to be someone from her mother's church. She'd stopped really looking at any of them since she couldn't do it without wanting to pluck out their nose hairs. Still, somewhere beneath the wrinkles in the tissue of this lady's skin was something familiar.

"I have something for you," the woman said.

She held out what appeared to be a Christmas card, sans envelope. That *was* familiar.

Catfish, what—are you having me followed? You would stoop to this to get the rent?

By then the woman was so close Sarah could see the fading shine in her brown eyes. She pressed the card into Sarah's hand with a trembling touch.

"Three visions," she said, voice high as if age had stolen her lower range. "The Lord will give you three visions."

Sarah looked down at the card now flattened into her palm. There was nothing there about the rent. Just a pen-and-ink drawing of the Holy Family with the three wise men gazing off into the distance. The inside was blank.

"Ma'am, I think you have—"

The wrong person died on her lips. The old woman was gone.

Sarah sagged against the wall. Okay. Get a grip. It was just a sweet old lady, suffering from dementia, who got away from her caretaker and was handing out Christmas cards and promising people visions from the Lord.

Except . . . she had known Sarah's name.

Sarah pushed the card into her coat pocket and took off for the elevator. The woman could have heard them call it out over the waiting room speaker—but she hadn't been in there then, and they'd read off "Ms. Collins."

Forget it. Just forget it. Sarah mashed the elevator button. She couldn't be trusted with anything that went through her head right now.

Megan had the car warm when Sarah climbed in. Her eyes, however, were below zero as she glared through the windshield.

"What?" Sarah said.

"The ubiquitous protestors. No wonder they have bullet-proof glass at the reception desk."

Sarah followed Megan's chilling gaze to the line of people on the sidewalk in puffy down jackets, scarves up to their noses, holding up signs that read, "It isn't a choice, it's a life," and "Don't stop a beating heart." They were the least of Sarah's worries.

But not, apparently, of Megan's.

"Why don't *you* get a life, you judgmental hypocrites?" She put a gloved finger on the window control.

"What are you doing?" Sarah said. "Megan—don't."

Megan jerked her chin up and squealed the Beemer away from the curb. Sarah clutched the seat, more from shock than fear of imminent death. Megan Hollister did not lose her cool.

"What was that about?" Sarah said when they were too far away for Megan to change her mind and hurl some epithet out the window that would land them both in court.

"I can't stand people thinking they can judge me."

Sarah blinked. "They were way more likely to be judging *me.*"

"Whatever. I'll get over it. Just give me a minute."

Megan clenched her jaw and fell into a silence that suddenly felt frightening. For the first time since Sarah had gotten into Megan's car that morning, no one was telling her what to do.

Because no one could.

Sarah tried to straighten her shoulders but they were too heavy, as if something were pressing down on them.

You cannot panic. You. Can. Not.

Think it through, SJ.

There it was—the whisper.

There's always a way to make a good choice.

Then she had no choice but to reach it.

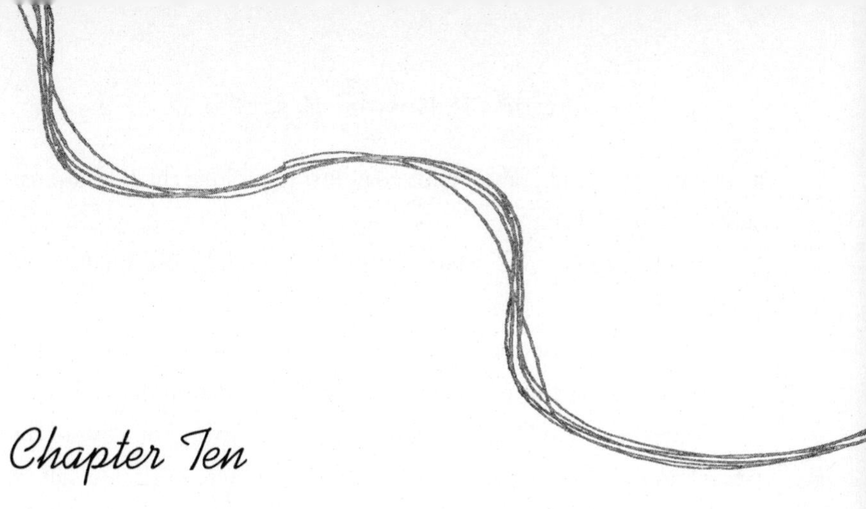

Chapter Ten

It promised to be a sweet deal.

Matt moved his uncle's Tahoe right after lunch and sneaked the keys back into Clay's coat pocket in his office while he was out at a supervisors meeting. The only person who got wise to him was Cherie. How she knew his every move when she never left her cubicle all day, who knew? But there was no way she'd out him. He could hear her snickering when he slipped back into his own cubicle and started the countdown 'til quitting time.

At six on the nose Clay poked his head into Matt's doorway and said, "You headed out?" Uncle Clay was nothing if not predictable.

"Yeah," Matt said. "And listen, I want to ask you some questions about the biz world."

"The biz world." Clay's face was deadpan. "Should I be encouraged by this or just wait for the punch line?"

"I'm totally serious."

Matt managed an all-biz look, but also took his time straightening a couple of files and grabbing his coat, just to prolong the now almost snorting from Cherie.

"See you tomorrow," Matt said to her as he followed Uncle Clay past her door.

"If you still have a job, Evans," she said.

It was Clay's turn to snicker. "The jury's still out on that, Cherie."

Once they were in the elevator, Matt pulled his phone out of his pocket and set it to camera mode. This would be too priceless not to catch it on film. Sarah was gonna love it, and with any luck it would take her mind off her stomach. He still hadn't decided whether not hearing from her after her doctor's appointment was good news or bad. He was counting on good.

"So . . . do you have a question?" Clay said. "Or should I just launch into the lecture I've been trying to give you for the last two years?"

Matt frowned at the elevator floor. "Here's the thing: how do you know who to trust in this business?"

"Simple. You trust no one. Keep your guard up—"

"Okay."

"Because the minute you let it down? Bam. They've got you by the short hairs." Clay gave Matt's face a full appraisal. "If you're serious about this, why don't we go to the Grille after work one day this week when we have more time to talk?"

"We're on."

Matt would have felt bad for letting the poor guy think he was finally getting through—if this wasn't so flippin' perfect.

The doors swished open and Clay took off out of the elevator and through the parking garage at his usual It's Miller Time pace. Miller Time, nothin'. Aunt Jerri was waiting at home with another four hours' worth of stuff for him to do. Matt felt himself grin. And it was only going to get worse in about seven months.

All the more reason to keep his uncle laughing. Which should start in about ten seconds . . .

Clay stood in front of his customary next-to-the-column parking place, which at the moment was empty.

Matt furrowed his brow, the look of concern he'd practiced in the mirror several times that afternoon. "Dude, where's your car?"

"I thought it was right here. I must've moved it after lunch."

"You went out to lunch? Without me?"

"Yeah. It's part of my live-to-be-a-ripe-old-age plan."

Matt licked his lips and watched Clay peer around the column. "I thought you *were* at a ripe old age."

"Where the devil is it—"

Camera ready . . .

"What the—"

Clay turned slowly to face Matt, the deluxe stroller Wes had snagged from his brother's garage in plain view behind him. Snap.

Priceless.

"Very funny," Clay said.

Matt's next guffaw echoed through the garage. "Not as funny as the look on your face."

But both the look and the laughter faded, and Matt found himself blinking at a weary expression he'd never seen his uncle wear.

"Y'know," Clay said, "I really didn't need this today."

Matt felt a faint sting somewhere, but he said, "Yeah, you did. I mean, c'mon, ever since Aunt Jerri told you there's another kid coming you've been walking around like Eeyore."

"Who?"

Matt grinned. "You definitely need to brush up on your Winnie-the-Pooh."

Clay's lips twitched. "And I hired you why?"

"Because you love me."

But again, the expected comeback didn't come back. Uncle Clay tilted his chin and looked at Matt as if he'd just noticed a mole growing on the end of his nose.

"Did you ever think that maybe this job isn't . . ."

He stopped.

"Isn't paying me enough?" Matt wiggled his eyebrows. "You thinking that too?"

Clay closed his eyes. "What I'm thinking is that I don't know where you got that stroller, but it's a nice one. I'm keeping it. We got rid of all our baby paraphernalia after Peter was born."

"Isn't Peter in middle school?"

"Shut up."

Clay shook his head and Matt saw the wit reappear in his eyes.

"Ya gotta admit this was classic," Matt said.

"Yeah. Classic Matt."

Matt raised both hands over his head. He'd scored. Even if Wes's brother would eventually go looking for his baby stroller.

Okay, so it hadn't gone as slick as he'd hoped. Matt sorted that out on his way to the Fourth Street Grille to meet Sarah. In spite of the *smokin'* pic he'd gotten of Clay with the stroller in the background, his uncle obviously hadn't appreciated the true hilarity of the thing. He could practically hear his father saying: *Nobody thinks you're as funny as you do.*

Nah. That wasn't it. The idea of being a father again must have thrown Clay farther than Matt realized. That was it.

He snagged the last parking space behind the Grille, next to Sarah's wreck, which he was surprised had made it. That day's spitting snow had thickened to a full-fledged storm, and the roads were like waxed glass. The minute she got that first promotion paycheck, he was going to talk her into at least getting new tires before she sailed the thing off an overpass. No wonder she'd stressed herself into an ulcer or something.

He *had* gotten Uncle Clay to lighten up a *little* with the stroller bit. Hopefully it would do the same for her. With some mild editing.

It didn't hurt that the Grille was one of Sar's favorite places. They'd gone there on their first date, if you didn't count their original rendezvous over out-of-a-machine cappuccinos in the break room at Carson the day they met. The Grille was always crammed with people their age, grabbing beers or burgers after a day of trying to make it and convincing themselves things would get better. A hockey game on the TV above the bar and Sarah across the table in a back booth—who wouldn't believe things were *already* better?

Sarah was in their usual spot, staring at a ginger ale. That didn't bode well for a decent report on the stomach thing. But he couldn't read anything in her face, which left him with a blank slate to draw on. First some laughs, then the diagnosis.

He kissed her cheek, making sure to get a little maddening snow on her hair, and hung his coat on the hook. Her arms were folded like she was freezing, which meant she probably hadn't been waiting that long, but an apology still made a nice segue.

"Sorry I'm late, Sar, but when I tell you why you're gonna love it." He slid into the booth. "Okay, so I told Uncle Clay I wanted to talk to him about the business world, so we walk to the parking garage together and he's, like, holding forth about"—Matt slipped into Uncle Clay—"never trust anyone because once you let your guard down, bam, they've got you." Matt's shoulders shook. "By this time we're in the garage and he's going, 'Where's my car?'"

He paused but Sarah just stared at him, two lines etched between her eyebrows like ditto marks. He went on.

"And he looks, and there's a baby stroller parked in his space instead of his car. The look on his face . . ." Matt sobered deliberately. "It was classic."

The look on Sarah's, however, was not. The lines deepened.

"That was meant to be funny?"

"Yeah. It was very funny."

Nothing.

"Okay, you had to be there."

"What if you were in Clay's position? Would that joke be funny to you?"

"Well, first of all"—Matt made an attempt to laugh—"I would never *be* in Clay's position."

Sarah's pause was interminable. She leaned back and closed her eyes and breathed until Matt's grin sank into his chest. Okay, so it was an ulcer. Or worse.

"Sar?" he said. "What?"

She opened her eyes and spoke in a voice so low Matt almost had to crawl across the table to hear.

"Guess what?" she said. "You *are* in his position."

"I don't—"

"I'm pregnant. *We're* pregnant. Seven weeks."

Matt had to hand it to her, if this was a joke, it was a good one. He felt like he'd been knocked against a wall.

"Say something, Matt!"

His mouth was paralyzed. She'd gone from inaudible to full-out explosion in a matter of seconds. This was no joke, and all he could get out was the disbelief that had frozen his brain.

"Are you sure?"

"*What?*" Sarah's voice was strangled. "What kind of question is that? Of course I'm sure!"

"You can't exactly spring this on me and expect a coherent response. I mean—"

"Then let *me* be coherent. There are only a couple of options, Matt." Sarah's fingers were tight, as if she wanted to claw her face. Or his. "I don't know how to say this except—you can give me one of two things: a wedding ring or a ride to the clinic."

"The clinic?"

Matt knew he was grasping at the unraveled strings of whatever was barely holding her together, but what else *was* there to grab onto? He sure couldn't hold Sarah at this point. She was turning into someone else right in front of him.

"Just give me a minute, okay? This wasn't part of the plan, so—"

"What plan?" she said. "I didn't know there was a plan."

"Look—I can see us together permanently, but not yet. I didn't think we were ready. You've got to give me a chance for this to sink in."

There was no chance in the clawed fingers and the choked-back voice and the tears she was fighting like a she-lion. In a year and a half he had never seen her this close to crying.

"Well, ready or not, we're there," she said.

Before he could say anything else pointless, Sarah jerked herself out of the booth and wove through the happy-hour crowd toward the exit.

Matt followed, blindly avoiding a collision with a tray of drinks and elbowing indignant ribs to get to her. By the time he reached the parking lot, she was almost to her Toyota. She didn't stop when he called to her.

"Sar, come on—"

"Leave me alone, Matt." She yanked the car door open, cracking ice and sending it flying in jagged directions. "Just leave. Me. Alone."

The words were almost lost in the sobs, but not their meaning. Matt stood helplessly as she slammed the door and cranked the weary engine to a start. Snow soaked his shirt and plastered the back of his neck but he couldn't move, even when she'd chugged the car out of the lot.

He told himself it probably wouldn't have mattered what he'd said, even if he could have thought of anything different. He should have seen she was wrecked when he sat down. He should've been able to fix it. He'd always been able to fix it with Sarah.

Bottom line, his father would be saying right now, *you screw it up, you fix it.*

Matt closed his eyes and let the thick flakes catch on his eyebrows. It wasn't okay. At all.

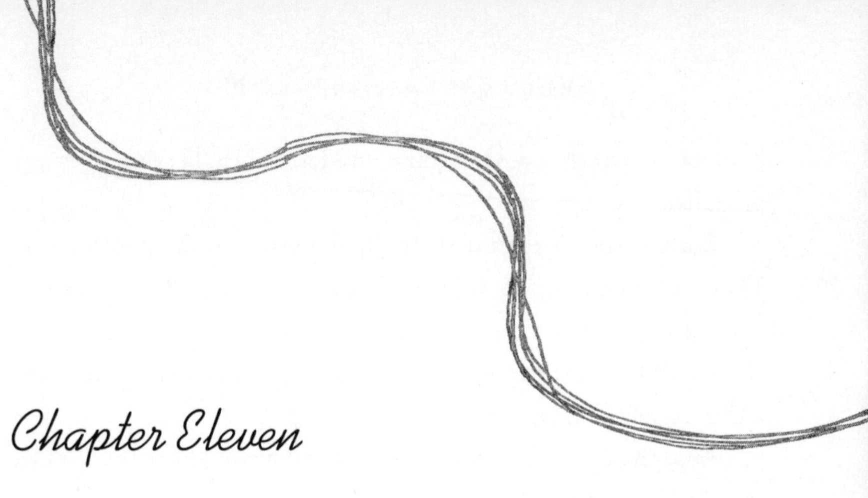

Chapter Eleven

Sarah didn't even check for Catfish when she half-ran from the car up to her apartment, the snow biting at her face like frozen fangs. All the more reason not to cry anymore. New tears would only turn to ice trails on her cheeks.

Inside she leaned against the door, eyes closed, and let everything that was too much melt away.

Too much arguing.

Too much waffling.

Too much . . . feeling.

When she'd thawed enough to pull off her scarf, she folded it with the deliberation of a flag at a funeral and pressed it hard against the kitchen counter top. The whispers she counted on were silent.

Sarah shook off her coat and hooked it on the overloaded peg. She had to get a grip on this. She couldn't make a decision based on how she felt at any given moment because that changed every time she blinked her eyes. Only one thing was clear, at least in this blink-of-an-eye: she couldn't count on Matt to help her decide. It was up to her.

But she sagged against the wall. She was probably too hard on Matt. No, there was no probably about it. She was. The anger had just burst open its drawer and clawed right at his face before she could stop it. That hadn't happened since the day her life was wrecked like a five-car collision on the Ike.

Anger had gotten her nowhere then, and it wouldn't now. She had to go with her strengths. That was somewhere on the list.

Sarah headed for the computer and slid on something on the floor. Already wishing Catfish a hideous attack of food poisoning, she realized it wasn't a rent notice but the three wise men staring off into space. The card must have fallen out of her coat pocket.

Speaking of weird. She tossed it toward the wastebasket.

She had to get to something that made actual sense.

But first she forced herself to get into pajamas and brush her teeth before she went for the computer. The idea was to get sleepy and fall into bed and not think about any of this after she got the information she needed to make a logical decision. There had to be one, right?

The idea that there might not be came at her like an arrow, but she dodged it and carried her laptop to her desk.

Two layers of late notices had to be shoved out of the way before she could even set the thing down, and that nettled at her. Good *grief,* this was a mess. No wonder she was confused: everything around her was in chaos. After finally finding a horizontal space for the computer, she pressed her hands to her temples. One thing at a time. That had to be on the list someplace too. Although *not* doing it that way would never have entered Megan's mind.

Neither would getting pregnant without the benefit of, oh, you know . . . a *husband.*

Sarah dodged that, too, and googled "abortion facts." The first site she clicked on announced that here she could see early fetal development.

"In other words, a wart," she said to the screen.

If that Michelle woman was right, she'd see no brain. No limbs. Just a clump of cells. It couldn't hurt to see that for herself.

Since the site gave week-by-week options, she clicked on seven weeks. Her phone vibrated on the desk. A text from Matt.

Actually several, each one more imploring than the one before it and the last one reading, *I'm coming over.*

Sarah squeezed the phone in her hand. She could still see his face, the way he looked at the Grille when she threw the whole thing in his face like a drink, ice and all. The shocked confusion made him seem more than ever like a little boy lost on the playground. And although that wrenched at her now, how was the next conversation going to go, when she didn't know any more now than she did an hour ago? She didn't want to scream at him again, and she couldn't be sure she wouldn't until that drawer was slammed shut and locked.

Don't, she texted him back. *We'll talk tomorrow.*

When the phone vibrated again, she turned it off and went back to the laptop screen, which now showed a round pink being that looked more human than she'd expected.

"'Arms and legs stretch out more and more,'" she read out loud to no one. "'Brain is developing.'"

That wasn't the picture the NP had painted for her. She definitely hadn't told her the lenses of the eyes were appearing. Sarah put her finger close to her own eye. That kind of detail was already happening? Something that tiny and real? And functional?

Sarah turned the image to see its small pink profile and caught her breath.

"You don't look like a wart to me," she whispered to it.

Okay, stop. Just. Stop.

It had been a long, exhausting, gutting day and she wasn't thinking any more clearly than Matt was. She needed sleep. She could almost hear her father saying what he'd always said when she wrestled with some tween-girl issue at bedtime: "Everything always makes more sense after you've let it rest." Then he would launch into "Tomorrow" from *Annie* until she begged him to stop without meaning a word of it.

She wasn't sure how this could make any more sense tomorrow than it did today, but she headed for the bed anyway. En route, she stepped on the wise men card again. She must have missed the trash can. The thing was more ubiquitous than Megan's protestors.

She was too tired to try to get it into the trash again, so she propped it on the bedside table and dropped into bed. She probably wouldn't be able to sleep, but she'd give it an hour . . .

In some amount of time she couldn't grasp, the edges of all she could see were framed in a faint amber light. Inexplicably she was at her mother's house, stripping off her coat and scarf in the hallway and calling out to Mom, who called back, "We're in here, Mommy." A baby was crying.

Sarah pressed her hand against the wallpaper. Its stripes were real. The smell of cheesy potatoes was real. The insistent wails of a tiny person were real. Maybe even more than real. Vibrant. That was the word.

"Mom?" Sarah said.

"There she is, sweetie. I told you she'd be back."

Sarah found her mother in the dining room by the window, arms around a bundle of pink that waved its protesting mini-fists.

"Daisy and I were starting to get worried about you," Mom said. "Were the roads bad?"

"Roads?" Sarah said. "What roads?" She didn't even know how she'd gotten there.

"Are you all right, honey?" But then Agnes didn't wait for an answer. She beamed instead at the squalling baby. "Daisy needs to be changed. You take her and I'll take your coat. Do you want some tea?"

Sarah couldn't even give her a head shake. Agnes deposited the infant—whose name apparently was Daisy—into Sarah's stiff arms and bustled happily through the swinging door to the kitchen.

Sarah stared at the baby, into the tiny scrunched eyes and the miniature tears and the red bow of a mouth that pouted between wails. "Mom, why do *I* have to change her?"

Agnes pushed the door back open a few inches and laughed through the crack. "Well, she's *your* baby. I'm just doing the grandmother things."

My baby?

Sarah bounced the baby girl, for lack of anything better to do. When that did nothing to quell the squalls, she tried patting. Unlike Denise, she'd never babysat as a teenager and she'd been away at college when her nephews were little babies. She'd definitely never changed a diaper in her life.

But somebody had, because there was a complete set-up on the dining room table. She had a master's degree, right? She could do this.

Her baby, though? Had she missed something? Something big—like an entire pregnancy, labor, and delivery—and about two months of this little thing's life? No wonder Daisy and Nana had wondered where she was.

When Daisy let out the ultimate scream, Sarah had to do something, even if it was wrong.

She laid the baby gingerly on the table on what appeared to be some kind of mat. There were tabs on either side of the diaper. Those obviously had to be pulled back, and . . .

The instant the soaking thing was pulled off, little Daisy stopped crying and peered at Sarah through tear-clouded eyes.

"I'd be crying, too, if my pants were that wet," Sarah said. "Ooh, not a good image."

It apparently worked for the baby because she locked onto Sarah with a trusting gaze.

"Don't put too much faith in me yet," Sarah said. "I have no idea what I'm doing."

One thing she knew: she wouldn't want to be put into dry clothes while her skin was still damp with her own . . . yeah. Those things in the plastic container looked like the wipes she used to clean her counters. On the rare occasion when she actually cleaned.

She pulled one out and eased it over the pink skin. If she wasn't mistaken, the baby sighed. Fighting off the thought that she was probably mistaken about this whole crazy thing, Sarah searched the table for the next step. The baby's eyes still tracked her, so Sarah kept talking.

"All right, the air's really dry so some lotion should feel good . . . here we go . . . don't need to hold it at such a high altitude . . . a little powder because I remember seeing that on a commercial . . . okay, probably not that much, we're not baking a pie here . . . not that I would know how to do that either."

Now to try to operate the diaper. She should have paid more attention to how the other one was put on.

"You'll let me know if I get this on backward, won't you?"

Daisy's eyes widened.

"I'll try not to . . . I'm just warning you . . . but I think I've got it. Yikes. We did it."

Sarah heard herself giggle, not a sound that came out of her mouth often, but it seemed to be a sound the baby liked. She searched Sarah's face with her dark little eyes, and then she smiled, faint and fleeting.

"Was that a smile?" Sarah said. "Was it real?"

Was it real?

Was it?

Sarah hugged the baby close to herself, but she was too soft, too squishy . . . because she was Sarah's extra pillow. She sat up in bed—not in her mother's house, but her own apartment. The first of dawn teased through the slats of the blinds. The amber frame was gone.

For somebody who didn't think she could sleep, she'd gone off somewhere deep and had a dream so vivid she couldn't believe she wasn't still standing in her mom's dining room holding a—her—baby.

As soon as she was finished throwing up, she was going to get back on the Internet to find out if bizarre dreams were part of pregnancy. Fighting down last night's soda, she climbed out of bed. Her eyes lit on that Christmas card she couldn't seem to get rid of—

Sarah heard her breath catch. "No. Way," she whispered.

Those three wise men had all been staring off camera yesterday. She knew they had. That was the one thing she'd noticed about the drawing.

But now, one of them was looking straight at her, eyebrows raised.

She moved the card, thinking she'd missed something before. Some drawings were made to change when you wiggled them.

That didn't happen. The first wise guy was still staring at her when she dropped the card and ran for the bathroom. And then she was definitely going back to that website. Forget weird dreams. Was certifiable craziness a symptom?

Matt switched off the first of the three alarms he always set to get him up every work morning. He didn't need it today. He didn't need any of them because he'd been awake all night. He hadn't done that since college when he was always disappointed that parties had to end at dawn. Back then the only six o'clock he knew was p.m.

That didn't seem all that funny anymore.

Nothing did.

Matt abandoned the beanbag chair and made his way through the dark to the kitchen. He didn't need intravenous coffee to wake up either, but maybe if he did some things the way he always did them, the things that were never going to be the way he always did them wouldn't freak him out so much.

He turned on the faucet and stuck the coffee pot under it. That was the one—the only thing—that became clear to him somewhere between 2:00 and 4:00 a.m.: most of what he'd thought was his life would never be the same again.

Not the confidence that he could fix anything if he could only find the punch line.

Not the belief that other people made life a whole lot harder than it had to be.

Not the idea that there was plenty of time to settle down and get serious later. That now was the time to be young and free and spontaneous.

And stupid.

Matt felt something cold on his hand. The coffee pot was overflowing its contents down the gurgling drain. He shut off the faucet and stared into the sink.

Sarah never believed any of that. He'd known it, but not how wide the gap really was between her system and his. Until 4:00 a.m. he thought he could still bridge it. She just needed time to get her head together. She said in her last text they would talk today.

But when that dark-before-dawn deepened and Matt was still awake, still searching for the button to push to cheer her up, the last truth hit him, the truth that crawled along his skin until he found himself in a cold sweat.

He couldn't cheer his Sar out of this one. And without the ability to do that, what did he have to offer her?

Looking at it again, now, with the gray light intruding under a bent slat in the blinds, it seemed even more stark and true.

And for the first time, so did his father's ever-nagging words: *Grow up or give up. It's time to choose.*

It was the only time he'd ever thought his father was right. About anything.

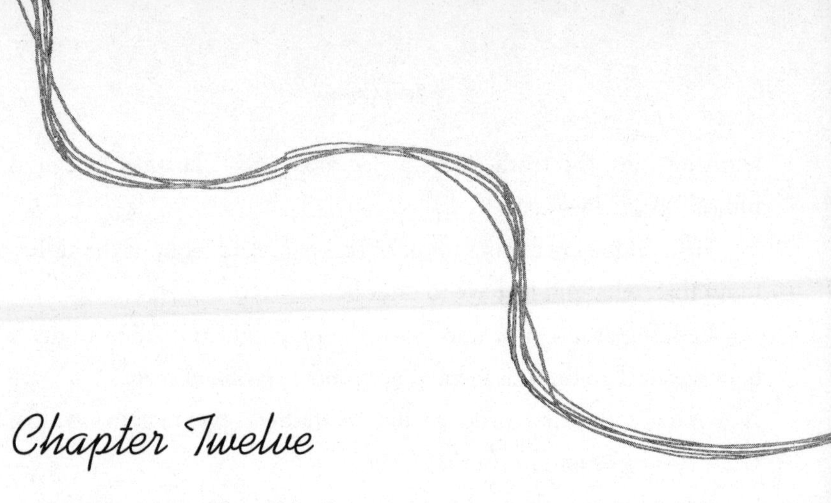

Chapter Twelve

Buzz Lightyear chose that morning to stay in hibernation. The fact that Sarah flooded the engine by furiously pumping the gas pedal only deepened the Toyota's determination to remain comatose.

So she took the train, which deepened her *stomach's* determination to spew its contents into the paper bag she had at the ready. The only saving grace was there was nothing left *to* spew. She gagged quietly and miserably until she got off at North Michigan and took the stairs to her office to avoid human contact. When she finally reached her desk, she dug into her briefcase for the crackers the Internet suggested she nibble on to stem the tide.

Surprisingly, it worked.

When she was calm enough, at least physically, to open her mail, she found a hand-written note with the letters JN embossed on the front. What was with the cards: Catfish, the senile woman at the clinic, and now Jennifer Nolte? Jennifer, the very one who'd said,

"You'd think they never heard of e-mail." Since it probably wasn't an eviction notice or a vision from the Lord, Sarah opened it.

I wanted to tell you this in person at lunch yesterday, Jennifer had written in cursive worthy of having a font named after it. *But since we couldn't get together, here it is—*

Sarah closed her eyes. Was this how they told you they'd given the promotion to someone else? Had they found *out—*

Okay, stop. The only people who knew were Matt and Megan, and neither one of them would chat it up with Jennifer. Pregnancy was definitely messing with her brain. She focused on the card.

Although your skills and creative ideas are enough to land you this promotion in my opinion, you would also bring considerable integrity to the table. That is a rare trait that would raise the quality of this company as a whole—

Sarah stopped reading again.

How was it that the same words—which two days ago would have wrapped themselves around her like an 800-thread-count down comforter—now slapped her across the face?

Integrity?

Where was that when she fell into bed with Matt without giving possible pregnancy a thought beyond, *You have the condoms? Great.*

Why hadn't she thought, *Gee, how will I pay Dad's bills if I have to take time off to have a* baby? Where was this so-called integrity then?

Her desk phone rang. Sarah slid the card from Jennifer under a stack of files and picked up.

"You need to come to my office," Megan said—in lieu of "Hi-how-are-ya?"

"When?" Sarah said. "I really need to start—"

"Now. It'll take five minutes."

Megan hung up before Sarah could tell her she didn't have five minutes. She stared at the pile of folders. The key to getting on top of this thing was what she'd always done before: lose yourself in those—get focused on the work—stay on one thing at a time.

And she was supposed to do that how? With this decision ripping open every drawer and dumping their contents out into one hopeless pile?

Maybe it did make sense to try to sort it through with Megan. Seriously, who else did she have to talk to about this?

Not Matt. Not yet.

Megan was in the doorway when Sarah got there and she closed the door, and locked it, behind her. She nodded at a steel-and-black-leather chair, but Sarah shook her head. It felt a little like martial law had set in, and she bristled. Megan didn't seem to notice as she leaned against the front of her glass-topped desk. Her hair was swept almost cruelly into a bun, which made her look like she was bordering on militant.

"So have you made a decision?" she said.

Sarah shook her head.

Megan nodded hers. "I knew it was going to be hard for you. I've been thinking about this ever since yesterday, and I think I can help you get things in perspective."

Sarah sat in the chair after all. "I could use some perspective. I don't usually get this confused over things."

"I can totally understand that. And you've got to take into consideration that your hormones are out of control right now."

That might explain the dreams. Maybe Megan's take-charge attitude *was* what she needed.

"Yesterday we just talked about your career and how having a baby was basically going to wreck it. But I think you need to consider that keeping this kid could also ruin your entire *life*."

Sarah opened her mouth but Megan said, "Just hear me out."

She reached behind her and produced her phone, which she proceeded to thumb. "What's the rent at that dump you're living in?"

"I wouldn't call it a dump, exactly."

"Trust me, it's a dump. What's the rent?"

"Eight hundred a month."

"Is it big enough for you and a baby?" Megan pulled her chin down to look at Sarah. "Take into consideration a crib, a swing, a changing table, a stroller, a dresser—"

"Okay, no. It's not."

"Which means you'll have to move to a bigger place, so let's double that rent." She thumbed in numbers.

"The woman at the clinic already said it would cost me eight thousand dollars the first year."

"Was she including the increase in rent? Day care? A new car?" Megan lifted one side of her mouth. "Are you seriously going to drive a baby around in that heap?"

Heap. Dump. It was like seeing her life boiled down to a junkyard.

"All right," Sarah said. "I get that it would be expensive."

"Not to mention completely confining. How often do you go to the Grille after work?"

"A couple of times a week."

"You going to take an infant in there?"

"No, but—"

"Your dining-out menu is always going to be on a board you read while you're standing in line with a kid on your hip. And forget sleeping. Do you have any idea how many times a night a newborn wakes up?"

"Do you?" Sarah heard the irritation in her own voice, and she didn't quite care.

"Not from personal experience, but I've seen enough post-maternity-leave women drag themselves in here in the morning with bags under their eyes they'd have to check at the counter if they were boarding a flight. And their productivity?" She turned a thumb downward. "In the toilet. Which means no promotions. No raises. No chance that their lives are ever going to get any better." Megan's eyes narrowed. "And, Sarah, those women had husbands."

"Why don't you just say it? You think I should have an abortion."

"I think you should have an abortion."

Again the words she had no plans to say came out: "I can't see myself doing it."

Megan took the chair across from Sarah and reached over the space between them to put her hand on Sarah's. It was as cool as everything else about her.

"Number ten on the list: 'The more you resist something, the more likely it is that it's exactly what you need.'"

She squeezed Sarah's hand and almost smiled at her.

Sarah wilted. "I'm not going to say that doesn't all make sense, because it does. But last night—"

"You talked to Matt, didn't you?"

"This was after that."

"I thought you weren't going to tell him until you decided what to do."

Actually it was *Megan* who thought that, but Sarah pushed that aside. "This weird thing happened. Just . . . just tell me what you think about it."

Megan shrugged and leaned back in her chair, arms folded. "Go for it."

"Yesterday at the clinic this woman gave me a card."

"Right. The number to call to set up your appointment for the—"

"No, this wasn't somebody who worked there. It was this older woman who looked familiar . . . anyway, she handed me a Christmas card and said the Lord was going to give me three visions."

Megan broke her own rule and rolled her eyes.

"That's what I thought too," Sarah said. "But last night when I went to bed, I had one."

"One what?"

"A vision. I thought it was a dream. Maybe it was. But it was more real than a dream. And there was this baby—"

Megan put a hand up. "Okay, stop. You can't let these religious people get to you. You're the one who's always complaining because your mother tries to shove the whole church thing down your throat."

"I know. But this—"

"Was a dream. Like I said, your hormones are totally off the charts. You can't make a decision like this based on something your messed-up body chemistry tells you. I don't even go *shopping* when I have PMS."

Sarah stood up. "I have to get to work."

"Just think about what I'm saying to you, all right?"

Sarah wasn't sure how she could think of anything else unless she got out of there. And right now that was what she had to do, before she melted down all over Megan's glass-topped desk.

"Sarah?"

She stopped, hand on the doorknob. Megan's voice was low.

"I admit my motives are partly selfish. I don't want you to leave Carson. You're the only friend I have here."

Once she was out in the hall, Sarah had to go anyplace but her tiny office where the tasks that were supposed to raise her to a new level would press down on her. That level seemed so far out of reach now, the only place she wanted to go was out.

She rounded a corner in the labyrinth of cubicles and spotted the glass door exit to the outdoor courtyard. Not even the smokers ventured out there when the temperatures dropped into the single digits, but Sarah headed for it now and let herself out. Frigid air cut into her face and seeped through the sleeves of her sweater, and she had to hug her body with her arms to get her breath. It hung in solid puffs before her as she walked, cold-stiff, to the latticework that shielded the courtyard from the city below.

Sarah clutched the diamonds of the wood lattice with her fingers and stared through the openings. Buses groaned and passed. Taxis honked and jockeyed for position in the traffic. People crossed the street in overcoats and lamb's wool scarves pulled over their noses and went about their business because they could. They weren't trying to make decisions that would haunt them forever like howling wolves, no matter what they chose.

Heaviness pushed down on Sarah's shoulders, the same heaviness she felt in the car the day before, when Megan fell silent and she was alone with the choice. Today she could name that heavy thing.

It was loneliness.

Sarah pressed her forehead against the frosty wood and let the cold shudder through her. Come to think of it, this pressure, this burden heavy as a load of cement blocks, wasn't new. She'd felt it with her family, even Denise. It had always been that way with Megan.

Even with Matt, the sense that she wasn't connected weighed on her.

But never long enough for her to give it a name this way. She always managed to shrug it off. Or pretend she could handle it. Or work so hard that surely it would be taken from her.

Below, the unmistakable sound of a car sliding on ice brought her attention back to the street. Snow was falling again, the thick powdery kind. Her dad called that skiin' snow. He didn't even have to ask if she wanted to go to Wilmont Mountain. He just loaded the skis on top of the Jeep and pulled his Cubs cap over his mass of hair so that the waves stuck out like wings, and grinned at her.

Sarah was the only person in the family who loved the slopes like he did. She was never sure whether she actually enjoyed skiing or just wanted to be alone with him. She mastered the higher, steeper hills because that meant more time together on the lift, dangling their ski-fitted feet and talking about things that only being in midair brought to mind.

Like the deepening God-questions they could only discuss when her mother wasn't there to pat her on the head and tell her all she needed was faith.

His encouraging her to keep talking about love, not rules. To keep asking why not instead of why. To keep praying what was honest. To keep listening.

It was that last conversation on the lift, just before the diagnosis, that was clearest right now.

"I know you have to go back to New York, SJ." He always called her by her initials; he said she'd been businesslike since she was two and that it fit. "But I'll miss you."

"I'll miss you too, Dad." She remembered now trying to turn sideways to look at him and swaying the lift chair. "But when I finish this degree and get myself established, I *am* going to help you start your own firm. Enough with working your buns off for somebody else to have it all. I'll do all your marketing."

"You've always had big dreams."

"This isn't a dream. You're talented, Dad, and there's so much you could do with that."

He'd tilted her chin with his gloved fingers. "And you always make me feel like anything is possible."

"It is."

"We'll see. I'm still praying about it. Ultimately that decision is up to God—"

Sarah pulled away from the lattice and folded her arms hard across her chest. It could be anger again. It could be the sharpening cold, but something shivered through her. She started for the door and found she could hardly move for the heaviness and the stiffness and all the other things that kept her from running.

Maybe coming out here was a stupid move. But it made her recognize one thing. Deciding for yourself was a lonely business.

And it was a business she'd been in for three long years.

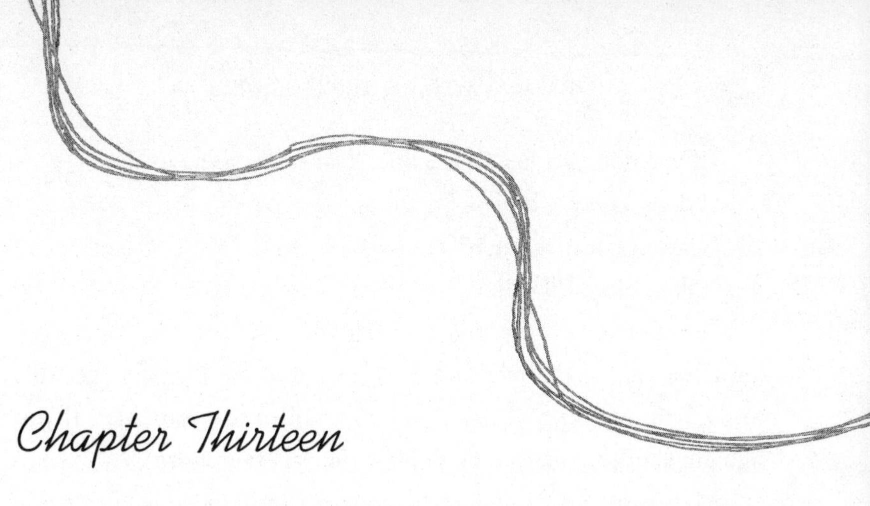

Chapter Thirteen

Matt was still putting off calling Sarah after lunch, although all morning he waited for Cherie to tell him she was on the line. She never was. Every time he came back from the restroom he paused outside Cherie's cubicle and said, "Any calls for me?" He did it so many times she finally said, "Did you ever think of calling *her*?"

"Who?" Matt said.

"Your girlfriend."

"How do you know that's who I'm waiting for?"

"Because you sure aren't anxious to hear from your parents. Who else calls you, Evans?"

She was right. No one else called him. No one else checked in either to tell him he was a useless excuse for a human being or make him feel like the only human being who could be of any use at all.

He sank heavily into his desk chair and parked his forehead on the heels of his hands. The chair squeaked as he rocked back and forth.

"If you don't get her on the line, Evans, I'm going to."

"I don't know, Cherie—"

"Carson Creative, right?"

"Okay, okay, I'll call."

"I'm putting on my headphones so I can't hear you. You've got until the end of the overture to *Phantom of the Opera* to get this worked out with her." Cherie's voice dwindled to a grumble. "If you sigh any harder, you're going to blow the partition down . . ."

Matt turned his back on the doorway and tapped Sarah's name on his cell. He alternated prayers—*Please let her pick up. Please just get me to her voice mail. Please let her pick up—*

"Hi," she said.

Matt almost cried. He swallowed hard.

"Hi, Sar. Are you—how are you feeling?"

"What about you?"

He stood up, turned around, turned back around. There wasn't room to pace.

"How am *I* feeling?" The honest answer was *terrified*, but he didn't think that was what she wanted to hear.

"I mean . . . have you made a decision?"

This time it didn't sound like she really expected an answer, which was a good thing because he didn't have one. He'd been thinking about nothing else all night and all day, and he knew partly what he wanted to say—but that edge in her voice, that un-Sarah-like bite threw him off balance, just like it had the night before.

"Don't make this all my decision, okay?" he said. "We can sit down and talk about it like responsible adults."

"I'm not sure we can even do that—"

"I don't want you to have an abortion."

Her pause was short. "Is that a proposal, then?"

Matt actually pulled the phone away from his ear and looked at it. This could not be his Sarah.

"I hate sounding like this, Matt," she said. "But I don't see what other options there are besides the two I gave you last night. Do you?"

"Yeah."

Her silence this time was long enough for him to rush on.

"You could have the baby, and we could give it up for adoption."

"As simple as that."

"I didn't say it was simple—"

"I can't even talk about this with you right now. Just . . . I have to go."

The phone went dead. So did Matt. *Consider thinking before you open that mouth,* his father would say. What a concept.

He knew he'd sounded like a dolt, and he couldn't let her go the rest of the day thinking he was—

His desk phone rang and he grabbed it.

"Look, I know I sounded like a jerk—"

"Matt?"

His mother's indignant punch of a voice shoved him into his chair. A bad day just got a whole lot worse.

"Matthew, is that you?"

"Yeah, Mom. Sorry."

"Do you always answer your business phone that way?"

Only when my life is circling the drain. Matt squeezed the receiver. "Look, Mom, I'm in the middle of something right now."

"I think you can take two minutes to tell us whether you're coming home for Christmas."

No matter what words Jolene Evans used, there was a demand tucked into every syllable. Unlike his father, who shot orders like they were coming from an AK-47, his mother had a full arsenal of less obvious weapons, everything from the Evans Family Standard that had to be upheld to her chart of illnesses, most of them imaginary. Today she'd chosen a guilt trip. Matt was a seasoned traveler when it came to his mother's guilt.

"Your *sisters* are both coming," she said. "If two *doctors* can get away—well, make that four, because Jarred and Bradley are coming, too, of course—then surely an investment assistant can tear himself away."

Matt didn't even try to interject.

"Your father wants the whole family together, Matt. He isn't getting any younger."

The man was sixty-one and never missed a day on a tennis court. She was projecting her pseudo illnesses onto him. Matt still didn't try to poke a stick in the spokes.

"And we're giving a party Christmas Eve. We've invited some people you should know. We're grateful to Clay for getting you started, but he doesn't have the connections your father does."

Matt stiffened. "Connections for what?"

"For better jobs, Matt. Possibly here. Or New York—

"No."

"You're saying no without giving it a chance."

She'd flipped the switch from guilt to accusation. He suddenly didn't care if she went with fingernails and teeth.

"I'm saying no to Christmas."

"You're not coming home? Is that what I'm hearing?"

"That's what you're hearing. I can't do it right now."

"You're going to have to explain that."

The light on the phone flashed.

"I've got another call coming in."

"You can take five minutes—"

"No. I can't."

Matt broke the connection and pressed line two.

"You owe me big-time, Evans," Cherie croaked.

"I do," Matt said.

That was the first time he had been honest with his mother since . . . ever. He'd charmed her, avoided her, and even lied to her to get out of whatever slot she tried to file him into. But he couldn't remember ever telling her the truth. For all the good it did. He'd be hearing from his father before the day was out.

He couldn't even think about that. The panic that had started to surge through him when Sarah hung up rose in him again. He pressed icy hands against the back of a clammy neck.

Okay, so blurting out an idea like "Hey, let's go with adoption" didn't work. Getting her to see the bright side didn't either, as if there was one.

He knew what not to do. But he still had no clue what *to* do.

Maybe this was also the first time he'd been honest with himself.

And the way it cut into him . . . no wonder he'd never done it before.

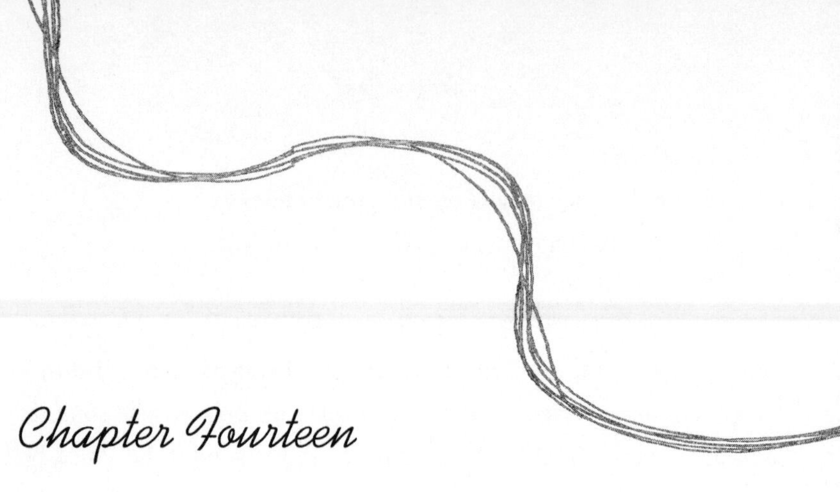

Chapter Fourteen

The next three days seemed less real to Sarah than the vision or the dream or whatever that was she'd experienced in her sleep. Diapering what was supposedly her baby was still bright and real and framed in light in her mind. But the things that posed as reality smeared across her brain like a finger painting.

She texted Matt after Tuesday's phone conversation and asked him not to call her again until she contacted him. She missed him, missed them together, missed the way he could reshape the circumstances until they bore no resemblance to anything real. That wouldn't work this time, and the realization that Matt couldn't give her any more than that was one layer of pain she couldn't handle.

Whether it was that or the saltines she'd just tried to eat, she didn't know, but the urge she'd learned not to ignore drove her out of her cubicle and down the hall. She barely made it to the nearest bathroom stall, and it wasn't until she turned to leave it that she realized she hadn't taken the time to latch the door.

She nearly slammed right into Audrey.

She was at the sink with her back to Sarah, but their eyes met in the mirror as Sarah stumbled across the floor. She considered skipping the hand washing, but since her aim hadn't been that good . . .

"Hey," Sarah said.

"Hey, Sarah," Audrey said. She tapped out what appeared to be her second helping of soap from the dispenser.

Sarah gave up any attempt to cover how miserable she was and splashed water on her face, right on top of her makeup. When she reached for a stiff paper towel, Audrey was still scrubbing. Sarah was surprised her hands didn't shrivel.

Okay, awkward. She really ought to say something. She decided on: "I'm sorry if I grossed you out. I just can't get rid of this bug I've had."

Sarah caught a glimpse of herself in the mirror. The words *I'm lying* might as well have been printed on her forehead.

Audrey finally dried her hands and headed for the restroom door. Sarah was just about to dive back into the stall when Audrey turned and said, "If you ever need a place to hide, my office has a door."

Can I go there right now*?* Sarah wanted to call after her. But the last person she needed to talk to was the person she was trying to replace. And a pregnant person at that.

But hiding. That sounded so good. Jennifer invited Sarah out to lunch on Wednesday, and despite her desire to do anything *but* eat, Sarah accepted. At least they went to a salad place a few blocks down that didn't reek of fried anything and had no pictures of greasy entrées on the walls. Just like everything else that Jennifer Nolte seemed to choose, it was tastefully understated and cost more per bite than Sarah made in a day.

"This is on me," Jennifer said when they were seated with bowls full of things Sarah never would have thought to put on a salad.

"That's nice of you," Sarah said. "But really—"

"I insist." Jennifer folded her hands under her chin, sculpted nails gleaming even in the subdued amber light from the wall sconces. "I'm not going to pretend I don't know how little you're currently making, but I think we're about to fix that."

Once again, the way Sarah would have felt hearing those words a week ago taunted her like a kindergartner's tongue. All she could manage to say was a feeble, "We are?"

Jennifer nodded. "As I said before, this is strictly off the record. As in, you tell anyone we had this conversation and I will take away that scarf you're always wearing."

Not her too.

But Jennifer smiled. "Actually I think it's rather charming. And I don't really care what you wear, and neither does Henry Carson. Nick doesn't either, as long as it's short and has a plunging neckline. And you didn't hear that from me either."

Sarah shook her head.

"What I care about is this. I want you to have this job because this company is in desperate need of people with integrity. Desperate."

Jennifer had lowered her voice almost to a whisper so that Sarah had to lean over her artichoke-spinach-and-pinenuts to hear her.

"You've been around long enough to know that the advertising business as a whole is all about getting people to spend money they don't have on things they don't need."

Sarah flinched. Those were almost exactly the warning words her father had spoken to her when she'd chosen her major.

"I don't usually have much of a problem with that," Jennifer went on. "I buy things I don't need all the time." She pulled back her sleeve. "Who *needs* a Cartier, right?"

"Well, right . . ."

"But I take issue with some of the means that are used on two levels." She put her fork down and held up one finger. "*Some* of our people—and I won't name names—are not above playing pretty serious head games with our clients, who in turn try to play their customers in the same way."

"I think I've seen that," Sarah said. Caveats hidden in the fine print on TV ads, implied promises in pharmaceutical campaigns, and half-naked girls on billboards advertising knee replacements all came to mind.

"I've done the research, Sarah, and the kind of advertising I'm talking about does not increase sales the way we as a company are telling people it does. I can't fight that alone, and people like . . . well, the established people at Carson aren't going to do battle alongside me. But I've watched you—even the way you handled yourself in that heinous meeting with Nick and Henry the other day—and I think . . . no, I *know* you have the kind of ethics that would make it impossible for you to do otherwise than to get on board with me."

Sarah could see her father's earnest eyes. *Learn the skills, SJ, so you can make people aware of products and services and issues and opportunities they do need—and steer your industry away from cheap manipulation.*

Jennifer was watching her, chewing her lettuce and, Sarah guessed, her thoughts.

"I'm honored that you'd say that," Sarah said.

"Don't be modest. You know it's true."

"It's what I work at anyway."

"And the ConEx account is the perfect opportunity for you to do that."

Jennifer pushed the half-eaten salad away and folded both hands on the table. Sarah had only taken two bites, but she gladly set hers aside too. What she wouldn't give for a ginger ale. For so many reasons.

"You've done the background work," Jennifer said. "You know ConEx is a reputable company with, to use your own word, honorable goals. For heaven's sake, they're in the business of helping the wealthiest of the wealthy find ways to give their money away. They're all *about* philanthropy. All we need is to get someone like Thad Nussbaum in there telling them they should show businessmen with trophy wives at their sides handing out iPhones to at-risk kids down in South Chicago. We'll lose that account and all chances Carson Creative has of developing any kind of decent reputation for honesty. Which we currently do not have in this industry."

She folded her arms across her crisp blouse. Sarah could have sworn she heard it crackle.

"I sound so jaded, don't I?" Jennifer said. "But you're still young and idealistic and so far you seem to be untouched by the seamier side of this business. I need you. We need you."

Jennifer leaned back and looked as if she expected Sarah to say something. What came to mind was, *Me? You're talking about me?* Because inside she felt old and disillusioned and very much in touch with her seamy side.

"Is there something you need for me to do now?" Sarah said instead.

"No. Well, yes, actually. Don't tell anyone we had this conversation. It's obvious I'm pushing for Henry Carson to promote you, but you aren't supposed to know that."

"Did we have this conversation?" Sarah said.

Jennifer smiled briefly and then she said, "Another thing. If I were you, I would spend less time with Megan Hollister. She's one of the very people I'm talking about. Associating with her creates entirely the wrong impression, and it's not one you want, trust me."

Sarah was grateful the check arrived just then. She was having a hard time wiping "stunned" from her face.

Thad wasn't hanging out in Sarah's doorway like a spider monkey when she returned from lunch. When he passed her in the hall, there was no sweaty handshake—just a hate-laced look. She was never going to breathe a word about her conversation with Jennifer, but the fact that they'd had one at all was obviously old office news before they even got back to the building. Nobody missed anything in that place. Which was a scarier thought than usual.

In fact, Sarah had barely gotten her scarf off when Megan came into her cubicle and whispered, "Let's go in the break room. There's nobody in there right now. I want to hear everything."

Sarah turned quickly to her desk and picked up a folder. Any folder. "I can't. I stayed out longer than an hour, and I've got stuff to catch up on."

Megan glanced up and down the hall and then came to perch on the counter. "What aren't you telling me?"

Everything.

"There's nothing to tell," Sarah said.

"You're a worse liar than a used car salesman."

Sarah had seen that for herself in the bathroom mirror. Although . . . Jennifer Nolte didn't think she lied at all.

But it wasn't just because Jennifer had told her to dump Megan that Sarah wanted her to go away. She needed some time to sort out that lunch conversation—all of that about the difference she could make. The compartments were confusing their contents again, and it was starting to matter more than ever.

"I can't talk about it," Sarah said.

"Not even to me?"

"I'm sorry."

Megan stared at her for a long moment, eyes boring. Sarah turned her head before they could get in too far.

"I get it," Megan said. "Okay, a back table at the Grille then. After work. My treat."

Sarah just shook her head.

"Fine. Do what you have to do."

As she listened to the heels tap importantly down the hall, Sarah closed her eyes and felt the weight of one less ally.

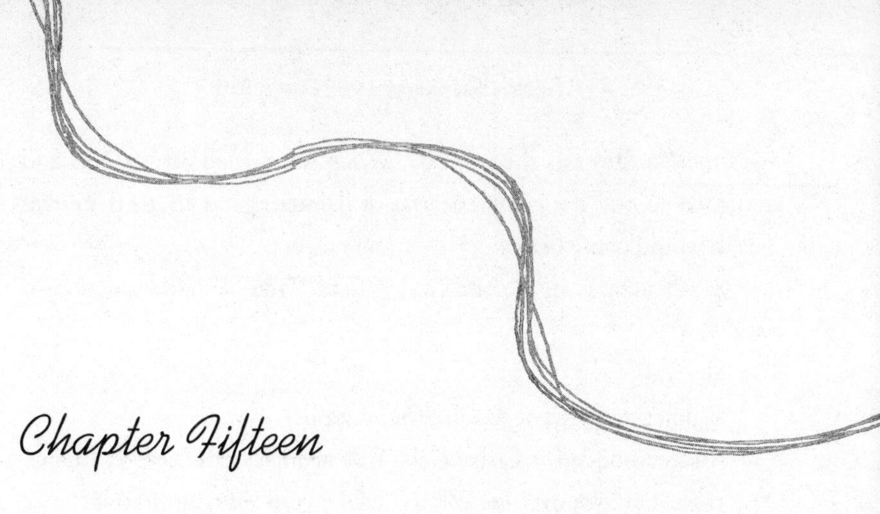

Chapter Fifteen

Thursday, Sarah had trouble sitting at her desk. It wasn't only the runs to the restroom now. It was the anxiety, the kind that wouldn't let her, the Focus Queen, be still for longer than seven minutes at a time. She'd never been this way.

Okay, maybe once—when she first moved to her tiny apartment in New York and found herself alone, facing graduate school and friendlessness and a refrigerator she couldn't afford to fill. That day she was melting from Independent Sarah into Daddy's Sarah so fast she could hardly talk when she got him on the phone. She'd curled into a fetal position in the closet of her apartment and listened to him pray for her.

Sarah lurched from her chair for the fifteenth time and took an aimless walk down the hall. All heads were bent over desks or inclined with phones pressed against them. Everyone was focused the way she always was. The way she couldn't be until she decided. And how could she decide when even she seemed to have abandoned herself?

Only one person looked up at her as she rambled past. Sarah's eyes met Audrey's as she went by. When she turned on her heel and returned to the doorway, she was still looking, as if she'd known Sarah would come back.

Sarah stepped inside and Audrey said, "You can close the door if you want."

She did.

"I don't really want to talk," Sarah said.

Audrey nodded, splashing the bob against her cheek. "I know." She swept her arm over her office. "Make yourself comfortable."

That would have been easy to do if she hadn't felt like she was about to come out through her own pores. Two stripe-cushioned wing-back chairs faced Audrey's desk and another cushier one hung out in the corner next to a small table with a teapot on it. It occurred to Sarah that she'd never even peeked into Audrey's office before. If she had, it would have surprised her. It looked more like a favorite aunt's sitting room than the place where an account executive made decisions.

Sarah chose the chair in the corner and pulled her feet into a cross-legged position. Then she thought to ask, "Is this okay?"

"It is. You want some tea?"

Tea. Sarah hadn't thought of that.

"I recommend the peppermint," Audrey said. "It will settle your stomach."

"Sure. Thanks," Sarah said, and watched Audrey hoist herself out of her desk chair and waddle cutely over to a kettle plugged in next to her printer. She spooned loose tea into some kind of tea-making gadget and put a small pitcher of milk into the microwave. Her movements made Sarah want to lapse into a nap.

Audrey said nothing as she handed Sarah a large mug with Rocky Mountain National Forest printed on it. When she went back to her desk with her own cup, Sarah looked around some more.

It was clear a great deal of work got done in here. Files were in neat slots and the out-box was fuller than the in-box. But it was as if Audrey were determined to work at home, even if she had to come here. Fresh poinsettias on the credenza. A lamp with a fabric lampshade on the desk, casting a cozy light. And a gallery of framed photos on the wall above Audrey's head. A life with a shaved-headed happy-faced guy was chronicled there. Hiking. Sailing. Toasting glasses over Italian food. In Italy. It was a testament to the possibility of happiness.

Sarah had to look away.

When she finished off the tea, she stood up. "Thanks for this."

"Come back any time. Sometimes ten minutes of hiding makes all the difference."

Sarah nodded and put her hand on the doorknob.

"You know . . . my husband's going to be out Saturday night. You want to come to my place for supper?"

Sarah stared at her.

"Just a thought," Audrey said, head tilted. "I'll e-mail you the address and you can let me know."

Sarah had no idea what to do with that. How could she spend an evening with a woman who rested her hand on her belly because there was no question that she loved what was inside? Somehow the offer made her feel lonelier than ever.

By Friday afternoon that aloneness pressed down so hard on Sarah's shoulders, she couldn't bear her own heartbeat. She decided to go to the tree-trimming party at her mother's. The strand upon strand of twinkly lights and the chatter and the pretense that the celebration could be what it had always been might take her mind off the absolute isolation.

And she might talk to Denise.

Sarah seldom went to her sister with her struggles, because Denise never seemed to struggle at all. She had always been "the easy daughter"—according to their mother, not to her—while Sarah was the "challenging" one. But Denise was the closest thing to a saint their family had now that Dad was gone. She had his patience. She never judged. She just listened with her whole body.

So Sarah might talk to her.

Maybe.

Buzz got her there, thanks to a trip to the mechanic Wednesday that carved a two hundred–dollar hole in her savings and left her with less than fifty in the bank. Sarah could almost hear Megan saying, *Would you be able to afford that if you had a kid to feed?* It didn't seem to matter whether she hung out with Megan or not; she was still in her head like a CD on how to live your life. Dad's whisper, on the other hand, was still silent.

Yeah. Sarah really did need a night of nonsense.

Her mother was over-the-top delighted when she walked through the door. Sarah had a cup of from-scratch hot chocolate and a plate of red sprinkled snickerdoodles in her hands almost before she got her gloves off. But the evening threatened to immediately go south when the scarf fell to the floor as Agnes hung her coat on a hook in the front hallway.

"I'm so glad you wear this, honey," she said, pressing it against her face. "I know it's not as sophisticated as your other things, but your father would be so pleased." Her voice choked.

Can we please not go there tonight? Please?

And as if that weren't enough, her mother's next words were: "Honey, where's Matt? I thought he was coming."

"He couldn't make it," Sarah said.

She must not be getting any better at lying, because Agnes's eyes drooped. "You're not having trouble, the two of you?"

"Mom—"

"I would hate to see that happen. He's a nice boy. Several of the women at church were very impressed with him. He looks people in the eye. Not many young people do that—"

Sarah raised the mug of chocolate. "Do you have any marshmallows, Mom?"

"Marshmallows." Agnes blinked. "Yes. And you're right. This is a happy night, isn't it?"

She was off to the kitchen before Sarah had to answer.

Sarah made it to the end table in the living room with the mug and plate just before Sean, chubby cheeks fiery from too much stimulation, tore through with a box of candy canes under his arm and Tim on his heels. Screaming, of course. Sarah grabbed her mother's nativity snow globe a mere shaving of a second before its dive from the table was inevitable. Sean left her and the sloshing globe in his wake as he careened across the living room and leapt onto his father's unsuspecting back, candy canes still in hand, Tim still squalling. Justin juggled his camera and let out a "Whoa, dude!" which was a whole lot more civil than what was about to come out of Sarah's mouth. Behind her, Denise put in a halfhearted, "Settle down in here," and went off after Tim, who was suddenly wailing that he had to go potty. From the smell of him, that announcement was coming several minutes too late.

If someone had put a gun to Sarah's head right then and said, "Are you going to have this baby or not?" she would have said, not no, but *heck* no!

Until she passed the still-naked Christmas tree and went toward the kitchen and the aroma of vegetable soup—and stopped dead in the dining room.

The table was piled with boxes of ornaments and trails of garland—not with a changing mat and containers of powder and lotion and stacks of diapers. Or a baby.

The last time she was in this room she was holding Daisy. That scene was far more real than the ghosts of Christmas past that flitted fitfully among the nativity scenes and the faded felt stars dotted with glitter, looking for a place to be put to rest. It was easier to believe she could kiss that sweet pink neck than she could bear to put those preschool-crafted ornaments on a tree one more time. Not without her father reclined in his chair saying, "Put that one that says 'Daddy' on it right in the middle." Her father who didn't care that she'd spelled it *Dady*.

Why had she thought coming here was a good idea?

"I'll be on social security before I get that kid potty-trained." Denise put her arms around Sarah's shoulders from behind. "Where's Matt?"

Sarah closed her eyes. "We're not attached at the hip. He had something else to do."

"Bummer," Justin called from the living room. "I got some great shots of you two at Mom's birthday party. My camera's on the table if you want to take a look."

For once her mother's timing was impeccable. The kitchen door swung open and she appeared with yet another plate of frosted, sprinkled goodies in one hand and a bowl of tiny marshmallows in the other. Heaven forbid you should serve them from the plastic bag.

"It's time!" she sang out. "Boys, are you ready?"

"Have you *met* them?" Justin said.

He was now on a ladder, stringing lights, while Sean wrapped a stray strand around a big-eyed Tim. The little guy's hair stood straight up on his head in spikes as if his brother had plugged it in. But, then, he always looked that way. His cuteness was depressing.

"Here's how we do this," Agnes said. And proceeded to give the same instructions she handed out every year. Lights first. Then the angel on the top. Then the adults would hang the breakable ornaments on the higher branches and the kids would hang the nonbreakables on the lower ones.

"Good luck with that," Justin said.

But Nana was undaunted. She somehow managed to make the whole thing happen and avoid any mini-man meltdowns and keep all the mugs steaming and marshmallow-filled. Even Sarah got into the hilarity of the concoctions she and Denise had made as kids, which became more misshapen every year.

"Mom, really," Sarah said, "this stuff makes the tree look like a Salvador Dali painting."

Denise hooted.

"Who?" Mom said.

Denise collapsed.

"Now *you* look like a Dali painting," Sarah said to her.

Agnes stroked the face of a lopsided cardboard snowman missing three-fourths of his cotton. "It's patina," she said.

Justin gave her a deadpan look. "I don't even know what that is."

Sarah started to tell him *patina* was a nice word for "This has seen way better days," until she peeked around the tree to find him propped up in Dad's chair, pointing to a bare lower branch for Sean to hook a clothespin reindeer onto.

Dad's chair. The wooden arms stripped of their varnish by his hands. The headrest rubbed raw by his head. The cushions recessed to the contours of his fading body even when he stood up and groped at the air for something to hold onto—

"Sarah," her mother said, "someday your children will be doing this with us."

The tree was almost done. Mom had her grandchildren to fill her up. Sarah could go now and not leave too much disappointment behind her. And if she didn't leave, she couldn't be responsible for what might burst out of her.

She collected her mug and plate and slipped into the kitchen. Denise was right behind her.

"You going to tell me what's up with you, or do I have to get out the bamboo shoots and start sliding them under your fingernails?"

Sarah evaded her eyes and went with, "It still feels wrong without Dad."

"Uh-huh. And?"

When Sarah didn't answer, Denise curled her fingers around Sarah's wrist and pulled her through the other swinging door and into the hallway. Beyond them the chirp of little-boy voices wove among their mother's murmurs, and the cassette player Agnes couldn't part with provided a Mannheim Steamroller Christmas album as backup. Around them the cozy darkness of the place they had always come to as kids to share secrets closed in. Denise's first crush. The only D Sarah ever received. Their plans for Dad's breakfast in bed for Father's Day.

Sarah leaned against the stair railing, her back to the living room. Denise perched on the edge of a step and waited.

"I guess I should tell you," Sarah said. "I'm pregnant."

The calm Sarah counted on was right there. Denise nodded as if Sarah had just announced she was having her brows waxed.

"I'm guessing this was an accident."

"A train wreck."

"So what are you going to do?"

"Not tell Mom, for one thing."

Denise zippered her finger across her lips.

"Thanks," Sarah said. "I can't handle that right now."

"Is this my sister Sarah I'm talking to? The one who can handle anything?"

"I know, weird, right?"

"Maybe not. Having a baby is a huge deal. It changes everything . . ." Denise touched Sarah's hand. "Even you."

Sarah stiffened. "You're assuming—"

"Are you and Matt getting married now?"

"It doesn't look that way."

"Sarah, I'm sorry." Denise pressed her hands to the sides of her face for a long moment. "You know we'll all be there to support you and the baby. Even Mom. You see how she is with the boys. This is her grandchild. Whatever the circumstances, that trumps everything."

"Denise."

Sarah knew it was her tone that froze her sister's smile. She couldn't seem to talk to anyone about this without turning into Cruella de Vil.

"This is just bringing out the worst in me. But you're assuming I'm having the baby. There is another option."

Denise pushed at her face again, as if she were trying to keep it from crumpling. "Sarah, no. Listen to me—"

"If I have a baby, I won't be able to pay off the loan they took out—or the IRS—or the medical bills insurance didn't cover—and who else is going to do it? I can't wait around for Matt to grow up. He goes from one ridiculous scheme to another and his 'real job' is with an investment firm. That could fold with the next dip in the stock market. I might not have a choice."

While Denise shook her head and visibly fought back tears, Sarah reeled. Where was *this* coming from? When she talked to Megan, she wouldn't even consider abortion. But with Denise, having the baby was out of the question. Megan would love what was coming out of Sarah's mouth right now.

Because it sounded just like her.

"All right, look." Denise was so obviously trying to be soothing.

"This isn't a decision you should be making alone. You're saying all these things about Matt, but what does he think? He's wonderful with children—"

"He's wonderful with children because he thinks they're toys. He thinks everything is a toy and life is one big playground. To me, being wonderful with children means you can support them. He's just not ready to have a baby."

"I said this to you before: is anyone ever ready to have a baby?" Denise's voice warmed. "It's difficult and demanding and messy and annoying and at the end of the day . . . it's just more satisfying and rewarding than you could ever imagine."

"And more expensive and—"

"Sarah, have the baby. We'll get the bills paid eventually."

"Before they take Mom's house?"

"Yes! And Matt will grow up if he has a reason to. And besides, he loves you."

"Enough to get me into this mess."

"Like you had nothing to do with it?"

Sarah raked a hand through her hair. "I know. That was a stupid thing to say. I don't even know *what* I'm saying anymore."

"Then don't make a decision right now that you're probably going to regret."

"I don't have that much time, Denise. I'm almost eight weeks along."

"There's still time. Keep talking. We'll figure this out."

"I *have* talked about it. All I can see is that my whole career has been leading up to this promotion. I had a plan. I wasn't going to let Mom lose the house, and I wasn't ever going to be in that position myself. If I have this baby . . . so much for the plan."

"Why?"

"Carson won't give one of their most profitable accounts to a pregnant woman."

Sarah felt like she was parroting Megan again. She clamped her lips. This conversation was pointless.

"You won't be pregnant forever. You can practically work up to the last minute. And I don't think you're employed by a bunch of jerks."

"You should hear what they say about the pregnant woman who's leaving."

For that matter, she should hear what Sarah herself had said. About that woman who breathed kindness. She wanted to throw up again, and this time it wasn't hormonal.

"Working women who get pregnant have legal rights. You can take up to twelve weeks off after a pregnancy and go back without losing your job."

"Twelve weeks without pay. I looked it up."

"So you don't use all twelve weeks."

"And then what? I go back to work with a baby strapped to my back?"

"Come on, Sarah. Like I said, this is you I'm talking to. The woman who got through college and grad school and came out with honors. And then sacrificed a job in New York to be here for Dad. And then took on his finances and yet is still thriving at work." Denise gave an elaborate shrug. "Look at this as life's next challenge."

"*Impossible* challenge. How would I pay for day care?"

"I could take care of the baby while you're at work."

"I wouldn't ask you to do that."

"You're not asking. I'm volunteering. I'm home all day anyway." She attempted a laugh. "Trust me, I wouldn't let my two have a bad influence on your baby."

"I don't want to punish you for my mistakes."

"You wouldn't be punishing me. This is my niece or nephew. If it's a girl, how much would I love *that*? And I know what to do with boys." She looked straight into Sarah's face. "Let me help you."

Sarah tightened her arms and stared hard at her boots. "If I decide to do it, would you still help me? Would you take me to have the abortion?"

She expected the silence, but not the horror on her sister's face when she finally looked up at her. Denise's eyes had shifted to something over Sarah's shoulder, and even in the dim light of the hall, her face was ashen.

"Mom?" Sarah whispered.

Denise nodded.

Let me die. Just let me die right now.

Sarah turned and watched her mother come to the bottom of the steps. Even the lines in her face trembled. Tears already gathered in the pockets under her eyes—eyes so wounded Sarah couldn't look into them.

The only thing she knew right then was that she had never hurt anyone this way before, and it stabbed at her.

"I'm sorry you heard that," Sarah said. "But, Mom, please don't—"

"You can't have an abortion, Sarah." Agnes whispered the word as if it burned her lips. "It's a sin."

Sympathy immediately began to seep away. "Please don't start with that."

"It's the truth. You would be committing—"

"I've already committed a sin by getting pregnant in the first place. I'm trying to fix it."

"But you cannot negate one sin by committing another. The Word of God says—"

"Don't talk to me about God!"

Denise was by now standing up, hand on her mother's arm. "Mom, now is not the time to preach at Sarah."

Agnes wrenched away. Sarah wedged herself between them. The tension that had pulled her apart for so many days snapped like a brittle rubber band. There was nothing left to hold her back.

"Do you remember the night I was sobbing on that couch in there and you sat next to me and you said, 'Don't worry. God told me your father's being healed. We just have to keep trusting him.' Do you remember that?" Sarah's temples throbbed. "He died the next day. The next *day*, Mom."

"Sarah, that doesn't mean—"

"So—what? God was lying to you? Or maybe this whole thing is in your head."

Denise said, "Sarah, you're—"

Sarah shook her shoulders from her sister's reach. "It doesn't matter. Daddy wasn't healed, and that's when I stopped counting on God for anything. God's not making this decision for me. I am."

Although her mother's face was all but frozen in shock, she still shook her head, still got out, "God knows what's best for us, Sarah."

"You know what, Mom? Right now I don't think God even knows I exist."

"No. Sarah, no, no, no—"

Denise clamped both arms around her. "Mom, you have to calm down."

"Nobody's going to calm down until I leave," Sarah said.

She grabbed her coat and managed to get herself out the door before the angry sobs erupted. She stumbled blindly down the steps, trying to jam her arms into sleeves and her anger and fear and confusion back into her chest. Neither attempt worked. When she fumbled her way into the car, her coat was draped crookedly around her shoulders, and her body shook so hard she had to grab the steering wheel to keep from flying apart.

She had never screamed in her mother's face before. Never slammed that front door in a fit of rage. Or left her sister to pick up the pieces she'd left behind.

Had that just happened? Or was it another 'vision from the Lord'?

The front door opened and Denise slipped, coatless and visibly shivering, onto the porch. She beckoned to Sarah with her hand, but Sarah shook her head and cranked the starter and stomped down on the accelerator. Buzz lurched forward and down the street, straight into a patch of black ice. The rear end fishtailed and Sarah steered, still sobbing, into the spin and managed to get the Toyota under control and around the corner. She pulled to the curb and pressed her forehead to the steering wheel and fought, hard, until she could breathe.

This couldn't go on. She was tearing Matt apart, tearing her family to pieces. Ripping herself in two for that matter. She had to make a choice. Even if it was wrong, at least this whole thing would be over. Wounds would get covered up, and she could move forward. Just like she'd done the last time she was in this kind of pain.

"This won't make you proud, Daddy," she whispered. "But I think I have to do it."

She felt for the scarf, but it wasn't there.

Sarah turned Buzz's brittle heater up as far as it would go and pawed through her purse for the card the nurse at the clinic had given her. She'd only looked at it long enough to see there was a number you could call twenty-four hours a day, seven days a week.

"Stop shaking," she said out loud.

But her finger still trembled as she tapped the number on her phone.

"Hello," the plastic recording said. "Thank you for calling the Lincoln Park Women's Center. We are now closed. If you'd like to make an appointment for a procedure, press one for our twenty-four-hour scheduling."

Good. She wouldn't have to talk to another person who would assure her she was just having a wart removal.

"Hi, this is Marsha. Would you like to make an appointment?"

Not a recording. A cheery live voice that should have been scheduling appointments for family photographs.

"Yes," Sarah said.

"And what is your name?"

"Sarah Collins."

"Hi, Sarah." The voice grew even cheerier, now that they were on a first-name basis. "Is this your first time for this procedure?"

"I'm sorry?"

"We just like to know if you've had this done before—"

Sarah hung up before she even knew why. Despite the failure of the car heater, her face burned.

Women did this more than once? Like it was nothing?

She closed her eyes, tried to imagine herself in a waiting room with newly pregnant girls who flipped through magazines and checked their text messages as if they were about to have a Botox injection, but she couldn't get it to come clear.

Sarah restarted the engine. She didn't know what she *was* going to do, but she couldn't imagine that.

The only thing she could imagine was to do just what Audrey said. Hide.

Hide just for a little while, someplace where she could get things to go back into their compartments.

She picked up her phone again and went to e-mail. Audrey had included her number with the directions.

Sarah tapped it and waited.

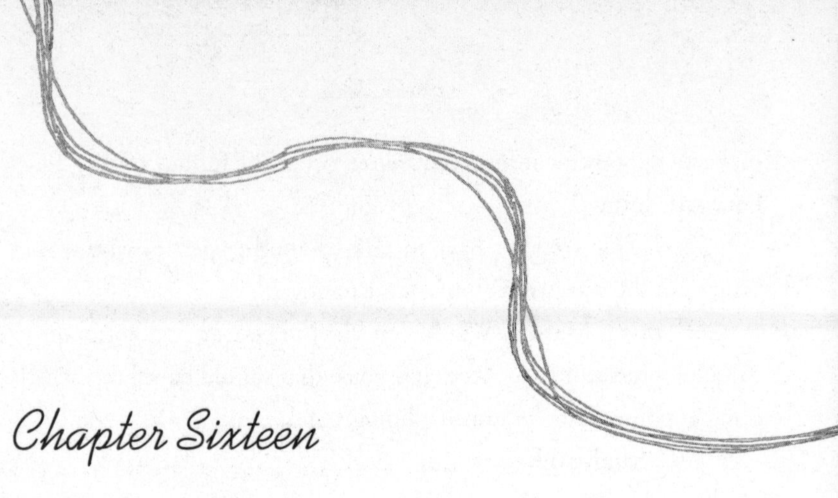

Chapter Sixteen

Saturday was snowless but bitter. Since Chicago seemed to be entering another ice age, Sarah decided to take the train to Wilmette instead of chancing the streets with Buzz Lightyear. His windshield thick with hardened cold, he looked as forlorn as she felt as she started the hike for the train station.

But once she was ensconced in a seat, face pressed to a warm window, Sarah sank into the cocooned feeling the train always gave her—a mixture of cradle-like swaying and rhythmic clacking and somebody else's driving.

And the memories. One in particular tonight, of coming back from a day of ice skating—she and Dad and Denise.

Dad always embraced anything she or Denise showed an interest in and took it to the limit with them. The year Sarah asked for ice skates for Christmas, when she was eight, he took them to the downtown rink on the train every Saturday and had them doing double salchows before the winter was over. Denise got more into it than Sarah and even competed for a while. Sarah could almost see them both leaning on Dad's shoulders on the train-rocking ride home from Denise's competitions, Denise asleep and Sarah wide awake asking him questions about anything she could think of, just to hear him talk. She knew more about term life insurance and church politics and the history of the Jeep than any kid in America.

Things were so clear then.

Audrey met her at the stop in her giant SUV with the baby seat in back. She had jazz playing on the car stereo, which wasn't what Sarah expected.

Neither was the house.

It was an original Craftsman bungalow in an older Wilmette neighborhood, probably built in the 1920s and redone in recent years. Sarah followed Audrey across the wide porch and stood inside the glass-paned front door while Audrey took her coat and hung it on a hall tree Sarah knew she had to have acquired either from an antique store or her grandmother's attic. Probably the attic. It was hard not to just stay there and soak in the gleaming wood floors and the earthy colors and the tiled fireplace where Audrey already had a fire going.

The whole place said, "Come in. Curl up. Be."

It was like an extension of Audrey's office.

By then Audrey, who had still said very little, had slipped into the kitchen Sarah could see across the open floor plan. More gleaming, from a copper kettle and pots hanging from the ceiling and the glass fronts of the cabinets.

"Does the nausea get better as the day goes on?" Audrey called out to her.

Sarah folded her arms and moved slowly to the sit-down counter Audrey motioned her to. Somehow a fat mug of hot cocoa had appeared there.

"It does," Sarah said.

"Well, just in case, I made the soup I was able to keep down those first few months. My mom's recipe." Audrey smiled her apple slice of a smile. "She had seven babies, so she pretty much had it down."

"You have six brothers and sisters?"

"Yep. We ate a lot of soup. You?"

"We ate soup too. Oh—you mean do I have siblings."

"You can answer either one of those. How are you with bread?"

Sarah nodded. She'd already sniffed the air enough to know it was homemade.

"So is there anything you *can't* do?" Sarah said. "You're amazing at your job. Your home is awesome. You obviously have a great marriage. And you cook from scratch. I feel like a slacker right now."

"Oh? This from the girl who's already had one promotion and is about to get another one—*and* dresses like a fashionista—*and* is put together so doggone sweet I have body envy every time I look at you—even before I turned into the Goodyear Blimp."

Sarah laughed. The sound was rusty. She probably hadn't let out so much as a real chortle in about ten days.

"You so do not look like the Goodyear Blimp," she said, and didn't add that she had once mentally compared Audrey to the Pillsbury Doughboy. Right now she was more reminiscent of a Rubens painting. That Sarah did say.

"I'm going to go with that until I deliver," Audrey said. She set two steaming bowls on a tray. "I thought we'd eat by the fire."

The scene couldn't have been more Norman Rockwell–idyllic, and Sarah settled into it, soup and bread on a wooden tray table in front of her, a sympathetic woman across from her, and the friendly spits and crackles of a fire beside her. This was true hiding. After an evening of this, she could absolutely get things sorted out and get this thing decided once and for—

"You know, I used to hate women like you."

Sarah froze, spoon halfway between the bowl and her mouth.

"You girls got pregnant without giving it a thought, and half the time you didn't even want to be. And there was me, ready to do just about anything to have a baby and seeing that dream recede further with every birthday."

Sarah set the spoon back in the soup. "I don't even know what to say to that."

Audrey shook her head, sending the bob into a light toss. "You don't have to say anything. I'm only telling you this because you've made me realize there's no reason to hate you at all."

"Well, no. I mean, you're about to *have* your baby."

"It's not just that. Seeing you this last, what, week or so since you found out, I've realized you aren't taking it lightly. It's not like, 'oh well, I can always have a kid later'—nothing like that. You're struggling with this decision. Or am I wrong about that?"

"Did somebody tell you—"

"It wasn't hard to figure out, at least not for someone who's recently been there. You're actually being very discreet. I don't think anyone else knows unless you've told them."

Sarah tore off a piece of bread and picked it apart and picked those bits apart, all while Audrey quietly spooned in her soup.

"So," Sarah said finally, "I still don't quite get why you invited me over."

"Because I have a lot of respect for you, for one thing. And I thought you might need a break."

"Then you're not going to tell me how having this baby or not having this baby is going to affect my promotion."

Audrey sniffed. "No. I'm sure you have Megan to tell you that. Assuming she knows."

"She does," Sarah said. "And I probably shouldn't have told her."

"In my experience, shoulda-woulda-coulda doesn't get you anywhere."

She drained the rest of the bowl like she was drinking a glass of milk and came up with a soup moustache as endearing as her overbite. If that baby looked anything like her, he was going to be one cute kid.

"We don't even have to talk about any of it," Audrey said. "I just thought we'd enjoy each other's company."

"Not to disappoint you, but lately I'm about as good company as Howard Stern in your living room."

Audrey laughed—a sound something like sand being shaken in a can. It was infectious.

"I'm serious," Sarah said. "I can't talk to my boyfriend without singeing his eyebrows. Last night I turned our family tree-trimming party into a scene out of some bad reality show—"

"You're killin' me." Audrey gave another sandy laugh. "I never realized what a sense of humor you have. You're *funny*."

"I'm just trying not to come apart."

Audrey surveyed her, eyes wise. "You look pretty together to me. More bread—since you decimated that piece?"

"No. I'm sorry, I just don't have much of an appetite."

"Understandable. Pardon me while I wolf down another half a loaf."

Audrey broke off a hot hunk and closed her eyes as she took a bite. The other hand rested as usual on her shelf of a belly, fingers spread out as protectively as hen's wings.

Sarah burst into tears.

Kleenex appeared, along with a blanket around Sarah's shoulders and another log on the fire. Sarah sat staring at it for long moments, until she could speak without drowning. By then, Audrey had pulled out her knitting and was rhythmically adding stitches to a tiny blue hat.

"I'm not some clueless teenager who never thought this could happen to her," Sarah said.

"Clearly not."

"And you're right, it's not like, 'oh well, I can always have kids when I'm ready.' I *know* the value of human life. Trust me."

"That's pretty obvious too."

"I hope you won't think I'm materialistic when I say this, but a lot of what I'm wrestling with in this thing is money."

Sarah looked at Audrey for any signs of disapproval. A nostril flare. A nose pinch. An invitation to get out of her house. She didn't see any. Audrey was curled up in her chair, hands working the needles. The light from the fire made her eyes shine.

"Do you really want to hear this?" Sarah said.

"I do, but that's not the question. Do you really want to tell it?"

Sarah pondered that for a few seconds and then nodded. She did want to, because suddenly it seemed that the only way to see it was to put it outside herself and look at it. Maybe then she could get it all to fit again.

"I'm in an unusual financial situation," she said. "I don't have credit card debt or student loans or a car payment—none of that. I wish it *was* that."

"Oh?"

"The only way I can describe it to you is . . . three years ago it was like I was involved in a five-car collision on the Ike. Not literally—it just felt like that. Car number one hit me: my father died from, well they said it was complications of lung cancer but he was only in treatment for a year and, yeah, he was sick from the chemo, but they were getting decent results. We thought we were looking at remission soon, and then . . . his heart just stopped beating."

"So it wasn't a shock, but it was," Audrey said.

"Yeah."

"And you were close to him."

"Beyond. He was my best friend. I know that sounds strange."

"It doesn't."

"So losing him was like, well, like I said, getting hit by a car. I was also plowed into by car number four when my sister and brother-in-law and I discovered the financial situation my mother was left in."

"What happened to cars two and three?"

Sarah felt her shoulders move up to her earlobes.

"Okay," Audrey said. "Number four works."

A nod of thanks, and Sarah went on. "The only even barely negative thing I can ever say about my father is that for an insurance guy, he was so inadequately covered—it was like he didn't even know what insurance was. Their health insurance didn't cover all the medical bills. When he first got to the point where he couldn't handle things, he asked a guy from the church to help my mother with the money, which none of us knew until we confronted her after he died. She said she was too embarrassed to go to him. Which was why no tax return was filed that year, and the interest and penalties accrued for another year before the IRS notices started coming in. They don't care if you're dead or not, somebody has to pay that. Then my dad's Jeep was repossessed because she wasn't making those payments. Or the payments on the loan they took out to try to keep themselves afloat."

Audrey's needles paused. "I am so sorry."

"We figured out that with just her disability, my mom needed to have my dad's life insurance money in the bank or she was going to go under. That left nothing to pay off all those bills. My brother-in-law has a decent job, but they have two kids and a mortgage. So the only thing left was for me to pare down my expenses and pay it off with payment plans."

"Or let your mother file bankruptcy. That's what that option is for."

"We'd have to put her in the psych ward if that happened. And I can do it and I need to do it."

"Because?"

"I just do." Sarah pressed her lips together. "I'm sorry. I didn't mean to bite your head off."

"You didn't. It's still there." Audrey focused on the yarn. "I might have been prying."

"Why wouldn't you ask that? I just can't—anyway, when I had the chance to go for the promotion and take over the ConEx account while you're out on maternity leave—"

"And be assigned to other accounts later."

"Right. It just seemed like the perfect opportunity. I could pay everything off in a year. I could almost see it, you know—me getting to actually start living again. Or maybe just start living, period."

Sarah cocked her own head to look at what had just come out of her mouth. Audrey seemed to be looking at it too.

"You weren't happy before that? I mean, I know you were grieving for your father . . ."

"I don't know, because I hadn't thought about it until I just said that, but maybe I wasn't. No, maybe it was that I knew I wasn't as happy as I used to be, before my dad died, but I didn't really think that was possible. And then it did seem possible, if I could just get financially stable. Then I could actually do the things that used to bring me joy. I'm not making any sense at all."

"Actually you are."

"It was probably stupid to hang so much on the promotion."

"Do you really think so? As far as I'm concerned, it's a done deal."

"Not now."

Audrey tucked a panel of the bob behind her ear. "Because you're pregnant."

"Yeah. I guess that was the stupid part." Sarah shook the blanket from her shoulders. "It's like I'm in this trap now. Do you mind if I try to describe it, because this is really helping."

"Go for it."

Sarah closed her eyes. "If I have the baby and keep her, my mother will probably lose her house and have to move in with Denise and Justin. Then everyone will lose their minds. If I don't have the baby, my mother will lose *me* because she'll never speak to me again." Sarah let her face drop to her hands. "Who am I kidding? *I'll* never be able to speak to me again. I can't just end my baby's life and then move on. So there's the trap: I'll never be happy no matter what I choose."

"May I ask a question?" Audrey said.

Sarah nodded. She needed a minute to catch up to herself.

"Is your boyfriend in this picture? Matt, isn't it?"

Sarah lifted her face. "How did you know his name?"

"Jack and I met him at the company picnic in August. I sort of floated in and out of the conversation, but they probably talked for thirty minutes about cars."

"Only thirty?" Sarah said.

"It would have been more, but I dragged Jack away. Another ten and he would have had Jack uncovering that '57 Chevy we have in the garage."

"I'm surprised Matt wasn't over here the next day with his tools."

"He offered." Audrey laughed. "I threatened Jack."

Sarah felt the tears welling up in her throat again. "He's a good, decent guy."

"He's precious."

"He's everything but responsible. He can't even decide whether to marry me or . . ."

Sarah bit the rest of it back. She couldn't imagine saying the word *abortion* in this house where the smell of new baby sweaters and delicious anticipation was everywhere.

"I'm not trying to garner sympathy," Sarah said. "I brought this on myself. But I've just never felt so alone."

Audrey looped a few more stitches. "I bet you wish your dad was here."

"I do. And I don't. He'd be so disappointed."

"That you made a mistake?"

"It's a pretty big one." Sarah pushed the blanket the rest of the way off of her shoulders. "I really should go. Thanks for listening to me. At least I can see what I'm dealing with now."

She waited for the question that begged: *So what will you do?*

But Audrey just tucked the tiny blue hat into the knitting bag and smiled at her. "I was right," she said.

Sarah grunted. "To hate me?"

"No. I do enjoy your company."

"Yeah," Sarah said. "Yours too."

Although Sarah offered to walk to the train, Audrey wouldn't hear of it and drove her there and waited until it arrived. When Sarah slid out of the SUV, she paused with the door open.

"Your baby is really lucky to have you for a mom," she said.

Audrey tilted her head one more time. "So is yours," she said.

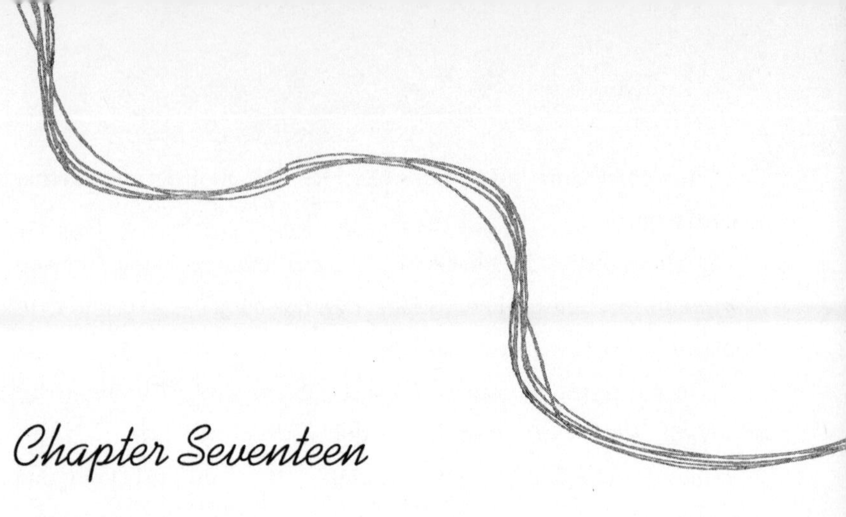

Chapter Seventeen

Although Uncle Clay had seemed a little off since the baby stroller prank, Matt still went down the hall to his office Monday morning and asked if he could take him up on that offer to meet at the Grille after work and discuss his future.

Clay continued to stare at his computer screen. "What's it gonna be this time, Matt? A mickey in my drink so you can watch me stagger down the sidewalk?"

"No. I'm serious."

Clay swiveled the chair and studied his face. Suspicion faded from his eyes. "Either you actually are, or you're a better actor than I thought—in which case you need to pursue *that* as a career."

"I'm a lousy actor," Matt said. "I'm starting to think I'm a lousy everything."

Clay stroked the rusty mustache. "Meet you there at six."

Matt nodded his thanks and started to leave.

"Matt."

"Yeah."

"You okay, buddy?"

"Never been worse, Uncle Clay," Matt said.

That may have been one of the truest statements he'd ever made. But knowing he could roll this all out for his uncle at the end of the day made getting through it seem like it could actually happen. He'd spent the entire weekend in his apartment—no football—with the TV off, actually—checking for messages from Sarah. Starting to text Sarah and then deleting. Punching in all but the last digit of Sarah's number and hanging up.

When he wasn't doing that, he was staring at a fetal development website and becoming more certain by the minute that if she had an abortion, he would never be the same. He already wasn't.

There were no nagging father words for that.

Sarah didn't question that she would spend her lunch hour with Audrey on Monday, until she was standing in Audrey's open office doorway with her box of saltines in one hand and her bottle of ginger ale in the other. She'd spent all day Sunday thinking about what they'd talked about and trying to get more clarity, and yet nothing seemed to come unless she said it out loud. But now, watching Audrey on the phone with what was obviously her husband—unless she called somebody else "sweet darlin'"—Sarah wasn't sure this was how Audrey wanted to spend hers.

And then Audrey put down the phone and looked up at Sarah and tilted her head in that way she had. She tilted and the world set itself upright.

"There you are," she said. "I'm warming up last night's leftovers for us."

Sarah closed the door behind her. "Are you sick of listening to me yet?"

"Are you kidding? We're just getting started, I hope. Try this chair."

Sarah sat in the wingback diagonal from the one Audrey sat in and took the mug she handed her. This time she downed several long sips before she set it down.

"Now that I'm here, I don't even know what I want to say."

"I know what I want to hear about."

"What?"

"Your father."

Sarah felt her eyes widen.

"I don't know why," Audrey said. "It just seems like somewhere you might want to go."

"I don't go there a lot."

"Too painful?"

"Not if I go way back. Those memories are good."

"You were a Daddy's girl, then?"

"Always. My mother says it was a good thing I wasn't her first baby or she would have been upset that I preferred my father to her, even as a tiny thing. She was actually grateful because Denise was sick a lot after I was born, so the minute my dad walked in the door after work, she handed me to him so she could tend to Denise." Sarah took another drag on the soup. "My mother has never been that emotionally stable; she can't handle more than one thing at a time even now."

"Good thing she had your dad."

"I can remember even at three, standing in the front window every day at 5:45, waiting for him to come down the sidewalk from the train.

As soon as I was big enough to open the front door myself, I was out there to meet him. I wanted to get close enough to smell him." Sarah looked through the steam at Audrey. "I guess that sounds a little weird, but really he had this combination of scents like nobody else."

"Doesn't sound weird at all. I could pick out my husband blindfolded in a crowd at a rock concert just by sniffing."

"Then you get it." Just like she seemed to get everything else. Sarah swallowed another mouthful. "I've heard smell is the strongest scent in terms of evoking memory, and I think next has to be touch. My dad had a heavy beard and by the time he got home from work in the afternoon, he had the five o'clock shadow guys try for now. You know the one I mean?"

"I do. Jack has more hair on his face than he does on his head."

"If he and my mother were going out again for the evening, he would have to shave again. I loved watching him shave. I'd sit on the edge of the tub and just gaze while he creamed up his face and worked the razor all around the contours. He'd twist his mouth so his cheek would smooth out on one side, and I'd giggle. When he dried off he would always let me touch it because it was so smooth. But I liked the end-of-the-day pricklies better because that meant he was home. A smooth face meant he'd be leaving soon."

Sarah drained her mug. Audrey still sat with her hands cupped around hers.

"You okay?" Sarah said. "You aren't going into labor, are you?"

"I wish. No, I'm just thinking how beautifully you put that. It's like you're there right now."

"I kind of do that when it comes to him. That's why I don't do it that often. When I come out of it, I'm sad because he isn't still here."

And then I get angry.

Sarah looked quickly at Audrey to see if she'd said it, but she didn't read that in Audrey's eyes. She only saw an invitation to tell her some more.

"If they did go out at night, he and my mother, I'd try to stay awake until they got home and usually I made it. Mom would check on Denise and he would come into my room and we'd do this thing we always did. I'd say, 'I'm happy to see you, Daddy,' and he'd say, 'I'm happy to see you, SJ.'"

"SJ?"

"Sarah Jane."

"I like it."

"It went without saying that we loved each other, and as I got older we actually said it less, but I felt it more. He was just so interested in everything Denise and I did. Even in high school, when I started playing around with photos on the computer and making the fliers for all the bake sales and car washes we did for clubs and teams. Denise was getting babysitting jobs and learning to cook, and I was joining everything."

"And being president of all of it."

"No. Publicity chairman. Dad got me all this software and arranged after-school time with the promotions guy at the insurance company. My father's the one who did the research to find the best college for me to go to."

"Northwestern."

Sarah looked at her. Audrey reached for the knitting bag.

"I looked you up when they asked for suggestions for my replacement. Your credentials are impressive. Bachelor's from there. Master's from Columbia."

"That was mostly him believing in me. There was never a doubt in my mind that I could accomplish whatever I set out to do."

"How 'bout your mom?"

"My mom."

Sarah watched Audrey stitch for a minute. A primary-colored hat this time. "Do you believe in God, Audrey?" she said.

Audrey didn't appear to miss a stitch. "I *know* God. And when I'm not sure I know, I do what I believe. And when I'm having a hard time believing, I just pray." She worked the needles for a few more seconds before she said, "Why do you ask?"

Because I don't want to offend you—because I don't want you to kick me out of the safest place I've known in . . . years.

Sarah opted for treading carefully.

"Every time my mother overheard my dad and me talking about my plans for the future—this was when I was still in high school and then in undergrad—she would ask me whether I knew those were God's plan for my life. She always said, 'Have you prayed about it?' "

"Had you?"

The question had no edge of judgment, so Sarah answered.

"I had, actually. Mostly I thanked God for all the opportunities I was getting. I mean, it seemed to be so right I assumed it was what God wanted me to do. And Dad said when you go with your God-given talents, you're being obedient to God. He used this image of doors. When doors open, you walk through them. When they close, you knock. When you hear the deadbolt slide into place, you go find another door."

Sarah tried to locate another place to look besides at Audrey. She hadn't thought about any of this for three years. Now she knew why.

"Too painful?" Audrey said.

"Kind of like a root canal."

Audrey tapped the knitting needles together.

"What does that mean?"

"Means it's time to change the topic," Audrey said. "Did he teach you about boys?"

Sarah let herself snort. "You mean did he teach me not to sleep with them so I wouldn't get myself into a situation like the one I'm in now?"

"Every father teaches his daughter that. Most of us don't listen." She stopped knitting long enough to give Sarah a wry smile. "I was no angel in my youth."

"I actually was," Sarah said. "Believe it or not."

"I do, but go on."

"I started figuring out that boys weren't aliens when I was about thirteen. It was more like I saw they could be fun, and it felt good to have their attention."

"Why wouldn't you have that attitude? That's the relationship you had with your dad."

"Right. I thought that was the way relationships were supposed to be. So until I was sixteen I just hung out with mixed groups—had a couple of crushes and was sad for about thirty minutes when they didn't work out. I don't think I was conscious of it at the time, but I see now that I was looking for a guy—"

"Like your dad."

"And I sure wasn't finding that at fifteen. Plus, I was trying to become a stronger woman than my mother. I didn't want a man to have to look after me the way he did my mom. During that time she was going through menopause and the hormones were wreaking havoc on her, when she was already struggling with depression to begin with. So anytime a guy started trying to make me into an adorable little baby doll, I was so out of there."

"So what happened when you were sixteen?" Audrey dimpled. "Let me guess—you thought you found mini-Dad."

"Oh, yeah. His name was Brick."

"You're not serious. Who names their kid Brick?"

"I know, right? Mom was in the hospital. Denise had already

graduated from high school, and she was in community college and dating Justin. It was just Dad and me, but he really had to focus on Mom, so I was a little vulnerable."

"Enter Brick."

"Yeah. He transferred in around November, and it didn't take him fifteen seconds to start fitting in—in our junior year, no less. He didn't look for friend slots to open up; he created them. It didn't hurt that he was so cute it took every girl at least three long looks to really appreciate the depth of his absolute hotness."

"You're killing me again, Collins."

"And as hard as I tried not to be, I was right there with them. It wasn't just his looks, although that was enough for Marilee Baltes, who went for him like a stealth bomber."

"I know the type."

"For me, it was more the way he was with people. He got respect from the teachers without acting like Eddie Haskell on *Leave It to Beaver*. He treated the not-so-cool kids like they were the in-crowd and the cool kids like his equals. I'd never seen anybody ignore the social castes like that, and I was impressed. Then—get this—he showed up at my church."

"No way."

"Marilee Baltes couldn't get to him there because Marilee Baltes couldn't have recited the Lord's Prayer if you threatened to take away her pom-poms."

"If you don't stop being hilarious, I'm going to have to take a pee break," Audrey said.

Sarah fell silent.

"Forget it. Keep going."

"Okay, so he joined the youth group and he did the same thing there. And that was saying something. We were really tight. We'd been together since the church nursery. There is actually a photograph somewhere of Candace Fogelberg and me sitting next to each other on matching potty chairs."

"Seriously, I do have to pee now. No—I don't. Continue."

"Kids before Brick had actually changed churches, I'm ashamed to say, because they couldn't break into our Christian Closed Club. Do you really want to hear all this?"

"Are you serious?"

"Okay, so Brick and I hung out at church, and then we hung out at school—much to Marilee's horror. She even cornered me in the girls' locker room one day after PE to tell me to leave her man alone."

"What did you say?"

"I said, 'Who's your man?'"

Audrey let go of her knitting long enough to high-five her.

"She confronted Brick about cheating on her and he broke up with her, just as if they'd been dating seriously for weeks. He made it so that she could tell people it was mutual and that, sadly, they had religious differences."

"Ya think?"

"It was pure finesse on his part, of course, but I saw it as the mark of a deeply caring individual, and I was smitten."

"Which was his plan all along."

"I loved him. He loved me. And there just wasn't anything else."

"And that's where it got complicated."

"That's where everything my father had taught me about physical relationships with boys stopped making sense. I couldn't go to my mom. And I sure wasn't going to discuss it with Denise. She and Justin were like the poster couple for purity. Besides, I thought Brick respected me and anything beyond your basic making out wasn't even going to be asked of me."

"So . . ."

"So Brick got his license and he wanted to take me out in his dad's car. My parents had told me I could date when I was sixteen, so I didn't actually ask my dad if I could go. I just told him."

Audrey winced.

"That was exactly the expression he got on his face." Sarah closed her eyes. She knew the scene would be there. "I actually prefaced the whole thing by telling him I thought I'd found the man I wanted to marry someday. His response was, 'Define *someday.*'"

"Did that surprise you?"

"Yeah, it did. I thought he'd say, *It's Brick, isn't it? He's a nice kid. I approve.* But he just sat there looking at me like he didn't know who I was. So I told him someday wasn't going to be any time soon and again, I thought he'd get that I'm-all-ears look and we'd talk about how perfect Brick was for me. Instead, he got all serious and he said, 'SJ, be careful with your heart. Go slow. Don't give it away too fast.'" Sarah pulled in her chin. "As far as I was concerned, that transaction had already been made. Brick had my heart, and I was sure he was taking good care of it. And even after I regaled Dad with all the reasons why Brick was husband material, he didn't say, 'Hey, let's have him over for supper and we'll shoot some baskets.' He tried to look interested, I know, but there was something different. It was an effort and it had never been that way before. I was so disappointed."

"Not to mention resentful."

"There was that too. He was pouring his love out on Mom, and Denise could be all about Justin, but I couldn't love who I wanted to love?"

"I take it he said no to the date."

"He said he'd have to think about it, and I was stunned. And then I lashed out. I had never yelled at my father before, and I definitely had never stormed out of the room and slammed my bedroom door. It took me about five minutes to figure out I'd just acted like a two-year-old."

"You're a fast learner."

"Well, he was my dad. I thought I'd blown our whole relationship for the rest of time. But he came in and said, 'Let's talk.'"

"What did he say?"

Sarah opened her mouth, but she closed it again. A sob was threatening in the wings.

"Time for another topic?" Audrey said.

"Time to go back to work, I think." Sarah picked up the ginger ale she hadn't opened.

"Do you have any idea why I just spent forty-five minutes telling you about a boy I haven't thought about since high school?"

"Well, I kind of do." Audrey tucked the bright hat, which now boasted a happy tassel, into the bag. "I just think you needed to go back to the beginning of why this decision is so hard."

"And I need to do that why?"

"So you'll have all the information."

"I'm not sure it's helping yet."

"That's because you're not there yet."

Sarah felt her brow furrow. "How do I get there?"

"Keep talking," Audrey said. "I'm thinking chicken noodle tomorrow."

Sarah left and paused outside the restroom across the hall, but there was no reason to go in. It was the first time in ten days.

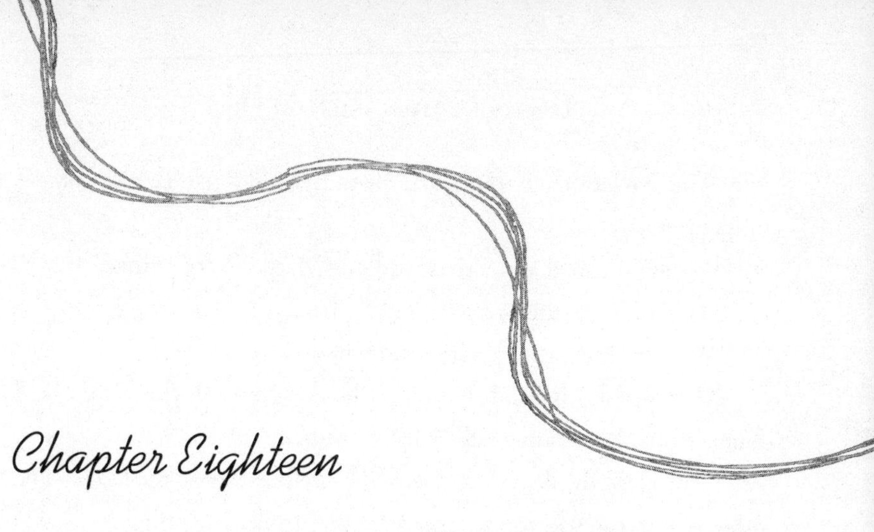

Chapter Eighteen

Matt didn't know what he was expecting from his talk with Clay, but spotting him at a bistro table in the dim corner of the bar section of the Grille was like seeing some kind of beacon. He sidestepped his way through the after-work crowd with their cast-off ties and jackets and sank onto the high stool across from his uncle.

Clay took a sip from his drink and squinted as he wiped off his mustache. "You look like you've been on a three-day binge. But since that's not your style, I'm thinking you're . . ."

"I don't know what to do, Uncle Clay."

It sounded lame, but it was the truth. Clay put up a finger to Matt and then waved at the ponytailed blonde with the empty tray on her hip who was chatting it up with a gathering of clearly out-of-town businessmen at the next table, probably hoping to change her own future.

"What are you having, Matt?" Clay said.

"Coke, I guess."

"You *are* serious. Large Coke, Brittany, and don't let his glass get empty."

Brittany flashed a practiced smile at Matt. "Party animal."

He couldn't bring himself to smile back.

"You mind if I start?" Clay said when she was gone.

Matt shook his head. Now that he was here, all the words he'd rehearsed had gone into hiding like cowards.

Clay set his drink aside and leaned both forearms on the table. "The other day in the parking garage, after the stroller . . . thing . . . I was going to say something to you, but I wasn't in the right frame of mind."

"Look, I'm sorry," Matt said.

"It wasn't all you. But that's beside the point. Now that you're obviously struggling with the future, I think I can say this."

"You're firing me."

Clay leaned back and smeared a hand across his forehead. "Will you shut up and listen. Please."

"Sorry." Matt said again. He'd already apologized more times in this conversation than he had in the last three years.

"I've seen you studying for your Series Sixty-Five exam and, hey, I'm all for that if that's what you want to do. But are you sure investment management is for you?"

"Am I that bad at it?"

"No. In those rare moments when you actually focus, you're *not* bad at it. For Pete's sake, Matt, you're not stupid. But you're also not happy, are you?"

This wasn't the direction he had in mind, but Matt shook his head. Going with this was better than pacing the cage like he'd done all weekend. He took the Coke from Brittany and motioned for Clay to go on.

"So what kind of work would make you happy?" Clay shrugged. "If you could do anything you wanted for a living, what would it be?"

"Are my parents in this equation or not?"

"Not."

"I don't know. I guess I'd either work with kids or work on cars." It was his turn to shrug. "Or teach kids how to work on cars."

"So why can't you?"

Matt poked at the ice in his drink. "Number one—and I know you said my parents aren't a factor—but my father would probably disown me."

Clay sniffed. "I don't think you're too far from that anyway. Your mother called me and said your father is *livid*, I think was the word she used, because you aren't going there for Christmas. So forget them for the moment. Come on, what else is holding you back?"

"I can't afford to quit my job and go back to school to get a teaching degree or my mechanic's certification."

"You can't work and go to night school? Take online courses?"

"Right now I can't even focus enough to brush my teeth."

Clay pushed his glass to the side again and folded his hands on the tabletop. "So you want to tell me what's going on?"

"Yeah." Matt lowered his voice, almost afraid to hear the words himself. "Sarah's pregnant. *We're* pregnant."

"Ah," Clay said. And then he was quiet, face smooth, eyes still.

"You're not going to tell me what an idiot I am?"

"Me?" Clay gave him a wry smile. "Nah. Where does it stand right now?"

"I love her. I don't want her to have an abortion." Matt stared glumly into the Coke. "That's all I actually know."

"What does Sarah want?"

"I don't know that, either. She's not talking to me. She won't even see me."

"And that's why you're talking to me."

"Yeah. I mean, like I said, I know I love her. She knows that, but it doesn't seem to be enough for her."

He'd punctuated the thing with so many sighs, Matt had to close his eyes and take a breath.

Clay looked up briefly at the knock-off Tiffany lamp hanging over their table. "Matt, Matt, Matt . . . do you think your Aunt Jerri and I love each other?"

"Yeah. Are you saying you don't?"

"Sure we do. We don't always *like* each other, though. Most of the time, yeah, but it takes work. Love isn't this . . . thing that just sticks to certain people. It's the result of fighting to keep a commitment you made." His face had come alive; his eyes gleamed in the lamplight. "It's living for somebody else. Do you want to do that with Sarah?"

"Yeah. I do." Matt felt hot color rising on his neck. "Right after she told me, I went out and bought her a ring."

"So what's the problem?"

"The problem is then she shut me out so . . . I guess I'll pawn it?"

Clay pulled in his chin. "You afraid to go bang on her door until she opens it and then ask her?"

Matt bent his head, fingers latched behind his neck. "If I had asked her before this and she'd said yes, I would have known it was because she loved me. Now if I ask her, it might just be because she needs me. For the baby." He knew his face was helpless as he looked up at Clay. "The night she told me, she said, 'A ring or a ride to the clinic.'"

Clay put up a palm. "Let's back up so I can get this straight. You want her to love you but you don't want her to need you."

"That's not what I mean."

"So ask yourself this: do you need her?"

Clay waited again. Matt floundered. Right now, yeah, he needed to hold her. He needed to know she was okay. He needed her to say, "Oh, come on, Matt. Grow. Up."

"I do need her," he said. "But I can't see how a marriage that starts like this can work. Right now I want to be with her and help her, but won't I feel resentment over time?" Matt latched his fingers again. "What am I saying? I know you can't really tell me that."

Clay reached across the table and tapped him on the forehead. "Okay, think: when is Katie's birthday?"

"Huh?"

"Trust me—I'm going somewhere with this. Katie's birthday."

Matt flipped through a mental calendar. He always bought his cousin some kind of girly heart thing for her birthday, so it had to be close to Valentine's Day. "February tenth?"

"Close enough. It's the eighth. When's our anniversary?"

"I remember sweating like a pig at your wedding, so it's sometime in the summer."

"July twenty-ninth."

"I don't get—"

"Do the math, Einstein."

"Math."

"Maybe you *are* an idiot. Count the months."

Matt did. Seven.

He felt a slow smile spread. "You're not serious."

"As a heart attack. Thank goodness your grandmother assumed Katie was two months premature . . . even though that kid weighed in at almost eight pounds." He gave Matt a lopsided grin. "People believe what they want to believe sometimes. The point is, it all worked out."

"And you've never felt like you had a gun to your head or something?"

"Is that how you're feeling?"

Clay paused to let Brittany survey Matt's glass and tell him to drink up because he was falling behind, and then move on to the now-rowdy businessmen before he leaned in to continue. Matt leaned in too. The light above the table formed a yellow disk around them.

"Look, Matt, for some reason, people these days, they fall in love . . . they get married . . ." He measured out the time line on the table with the side of his hand. "They fall out of love . . . they get divorced. We said we weren't going to do that. Granted, it was hard. But you know what?"

Matt shook his head.

"I wouldn't trade it for the world. Most people give up before they get to the good stuff. And the good stuff isn't good. It's great." Clay tapped Matt's arm. "You could have the great stuff, but you can only get it by going through the hard stuff. Because that's where the great stuff is." His eyes burned into Matt's. "It's called being a man, buddy. I don't regret a thing."

"Not even having another kid on the way?"

Clay waved him off. "Women should learn to tell their husbands they're pregnant on a Friday. That way they have all weekend to let it sink in—y'know, have their nervous breakdown before they have to head back into the world."

"So you're cool with it?"

"I am."

"Even the whole college thing?"

"Hey, I'm thinking of it as my retirement plan. They'll all need a good education to support me in my old age." Clay raised his glass. "I have expensive tastes, you know."

"What is that anyway?"

"7UP. Listen, this is on me so get a fresh Coke. That one's watered down."

Matt nodded but his mind was far from a soda refill. It all made sense, what Uncle Clay said. But did he have what it took for a long haul? When had he stuck with anything?

Clay was watching him. "I get that it's overwhelming right now. But think of it like your desk when it's covered with paperwork. What do you do? You take it one piece at a time and decide what's important to do now."

Matt had to grin. "That's not exactly something I can relate to."

"Right. Which brings me back to what we were talking about before." Clay put both palms up before Matt could protest. "We'll get to that another time. Look, I know I give you a lot of grief, but you can come to me whenever you need to. I mean that, buddy."

A new Coke arrived, and Clay bantered with Brittany while Matt waited for the surge that usually happened when somebody said, "Hey, do this."

Right. The same surge that had thrust him into flimsy money-making schemes and juvenile practical jokes. The take-the-risk surge that kept him moving . . . where? Forward?

Or around in circles?

There was no doubt Uncle Clay's advice was good. But he couldn't just take it and run with it this time. Not yet. Because this time he'd be running with Sarah's life too.

And their baby's.

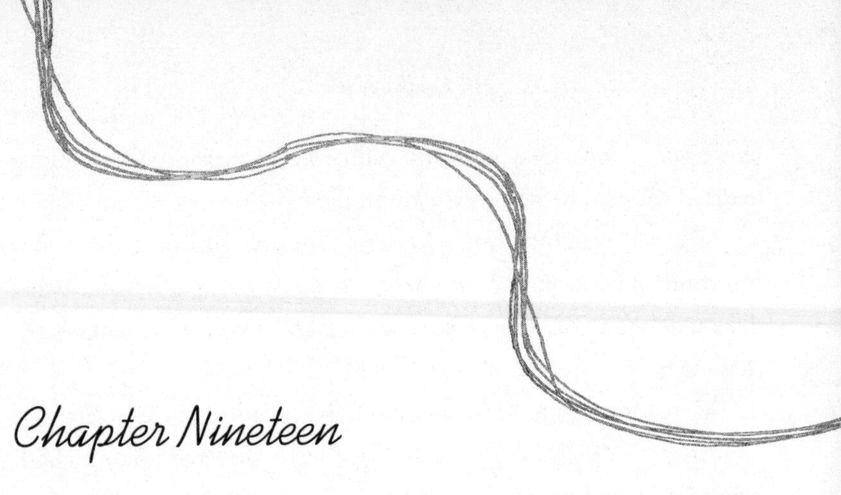

Chapter Nineteen

Sarah had just finished trying to eat a can of soup that couldn't hold a birthday candle to Audrey's when the doorbell rang. She ignored it and waited for the inevitable rent notice to appear under the door. What would it be this time? A wanted poster with her picture on it?

She was just about to yell that she'd pay Catfish with interest tomorrow if he would just go away, when a voice throbbed through the door.

"Sarah. It's Mom. I need to talk to you."

Biting back, *What in the* world *are you doing driving in this storm?* Sarah unlocked the bolt. It was snowing too hard to make her mother wait outside while she prepared a statement.

Agnes stood there, diminished and frail, as if she'd aged ten years since last night. Sarah knocked back the guilt and said, "Come in, Mom."

By the time she got the door closed and re-bolted, her mother had wandered into the bedroom/living room/everything else room. Sarah shoved her boots against the wall with her foot and grabbed the skirt and top she'd shed onto the floor when she got home from work.

What was she doing? Tidying? As if her mother wasn't already staring into the kitchen with an appalled look on her face. Sarah noticed for the first time that the trash can was overflowing onto the floor mat, whose original blue had morphed to a winter-street gray.

"I know it's a mess," Sarah said.

Agnes turned to her and shook her head until strands of gray separated from the always-neat curls as if they, too, were frantic. Sarah could see her Adam's apple struggling as she tried to swallow.

"Are you okay, Mom?" she said. "Do you want some tea?"

"I want to talk. Like two grown women."

Sarah dumped the contents of the chair onto the floor and nodded for her mother to sit. "I'm willing to try that, as long as you leave God out of it."

Agnes took a breath and held it in for a long moment. Then she reached into her coat pocket and pulled out Sarah's Dad-scarf.

"You left this last night. I knew you'd want it back."

"Thanks. Let me take your coat—"

"Sarah, have you thought about what your father would say about this? You always trusted him—"

"I can't go there either, Mom. I'm sorry."

"Well, you have to go *somewhere*! You're obviously not able to think this out for yourself."

The tension that had drained out of Sarah after her lunch with Audrey threatened to snap again. But she pulled back on it. She couldn't put that wounded look on her mother's face twice. The frenzied one she wore now was pained enough.

"Sarah," Agnes said, "you haven't thought at all about what your father would say to you?"

"I have, actually." Sarah went to the hook by the door and hung the scarf. She kept her back to her mother. "I was standing out in the snow the other day, thinking about how we used to go skiing together. And you know what I think he might say to me right now?"

"I think I do."

Sarah faced her. "I think he might say, 'Go for your dream, Sarah. I never got to go for mine.'"

Agnes stood up so abruptly Sarah took a step back. "Have you ever thought this isn't all about *you*?"

Sarah jerked her arms into a fold across her chest. "Who *is* it about, Mom? You? Are you afraid of what the people in the church will say?"

"What I'm afraid of is . . . I've already lost my husband. I can't lose you too."

"The only way you're going to lose me is if you keep driving me away."

"But I can't accept you having an abortion, Sarah. It's wrong."

"I don't know if I'm having an abortion!" Sarah pressed her palms together and breathed. "Whatever I do," she said, "I have to do it alone."

Her mother put her hand to her face as if Sarah had slapped her. "Then you *will* be alone. I can't . . . I'm done."

Agnes somehow pushed past her and fumbled with the bolt.

"Mom—"

"Just let me out, Sarah. I have to get out."

Sarah turned the lock, but she couldn't get to the doorknob before her mother twisted it with a shaking claw and thrust herself into the cold. Sarah went after her.

"Mom, don't leave like this."

Agnes halted at the top of the stairs leading down to the parking lot, but she didn't turn to Sarah. She poked at her phone and pushed it against her ear.

"Denise!" she cried into it. "It's happening again!"

Before Sarah got to her, Agnes grabbed at her chest and sank against the railing. Sarah caught her before she could hit the frozen concrete. She heard her sister shouting through the phone Agnes still clutched in her fingers.

Sarah pressed her mother's body against hers and pried the cell from her fingers.

"Denise!" she said. "I think Mom's having a heart attack."

"No, she's not."

"She's holding her chest, and it sounds like she's having trouble breathing."

Agnes groped for the phone. "Let me talk to Denise!"

"Mom, I have to call 911—"

"Sarah, don't. She's having a panic attack."

"How do you *know* that?"

"Because it happened Friday night after you left. Let me talk to her."

Sarah didn't have much choice as Agnes somehow managed to snatch the phone from her. By then Sarah was sure her mother was hyperventilating, and she tried to guide her back toward her still-open doorway. Agnes dug her heels in with surprising strength and shook her head at Sarah with a vehemence she hadn't seen since she was twelve.

"I have to stay outside—"

"It's snowing, Mom. You don't even have gloves on—"

"Just until I can breathe."

She pulled away from Sarah, phone still at her ear, and nodded at whatever Denise was telling her, which was apparently to walk and breathe and say over and over, "I'm going to be all right. Everything will be okay."

Sarah watched her own breath heave dense puffs into the night air. She felt like having a panic attack herself. Because they were all so far from okay.

Denise was right. Sarah only vaguely remembered her mother's attacks back when Sarah was in high school. It was always Denise and her dad who handled them, and, true to form, Denise oozed at least a temporary calm into their mother now until Agnes said she could get in the cab Sarah reluctantly called for her. The driver careened in about thirty seconds later; he probably hadn't gone far after he dropped her off. If Agnes had driven herself in her fifteen-year-old Mercury, there was no way Sarah would have let her leave. Even so, setting her out with her hands still trembling like dry leaves and her nearly blue lips still murmuring, "I'm all right," was against her better judgment.

But then, how much had she been able to trust her judgment lately, anyway?

Her mother's shoulder hardened as Sarah tried to assist her into the backseat, but still Sarah said, "Call me when you get home. I want to know you're all right."

Agnes abandoned her mantra and looked up at Sarah with wet, red-rimmed eyes. "I won't be all right until you do the right thing."

Then she stared straight ahead until Sarah closed the door. The driver took off and shot a pile of gray icy slush across her feet. She didn't realize until then that she wasn't wearing shoes.

She'd long since lost feeling up to her ankles. Her feet were mere stumps as she plodded her way back toward the building with her arms wrapped uselessly around the thin, snow-soaked hoodie that clung to her ribs. Head down against the blistering wind, she headed toward the steps—and plowed into a scrawny body that materialized among the flakes.

Even through a nearly frostbitten nose she could tell it was Catfish.

"I am *so* not in the mood," she said, and tried to maneuver around him, but she was too cold-slow. He planted himself on the first step and poked a finger close to her face.

"Two months," he said.

Sarah grabbed for the digit and missed, which was fortunate because she was sure she would have bitten it off in the rage that bulleted through her.

Apparently Catfish sensed none of that. It was his face he poked close to her this time, so close she could see the cobweb of red lines in his eyes.

"You owe for two months."

"I *know.*"

"Then why haven't you paid?"

"I told you I was going to. And I will. Look, just let me by. My feet are frozen up to my knees—"

"I'll follow you to your apartment and you can write me a check."

"Get out of my way, you heartless little . . . hipster."

An expletive slipped between his lips. "Heartless? Look, I've cut you more slack than anybody—"

"Then cut me some more!"

Sarah tried to shove him, but the wraith look was deceptive. He didn't budge, and panic and anger and the horror of losing her toes gathered like a fist.

"I'll get you the stupid rent tomorrow."

"Tomorrow's too late. I get it tonight, or the landlord's getting involved—and you don't want that, trust me. Look, I can't help it if you blow your paychecks on—"

"Shut. Up. Just shut up! My mother just had a panic attack in front of my apartment—my boyfriend is like a twelve-year-old—and I'm *pregnant.* I said I'll pay you tomorrow, and if you don't get out of my way right now, I *will* punch you in the face."

Catfish blinked and stepped mutely aside. Sarah tried to rush forward but her feet would only hobble up the steps. When she reached the top, Catfish called to her.

"Hey. Are you really pregnant?"

"No," Sarah said without turning around.

"Oh. I was going to say congratulations."

Sarah wasn't sure which part of that tipped her over the brink. She hardly made it inside her apartment before she went to the floor. Cold air bit through the doorway and she kicked the door shut. Her body was numb, but she still felt the blows of the sobs that hit her hard. She couldn't fight back. She could only crawl to the bed and tear off her half-frozen clothes and hurl herself under the covers until she stopped shaking and sobbing and submitting to the punches of someone beating herself up.

Why had she blurted all of that out like projectile vomiting—and on Catfish, of all people? She owed him the rent. She should have paid him a month ago, for both months. But everything had pointed to her getting the promotion and being able to leave this dump, as Megan called it. It was, in fact, Megan who advised her to put him off so she could buy the necessary professional accoutrements. Spoken with a French accent.

Sarah sat up and dug her fingers into the hair that hung like melting icicles on her shoulders. How long had she been letting Megan influence everything she did? Influence? She'd practically been controlled by her. She had even blotted out Dad's whispers. In a way she was no better than Schmoozing Thad, allowing Megan to hand down edicts and scurrying to carry them out.

Until the day Sarah said she couldn't have an abortion.

Yet here she was tonight telling her mother she still didn't know if she would or wouldn't and driving her to the far edge of her sanity. And her own, for that matter. Who runs shoeless into the snow? Who threatens to take out her building manager? Who calls her boyfriend an adolescent when she herself can't make a decision to save her soul?

Sarah extricated herself from the damp covers and made her way to the floor by the chair for a pair of sweats she'd dumped there when her mom came. As she fumbled her way into them, still shivering under her skin, she caught sight of herself in the mirror she checked herself out in every day, last thing before she went out into the world she thought she could conquer.

Bleak. There was no other word to describe the thin, pallid creature who stared back at her from sunken brown eyes. Even without the lips still colorless from the cold or the gooseflesh pimpling her skin, she would have seemed pathetic.

Sarah hastily pulled the sweatshirt over her head. The fabric brushed against her sore breasts, and she winced. She looked down at her still-flat stomach and spread her hands across it.

"This is all because of you, Daisy," she said.

She was suddenly cold again, this time from the inside. She couldn't do this. She couldn't give this person a name until she came to a decision. She'd made it hard enough on herself when she'd accepted that she—it—was a baby. Besides, the name was a dream.

Just like she wished all of it was.

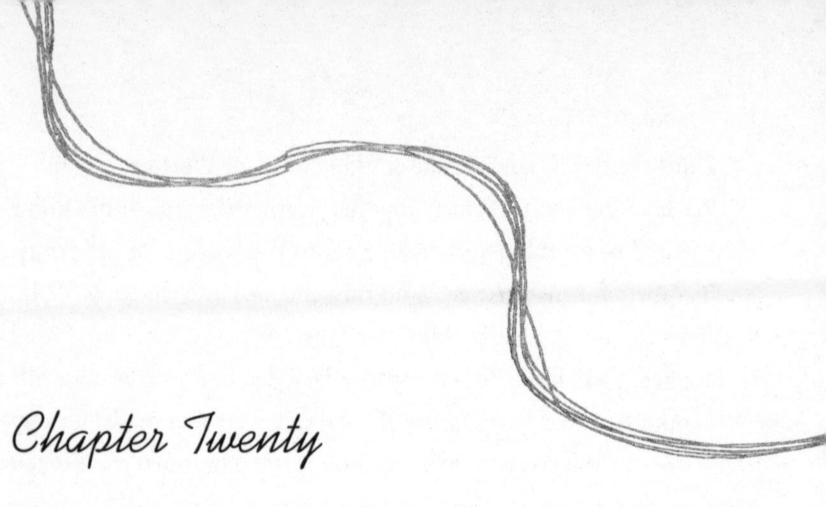

Chapter Twenty

Sarah found a pair of socks and a dry blanket and crawled back into bed. She'd felt far too much for one day. Emotions were exhausting when you weren't used to letting them out.

She was immediately asleep and just as abruptly awake again, as if she'd slept hard through the night. She had to rub her eyes three times to realize she was in, not her apartment, but a bright bedroom with the unmistakable light of a blue-skied morning beckoning at a bay window framed in misty gold.

Sarah put her feet on the rug and stepped on one of a pair of frog slippers—*frog* slippers?—that seemed to wait for her to stuff her toes into them. She did, and followed the smell of slightly burnt pancakes like a trail down a flight of polished wood stairs and into a kitchen. Although the cooking area gleamed with every stainless steel appliance and Pampered Chef utensil known to the culinary world, the counters were a complete disaster—worse, even, than her apartment. Two dozen eggs had apparently been used for something because their oozing empty shells formed a trail from their sticky cartons to an overturned box of Bisquick and several spoons and spatulas, each coated with a gooey-looking substance that made Sarah wonder why her stomach wasn't threatening to erupt.

But across the room the scene was far different. A table in another sun-filled bay window was set with a bouquet of construction paper flowers on pipe cleaner stems and a card propped up against them that said, in painstakingly formed crayon letters, "Hapy Birthday Momy." Those letters could only have been made by someone whose tiny tongue poked out with the effort.

A cherub with a mop of mink-colored curls approached with a plate piled almost comically high with hot cakes. The pink tongue was indeed visible as the little girl of maybe six set the plate on the table. The cakes were misshapen as mud pies and singed around the edges, but the hopeful wrinkles in the child's brow made Sarah say, "These look delicious." And kept her from saying, "Honey, who *are* you?"

"Sit down," the cherub-child . . . chirped. There was no other word for the sound of her voice. "I'll get you the syrup. You want whipped cream? I have some. And strawberries."

"Just syrup, I think," Sarah said.

"You should have everything." She nodded wisely. "It's your birthday."

Sarah could only nod back. The little girl dashed for the refrigerator, and Sarah peeked inside the card. More careful work with a big crayon had produced: "I lov you Momy. Lov Daisy."

Sarah sucked back a gasp.

The child skipped to the table with a bottle of syrup under one arm and a container of Cool Whip under the other. "I hafta go back for the strawberries. I couldn't carry them."

"Wait—Daisy?"

The face wreathed into a smile of miniature white teeth. All except two big ones in the front which were as perfect and shiny as Chiclets. It was the same smile that had sprung toothless to a baby-chubby face in her mother's dining room.

"They're okay to eat, Mommy," Daisy said, her brown eyes now round with concern. "I already ate the ones that didn't work out."

Sarah couldn't speak the questions she'd been about to ask. She smiled because that was all she *could* do in the presence of this child and said, "And how many of those were there?"

"Five. Or six." A giggle bubbled out. "Maybe seven."

A laugh bubbled from Sarah, too, as if she'd been magically enchanted. "I don't think I can eat quite that many," she said, "but I'll try."

To be on the safe side she smothered the pile with syrup before she cut her fork into them.

"Aren't you going to say the blessing?"

The small face was serious. Sarah felt like she was drowning. When was the last time she had said grace at a table? And what had this trusting little thing's "Momy" taught her? Obviously something, or she wouldn't already be folding the chubby hands. Sarah floundered for the one she always said as a kid when it was her turn, but all she could come up with was, "Now I lay me down to sleep."

A tiny waterfall of laughter spilled from Daisy. "No! That's not right!"

"Um, why don't you say it for us," Sarah said. "For my birthday."

Daisy nodded soberly and bowed the curly head, eyes scrunched closed. Sarah couldn't close hers. She had to watch the bow of a mouth shape the words. Any time now this gold-filled life would disappear and reality would return. She found herself clinging to the moments.

"Dear Jesus," Daisy said, "thank you for this food, and bless it to our bodies." A smile pulled her cheeks into round, red blooms. "And please make this Mommy's best birthday ever. In Jesus's name we pray. A-men."

Sarah murmured her own amen. Daisy's eyes popped open and she pointed to the plate. "Go ahead," she said.

Sarah added a dollop of Cool Whip before she popped a forkful into her mouth, all under Daisy's expectant gaze. It ranked among the best things she'd ever tasted.

"They're so delicious I might just eat seven after all," she told the beaming face.

"And then what do you want to do? It's your day, so you get to do whatever you want, just like you let me do on my birthday."

I do? Oh, baby girl, I don't even know you. How could I—

"I think I can guess what you want to do." Daisy got to the window in two skips and pressed both hands and her nose to it, leaving warm little smears on the glass. "I think you want to go—"

Sledding, apparently, because as abruptly as she'd been transported to the happy house with the bay windows, Sarah was with Daisy on a hill above it, bundled in down everything—mostly pink for the cherub—their faces almost covered in woolly scarves.

Sarah's was the one she always wore.

Daisy squealed and jumped onto a well-used red sled. The purple flannel tassels on top of her pink hat tossed as she looked up at Sarah and said, "Come on, Mommy! I'm gonna take you for a *ride*!"

She patted the space behind her with a mittened hand, and Sarah climbed aboard. She could barely distinguish between this downy bundle of energy pressing against her and herself at six, back molded to her father's chest, the mingle of delicious fear and almost unbearable excitement coursing through her. And trust. Complete trust that he would take them safely down even the highest of all hills.

"Are you ready?" Sarah said.

The tassels bobbed in her face.

"Then here we go!"

Sarah gave a push with her feet, and the sled flew down the slope. Squeals mixed with the wind in their faces. They were halfway down the slope before Sarah realized half of them were hers. Daisy raised her hands in the air, the way Sarah and Denise had always done on the rides at the Navy Pier. Sarah tightened her own arms around the tiny middle and opened her mouth wide—to take in the sparkly confetti of snow they startled into the air, and to let out the joy she'd forgotten was possible.

The sled reached the bottom and Daisy, still shrieking in that octave only little girls can reach, snuggled her face next to Sarah's.

"Again?" Sarah said.

"Again!"

Sarah told Daisy to stay on the sled while she pulled it uphill. Maybe it was the exhilaration or the fact that truly this had to be a dream. Whatever it was, Sarah had the energy of a woman who'd been a slave to aerobics.

Or one who did this laughing, squealing, freeing thing all the time.

That part had to be true. Daisy knew how to hold on, how to knock the snow from her furry mini-boots, how to plant them again on either side of the sled until Sarah got on. When she leaned back into Sarah, there was no doubt that she fit there.

At the end of their third run, Sarah purposely tipped the sled over and ran from the doubled-over-giggling Daisy to scoop up a handful of perfect snowball snow. When Daisy ran toward her in her delightfully clumsy little-kid way, Sarah pelted her with a powdery ball that smashed lightly on the front of her coat and sent flakes twinkling like stars in the sun.

"Is it on?" Daisy cried.

Sarah froze. What six-year-old said that? She sounded like—

"Oh, it's on!" Daisy said, and hurled a clump of snow that missed Sarah by a yard.

Sarah collected herself and moved closer so that Daisy's next attempt would hit her square in the face.

"You bet it's on!" she said, and this time threw *herself* at Daisy and rolled with her into a feathery drift.

Daisy's face lit up brighter than the snow. "Snow angels, Mommy!"

Of course. Sarah went spread-eagle and made giant wings as Daisy scrambled to her feet and watched from above. Sarah might have made an angel, but the form watching her with her curls poking from her zany hat was the real thing.

The sun chose that moment to push a cloud aside and shine down with Daisy.

"Mommy," she said, "I *love* you."

Sarah wanted to see her face when she said she loved her too. But the sun blurred Daisy almost from sight. Sarah shielded her eyes with her hand and blinked. Daisy wasn't there. Only the light slanting in bars between the slats of Sarah's blinds looked back at her. The blinds in her apartment.

Sarah found herself up on one elbow, squinting, yearning. It was harder than before to sort herself out from the dream. And it took longer to swallow the disappointment.

She was still a single, broke, pregnant woman with four days to make a choice that no matter which way she went, her life would bear no resemblance to anything she'd planned.

Anger started its upward rush, just like it had with Catfish the night before. Sarah swung her legs over the side of the bed and shook off the image of big, warm frog slippers and reached for the clock to see how much she'd overslept. Her hand brushed the Christmas card still propped on the bedside table. She didn't bother to wonder how it had gotten there again. She snatched it up and glared at the wise men.

Now two of them were looking at her instead of at that far-off dream. The anger made the rest of its way up.

"Visions from the Lord?" Sarah flung her head back to search the ceiling. "*Now* you care? Aren't you about three years too late?" Sobs threatened but she cried out through them. "You wouldn't save my dad, but you want me to have a *baby*? Really?"

Sarah ripped the card in half, and then in half again, and hurled it away from her. No more visions.

The wouldn't-that-be-nice of her dreams wasn't what God gave. Not to her. Not then. Not now.

Not ever again.

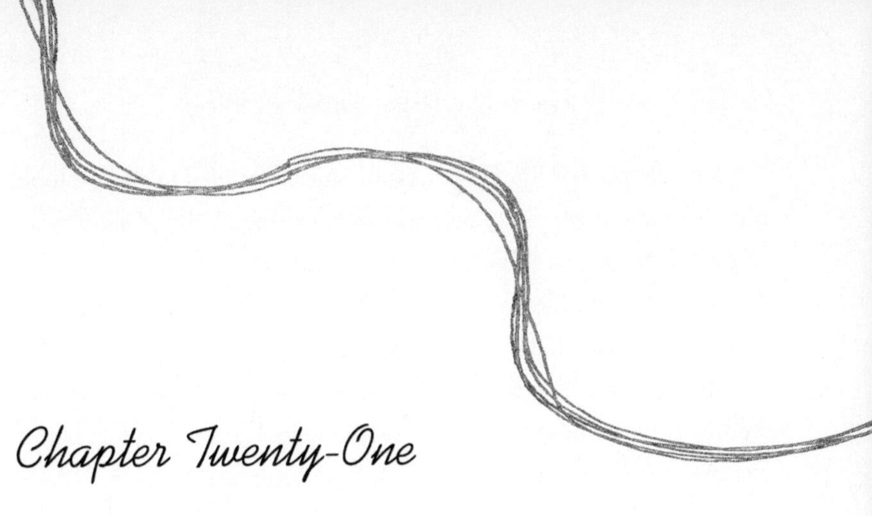

Chapter Twenty-One

Sarah decided not to go to Audrey's office for lunch again. What would be the point? She'd thought talking things through would help, but it was obvious that wasn't going to get her anywhere. Not after the confrontation with her mother.

And the one with God.

The problem was that Audrey was expecting her. Sarah felt like she'd plastered disappointment across enough people's faces. She had to at least give Audrey an explanation.

She was on her way out of her cubicle, sans crackers and soda, when Jennifer Nolte was suddenly there, walking with kitten-heeled briskness as always, yet stopping as if Sarah were just the person she was looking for.

"I hoped I'd catch you before you left for lunch," she said.

Sarah held her breath. Audrey said she didn't think anyone else knew, but Sarah still wondered when somebody was going to notice that she spent most of the workday with her head in the toilet.

Jennifer put her lips close to Sarah's ear. "I'm glad to see you took my advice about Megan. I'm very close to getting Henry to go my way instead of Nick's, so every little thing counts now."

Sarah had no idea what to say. Which wasn't a problem because without another syllable, Jennifer was gone.

By the time Sarah reached Audrey's office, she was a wreck. Audrey turned from the chicken noodle to look at her and had her in the chair with the mug in her hand before Sarah could get out, "I have so screwed this up."

When she did, Audrey shook her head.

"Have you made a decision yet?"

"No."

"Then you're no worse off than you were yesterday."

"You have no idea. Audrey, I have this promotion if I want it."

"I know that."

"If I give it up and have this baby, I'm not going to be able to give her everything she should have. And you know what, I'm not sure my dad would disagree with me."

Audrey motioned for her to drink the soup. She took a sip.

"Drink some more. You're losing too much weight, and no matter what you do, you're going to need your strength."

Sarah drank half of it. The shakes began to settle.

"I wasn't going to come in here and talk to you today," she said.

"Am I being too pushy?"

"No! That isn't it at all. I just didn't see how it was helping, but now that I'm here and I'm calm like I always am when I'm with you because you're like Mother Earth or something—"

Audrey laughed her sandy laugh. "You crack me up, you know that."

"I don't know . . . it just seems like if I could stay as sane as I am when I'm talking to you, somehow it'll come to me. You know, what to do."

"You have no idea how glad I am."

"Why?"

"Because I want to hear what your dad said when he came in to talk to you. After you pitched your fit."

"Okay."

Audrey waited.

"Aren't you going to knit?" Sarah said.

"I thought I'd just listen."

"I don't think I can talk if you don't knit."

Audrey laughed and reached for the bag. "We can't have that."

Sarah collected herself while Audrey cast on a mint-green yarn. This kid was going to be nothing if not well capped.

"I thought my father was going to give me another guard-your-heart lecture," Sarah said. "The extended version."

"But he didn't."

"No. He told me a story and it just absolutely rocked my world."

Sarah stopped.

"You okay?"

"Yeah. I just realized I've never told anyone else this. I don't even think Denise knows."

"Did he ask you not to tell anybody?"

"No. I guess I've always felt like it wasn't my story to tell. And that maybe he told me just for that situation."

"Do you think it could be for this situation too?"

"I guess I'll find out." Sarah drank a few more sips of soup and picked up the spoon for the noodles and chicken chunks at the bottom of the cup. "You know you've ruined me for Campbell's for all time," she said.

"That was my plan."

"Okay, so here's what my father told me. He said he was married to someone else before my mother."

Audrey stopped knitting. "You didn't know before then?"

Sarah shook her head. "He said he was eighteen, barely out of high school, and he'd been in love with this girl since he was sixteen."

"Your age at the time."

"She was the girl all the guys wanted, and for some reason she chose him. *I* could totally see it, but he didn't. Anyway, they started making plans for marriage their senior year. They both had full scholarships, so they figured they could each work part-time and make a go of it living in her parents' garage apartment."

"They had it all worked out."

"Except that his parents were against it. So were hers, but she was an only child and used to getting exactly what she wanted when she wanted it."

"And she wanted your dad, and she wanted him then."

"Yes. So they gave Dad and First Wife—he never did tell me her name—a wedding in August, and they started their new life."

"I almost don't want to know what's coming," Audrey said.

"I almost don't want to say it. Before the first semester of college was over, he knew he was losing her."

"I hate that."

"She found out it wasn't any fun to go to the parties together and come home to dirty dishes and a pile of laundry. She didn't get to join a sorority with all her friends or hang out with a gang of girls talking about guys. She and Dad were cooking their own meals instead of eating in the commons complaining about the food with all the other freshmen."

"You're remembering these details like you were there."

"That's the way he told them to me. She was missing everything her parents had warned her she'd miss. By June, she wanted a divorce."

"Your poor dad."

"At that point in the story, I was so ticked off at First Wife, I was ready to go after her and pinch her head off. Even however many years later, I could still see the hurt in his eyes."

"I get why he wanted you to know."

"Oh, that wasn't all." Sarah rubbed her chest. It burned there, the same way it did the night he told her. "He went to his parents and they were furious, not with him but with the girl. His father said Dad should sue her because her family had a lot of money and she shouldn't get away with it without paying."

"Nice."

"My dad didn't want to do that. And even he knew he didn't have grounds. Besides, he still loved her and he just wanted to set her free so she'd be happy."

"No wonder you were looking for a guy like him. The man was a saint."

"My grandfather thought he was a fool. When my dad told me that, I was ready to pinch *Grandpa's* head off, except that he'd already been dead for five years. Anyway, Dad didn't know at the time that his father went into debt to hire a private investigator to basically spy on First Wife. It didn't take him long to come up with the evidence that she was sleeping with not just one other guy but several. He had the photos to prove it."

"Are you serious?"

"So my father was not only heartbroken, he was humiliated. If he sued her it would be big news, and how was he supposed to stay there on campus with everyone knowing that?"

Audrey had stopped on the first minty green row. "What did he do?"

"He broke off ties with his father. They didn't speak until Denise was born. Dad left town, gave up his scholarship, and took the first entry-level job he could find, in insurance. First Wife served him for abandonment, and he signed what little they had—a lot of useless wedding presents, you know, like silver tea sets—over to her and tried to forget."

"Which, of course, he couldn't."

"Especially when he found out she was pregnant."

Audrey's eyebrows went up. "His?"

Sarah shook her head. "I asked him that, and I would sell my tongue to take it back. He said, 'No, SJ. The possibility of that was over months before I left.' I could only imagine how having to say that to me humiliated him all over again." Sarah squeezed the now-empty soup mug. "I may still go after that chick."

"She's the one who lost out, though."

"True that. Anyway, I said, 'Dad, I'm so sorry.' And you know what he said?"

"What?"

"He said, 'So am I. I have never forgiven myself for the damage I did when I married her.'"

"The damage *he* did?"

"That's what *I* said. But he pointed out that he put his parents through total hades. And abandoned his young wife when she was probably as mortified as he was."

"She kind of deserved it."

"She didn't deserve for my grandfather to send those pictures to the papers."

"Oh. My. Gosh."

"And—this seemed to bother him the most—he never told her he forgave her."

"Did he ever try to contact her, do you know?"

"He said no. When it occurred to him to do that, he was already married to Mom and he just wanted that marriage to be different. Y'know, I was wrong—what really bothered him the most, what he could never get over, I think, was that like he said, he let his pride cost him his education. A lot of those doors he talked to me about were closed to him because he never went to college and always had to settle for jobs beneath his ability. And that meant he couldn't provide for Mom and Denise and me the way he really wanted to. I started to protest about that, but he wasn't having it."

"Really."

"He got right in my face, right where I could see that deep hurt still in his eyes, and he said, 'Do I have to explain to you why I've told you all this?' I said no."

Sarah let that settle in the soft air between her and Audrey. In it she could still feel her father kissing her hair, still hear him leaving her there to know what she had to do.

"So what did you do about Stone?"

"Stone?" Sarah laughed. "You mean Brick."

"I knew it was something like that. My next guess was going to be Rock."

"I didn't have to do much about him, actually. I still thought he was the greatest thing since the iPod, but two things happened. One was that every time Brick vowed his undying love for me, I closed my eyes and saw the hurt on my father's face."

"What was the other thing?"

"Brick kept pushing for us to have car dates—which I didn't ask my dad about again—and I got the feeling he was getting impatient to get me alone."

Audrey's eyebrows practically became one. "Really, Sarah? Really?"

"I know, what was my first clue, right? Then one night after youth group when I was waiting for Dad to pick me up, Brick just pretty much shoved me into his car and started driving off. It was funny at first until he pulled in behind the Dairy Queen and tried to put his tongue down my throat."

"Eww."

"Exactly. And he said, 'This is what it could be like, Sarah.' Then he took me back to the church and I got to the pickup stop just in time for my father to drive up. Dad kept looking at me every time we stopped at a light, but I didn't say anything. Except, 'Dad, you were right.'"

"So no more Brick."

"He stopped pushing, stopped calling. Stopped smiling. I didn't get the respectful breakup thing he did with Marilee Baltes, and I was okay with that."

"Because . . ."

"Because I started to see how he pulled off being all things to all people. He manipulated them like some kind of crafty chameleon. When I realized that even the jerks liked him, I finally got it. And what do you know: he stopped coming to church."

"Shocking. You really dodged a bullet."

Sarah shook her head. "No. I think my dad reached up and caught it with his hand."

They were quiet for a minute. In it, Sarah longed for a whisper.

"I can see why you miss him so much," Audrey said.

"There's never been anybody else like him in my life. Can you blame me for wanting that in a life partner? I don't mean a guy has to *be* my dad, but I want the qualities that I had in that relationship." Sarah thought back. "You know, my father and I actually had a conversation about that. If you want to hear it."

"I'm only two rows in. Of course I want to hear it."

"I was in college by then, undergrad, and I was dating this guy named Ben. Great guy, really. We liked the same things. My family liked him. My mother especially. I think she wanted me to drop out of college and get married and have babies like my sister. Anyway, Ben was like my dad in some ways."

"But . . ."

"But he just couldn't understand why I didn't want to have sex."

"How old were you?"

"Twenty."

Audrey lifted her eyebrows at the needles. "Impressive. So what happened?"

"I told him I couldn't understand why he couldn't wait a year until we were out of school, and he cut me off with, 'You mean and get *married*?' That's when I knew we were not on the same page."

"At all."

"We weren't even in the same chapter. So instead of going to the UP with him for a week after the spring semester like we planned, I went home to talk to Dad. That's when I told him I wanted a man like him. He wasn't at all flattered. In fact, he got really stern and said that wasn't fair either to the men in the world or to myself."

"I'm liking this man more all the time."

"He said I didn't need to find a man like him. I needed to find a man who was right for *me.* He made me promise I would stop trying to find a younger version of him."

"And did you?"

"Yes. That was the first and only time I ever lied to my father."

Audrey took a sudden intent interest in the knitting and purling Sarah now knew she could probably do while simultaneously kneading bread and doing the Hokey Pokey.

"What?" Sarah said.

"I was just wondering if you wanted to talk about Matt."

"No," Sarah said. "I don't." She sighed. "Sorry. Was that rude?"

"No. It was honest."

"I should go."

"I won't push you on that."

"I know. I just need to hit the restroom."

Audrey's eyes looked concerned. "Are you still nauseous?"

"Actually, no. I just want to look in the mirror and see if I'm the same person I was last time I looked. This is all so . . . I don't even know."

"Very cool," Audrey said.

"Very *cool*?"

Audrey shrugged. "I don't think she was really you anyway. It takes the real you to make a decision like this."

"Then I'd better hurry up and find her," Sarah said.

"I think you're getting there. How do you feel about minestrone?"

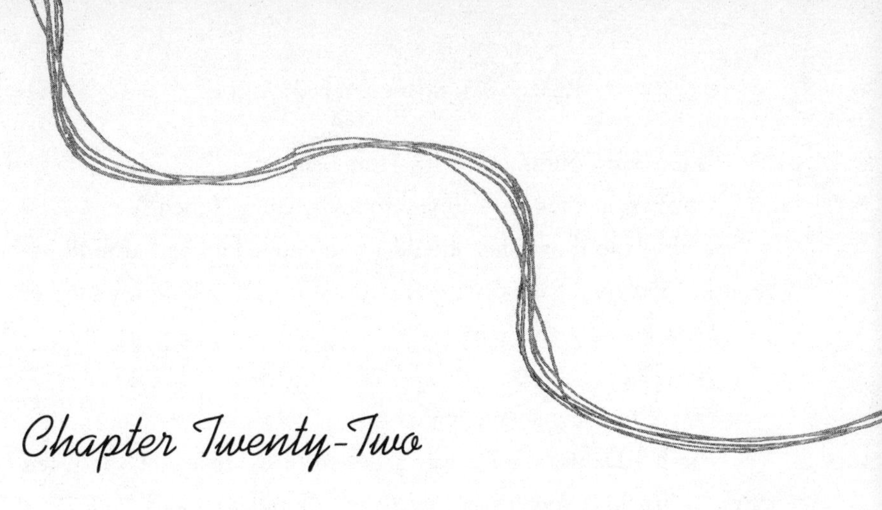

Chapter Twenty-Two

Something about her talk with Audrey made Sarah hope she would hear from her mother that night. Maybe, she thought, it was a more real Sarah who wanted to mend things.

But she didn't get a call, at least not from Agnes.

Matt's Aunt Jerri called, and when Sarah didn't pick up she left a voice message.

"So—Sarah . . . thought you might want to talk . . . just about, you know . . . things. Text me and we'll get together."

Matt had obviously found someone to talk to. Why wouldn't it be Clay and Jerri? They loved Matt like a little brother—wanted him to have the life he deserved. Sarah wouldn't mind getting some of that love herself . . . if Jerri wasn't convinced Sarah was the one who could give him that life.

She didn't call her back.

The one call she did take was from Denise at work Wednesday morning. Denise never called her there.

"Is it Mom?" Sarah said. "It's Mom, isn't it?"

"Can't your sister just call you to invite you to lunch?"

Sarah glanced over her shoulder and cupped a hand around her mouth. "She can, if she's not going to tell me I'm giving my mother panic attacks. I got that part."

"No—"

"Or try to convince me not to—"

"Sarah." Denise's voice was a determined version of the usual calm. "I just have something I want to talk to you about, and, no, I will not try to convince you to do or not do anything." Her laugh was light. "Like I could anyway."

Sarah swallowed down the tears that were now as ever present as the nausea and the urge to snatch people bald-headed at the slightest provocation. "I'm sorry. It's these stupid hormones."

"Then you're still pregnant."

"Uh-huh."

In the pause, Sarah heard a relieved sigh.

"I still haven't made a decision," she said.

"Do you mind if I tell Mom this much? That you haven't had the abortion yet?"

Sarah pinched the bridge of her nose. Every time she closed her eyes, she saw her mother clinging wild-eyed to the railing with a blizzard swirling around her. She could at least give her a few minutes of peace.

"Sure," she said.

"Thank you."

There was a wobble in Denise's breath. Maybe Sarah was giving her sister a few minutes of peace too.

~

Sarah left a note for Audrey and arrived at the Wildfire before Denise. She got them a table and ordered a ginger ale. When this was over, one way or the other, she was never going to touch the stuff again.

The place hadn't changed since the last time Sarah ate there, but the classy nostalgia of the 1940s dinner club atmosphere didn't do anything for her today. It had when she and Denise had brought their mom here to celebrate Agnes's forty-eighth birthday. It was only a year after Sarah's father died, and she remembered the quiet stream of tears on her mother's face, whether she was reading one of their cards out loud—a practice she insisted on, no matter how sappy the verse—or soaking in one of Denise's stories about the boys like the classic grandmother she was, or biting at her lip because Sarah and Denise picked up the check.

Sarah remembered that part of the conversation as if it were currently taking place at the next table.

MOM: I know you girls can't afford this. You're already taking on too much of my financial burden.

SARAH (holding the check out of her reach): Give it up, Mom, it's your birthday.

DENISE (covering Mom's hand with hers): After all you've done for us through the years, it's our turn to have some of that joy, okay?

Sarah took a sip of her soda. If left on their own, she and her mother probably would have argued about the tab for the rest of the afternoon. But all Denise had to do was say one silken sentence, and Mom acquiesced with the grace of a queen.

It had always been that way from the time they were old enough to know they weren't just appendages of Mommy. Sarah would stand in the middle of the kitchen with her fists balled at her sides and debate everything from having another cookie to extending her curfew. Just when Sarah was about to be banished to her room, a convent, or simply the streets, Denise would inevitably appear between them like Glinda the Good Witch and purr something soft and reasonable that Sarah never would have thought of, and everyone went away thinking they'd won. Later Sarah always realized she hadn't scored a *complete* victory but at least Mom was back to humming and packing lunches and regaling her friends with how wonderful her daughters were.

Sarah never figured out just what secret Denise possessed, but as she watched her now greet the hostess with the guileless smile few people still had at thirty, she hoped that secret was still there. If she decided to end this pregnancy, both Sarah and her mother were going to need for Denise to use it.

Denise blew a kiss onto Sarah's forehead and plumped into the leather-backed captain's chair, rosy-faced and breathless. She pulled off a floppy knit hat and let her blonde hair fly out. Denise could make even static look good.

"Sorry I'm late. Just as I was walking out the door, Tim pitched a fit. You know, the kind where they hold their breath until they turn purple?"

"Fortunately I don't know," Sarah said.

"You will."

A small curly-haired person with cherub lips smiled her Chiclet teeth into Sarah's mind. Daisy would never pitch a fit.

She was definitely losing it.

"I'm sorry." Denise curled her fingers around her wrist. "I promised I wouldn't pressure you."

"It's fine. Let's order."

Denise opened the menu, blocking her face from Sarah's. "You never could lie very well. I actually don't think you ever tried to."

Sarah closed her own menu and sighed. "How can we help talking about it? It's like this elephant in the middle of the table."

"I think I have a way to get rid of it." Denise peeked at her. "After we order, I'll tell you."

The waitress took the downed-menu cue and was there with an endless verbal list of specials. The very sound of a horseradish-crusted filet made Sarah feel green.

She cut her off at the Asian duck quesadilla with, "Just a cup of your chicken soup, please. And crackers. Lots of crackers. Okay?"

She did get a smile out and hoped she hadn't come off like a diva.

"Still sick to your stomach?" Denise said.

Sarah watched the server retreat to the kitchen, probably to tell the cooks to put extra salt in that soup order because the woman at table 5 was a pain.

"It gets better in the afternoon. Okay, I want to hear about Mom first. Is she okay?"

"Physically, yes. But she's mad at me right now."

Sarah's eyes widened. "Mad at *you*? Why?"

"Because I said I could understand why this decision was so hard for you. To her it's black and white." Denise poked at the lemon in her water with a straw. "I'm sure she expected me to completely side with her, but I told her I also had to support you. As my sister."

"I hate that this is messing things up for everybody," Sarah said.

Denise set her drink aside. "Some of this doesn't have to be messed up, you know. I tried to tell you this the other day at Mom's: Justin and I are not as bad off financially as you think we are. He just got a raise, and I've started working part-time in the church office now that I can take the boys to Mother's Day Out."

"No," Sarah said.

"You don't even know what I'm going to say."

"Yes, I do. And I'm not going to let you and Justin take on any of the financial burden. This is something I have to do."

Denise pressed her fingers to her temples. "That's what I don't understand. Why does it have to be all on you? It's not your fault things were such a mess when Dad died."

"Stop—"

"And it's definitely not your fault that Mom and Dad had no savings to fall back on—"

"Yes, it is!"

Sarah could feel heads turning. She wanted to smack all of them.

"I'm sorry," she said. "Denise, can you just drop this?"

"Not now. What do you mean it's your fault?"

Denise was looking at her the way she did her sons when they'd crossed the mommy line. Sarah tried to look away.

"Tell me," Denise said.

"If I do, will you leave this alone?"

"Maybe. I don't know."

"All right—look, when I got the scholarship to Northwestern, it wasn't a full one. There was still a quarter of the tuition to pay, plus room and board and books. It was going to be a lot of money and Dad wouldn't hear of me taking out any student loans. He said unless I became a brain surgeon or something, I'd never make enough to warrant that kind of payback."

"I know all this."

"You don't know that he assured me they'd saved enough to cover it."

"They obviously had."

Sarah dug her hands into her hair. "Don't make me say this, Denise."

"Say what?"

"My education depleted it. All of it. I got scholarship money for grad school, too, but Dad sent me money every month to help pay for the apartment."

"You always worked."

"For incidentals. So I could buy lip gloss." Sarah heard her voice rising again, and she caught it back. "They spent everything they'd saved on me, Denise. While you got nothing. Nada. You didn't even get to finish community college."

"By choice!" Denise lowered her own voice. "Do you really think I hold that against you, Sarah? Do you think Mom does?"

"No. But don't you see? Mom wouldn't be in the position she's in if she had at least a cushion to rely on. I have to do this. I owe it to her."

Denise was obviously fighting back tears. Why not? Sarah had just hit her with car number five.

"I wanted to die myself when I found out," Sarah said. "But I thought at least you never had to know. And I wouldn't have told you if I hadn't gotten myself into *this* mess. I probably shouldn't have told you."

"Do you have anybody else to stand by you?"

Sarah opened her mouth to tell her about Audrey, but Denise wasn't finished.

"Besides Matt?" she said.

"Matt is not . . . no, Denise." Her jaw tightened. "But I don't want to come between you and Mom either. She needs you."

Denise shook her head. "She hasn't turned me away completely. We're still talking."

"Mom mad at you is different from Mom mad at me. She wouldn't even look at me when she left the other night."

"Part of that is fear."

Sarah waited for the server to leave the soup and a mountain of crackers on the table before she whispered, "Fear that I'll go through with it?"

"That. And she's afraid you and she will never be close again."

"If I do this."

"Or if you don't. She just feels like too many things have been said that can't be unsaid."

Sarah parked the spoon in the cup and squeezed her hair back to the nape of her neck. "I'll try to find a way to fix that. I will. But right now . . . Denise, I'm no closer to making a decision than I was the day I found out."

"That's why we're here. I think I can help with that."

Denise dabbed at her mouth with her napkin and focused on refolding it next to the chicken salad she hadn't yet touched.

"How?" Sarah said.

"All right, just hear me out, okay? At first this may sound too far-out, but listen to the whole thing."

You want me to take a leave of absence and send me to a home for unwed mothers and give my baby up for adoption. You want me to have the "procedure" and tell Mom I had a miscarriage.

Sarah had to cover her mouth with her hand to keep from spewing out the possibilities she'd already wrung out so many times they hung like limp rags in her brain. She nodded for Denise to continue, but she was sure there was nothing she could say that Sarah hadn't already thought of and tossed aside.

Denise's soft blue eyes waited for Sarah until she met her gaze. "Justin and I have been talking about this—"

"You told him?"

"I tell him everything. He's my husband." Denise blinked at her as if any moron knew that.

"I'm sorry. Go ahead," Sarah said.

"Last night we were up all *night* talking about it, and actually he wanted to be here to help me tell you, but I thought it would be better if it was just the two of us."

She looked like she needed for Sarah to agree that, yes, that was a fabulous idea. Whatever this was, Denise was having an uncharacteristically hard time getting it out. Uneasiness stirred in Sarah's stomach with the soup.

"We've prayed hard about it, and we've been realistic about how we can do it financially and—" She took Sarah's hand into both of hers, clammy with nervous sweat. "Justin and I want to adopt your baby."

Sarah stared.

"We want to have another baby anyway, so this is perfect for us. And for you, I think, Sarah. You could be involved in his life as much you wanted . . . listen to me. I think of all babies as boys . . ."

It's not a boy. It's a cherub-cheeked little girl who chirps and giggles and doesn't care that she can't spell *Mommy* because she loves her.

"Sarah? Are you okay?"

Denise anxiously searched her face. Disappointment already tugged at the corners of her lips.

"I'm sorry," Sarah said.

"I know it's a lot to take in—"

"No, I mean, I just can't do that. I can't."

"We would do everything we could to make it easy for you."

"It wouldn't be easy! It would be agonizing!" Sarah felt the stares from the nearby tables, and she lowered her voice to a tear-thick whisper. "You're a great mom, Denise, but I couldn't live the rest of my life watching you be her mom and having her know I chose not to. I can't."

"But you can consider ending her life before it even starts?"

Sarah startled and knocked her water glass over. The server rushed over with a towel as if she'd merely been waiting for such a thing to happen at table 5, but Sarah waved her away. All empathy evaporated from Denise's face. It was replaced with something firm and strong.

"I told Mom I supported *you*, Sarah, as my sister. No matter what you do, I will still love you and I'll be there to help you. But support *that*? *No.*"

Sarah fixed her eyes on the stream that trailed from the overturned glass to the edge of table, soaking the cloth on its way. "So support doesn't include going with me if I decide to terminate?"

"No," Denise said. "I'll take care of you afterwards if you want, but be a part of it?" She paused until Sarah looked up at her. "That's what *I* can't do."

Her eyes filled and she fumbled in her bag.

"I'm sorry I dashed your hopes," Sarah said.

Denise pulled out her wallet and shook her head. "It's not *my* hopes you need to be worried about."

She motioned for the server, but Sarah pulled her hand down. "You're upset. Go. I've got this."

Denise shoved her wallet back into her bag, but she still sat there. Sarah could almost see soothing hands in her sister's head, stroking her thoughts into place.

"You really need to talk to someone besides us about this," she said finally. "I know you're going to toss this aside, but I'm saying it anyway."

Sarah didn't stop her. She'd already hurt her so much she wanted to remove her own tongue.

"When I'm struggling with something, I still go to Reverend Smith—not because he can quote me chapter and verse—but because he's our oldest family friend. When I wish I had Dad, I call him."

"I'm sure Mom's already gone to him."

"No. She hasn't."

Denise averted her eyes.

"It's because she's embarrassed, isn't it?"

When Denise didn't answer, Sarah said, "Okay, thanks."

"You won't go see him, will you?"

"I don't know."

Denise gave her one more crumpled look and hurried for the door. Sarah stayed and mopped up the water from the table.

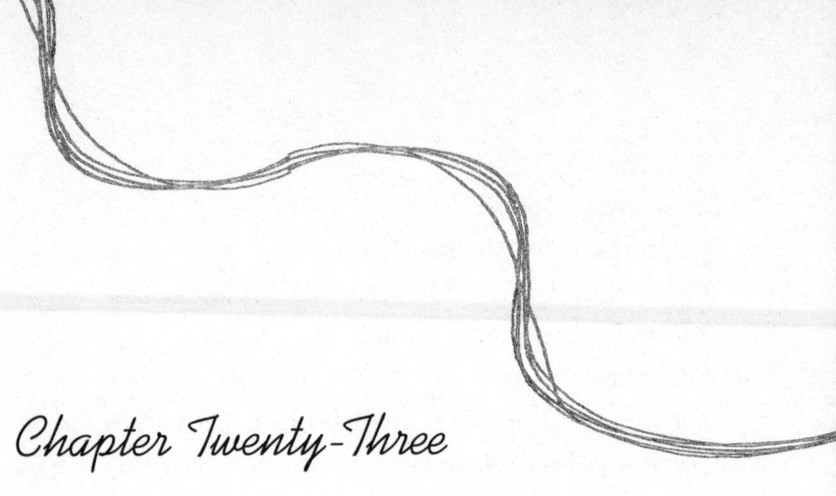

Chapter Twenty-Three

Sarah barely had time to take off her coat in her cubicle before her phone buzzed.

"Sarah?" Jennifer said. "I'd like to see you in my office."

This was only Wednesday. Friday was the day they were supposed to announce their decision, right? Sarah's stomach seized. Her deadline was Friday too. If they told her now—

"Sarah?"

"I'm sorry. I'll be right there."

Wonderful impression of someone under hypnosis. Sarah tried to straighten her shoulders and get her game face on. But the pounds of loneliness were immovable now. Now that she'd lost Denise too.

Jennifer's office was as stylish as she was, everything gray and black and smooth, from the stapler to the sleekly framed ad for a perfume line Jennifer had headed up. Sarah would have appreciated it all more if Jennifer hadn't rounded her desk like a high school principal and led Sarah by the elbow out the door and around the corner.

"I want to show you something," she said into Sarah's ear.

What? A guillotine? What happened to *Sarah, you're a woman of integrity*?

Jennifer stopped her at the corner and nodded toward the end of the hall. All Sarah saw there was Nick with somebody.

Thad.

Thad and a bag of golf clubs, which Nick was obviously admiring in spite of himself. Thad pulled out a—what—a nine iron? Who knew? Nick clearly did because he gripped it like it was an extension of his arm and took a practice swing at an invisible ball.

"Do you see what's happening down there?" Jennifer said, lips barely moving. "Thad figured out that the way to Nick's heart is through his golf bag."

In other words, he was schmoozing. And?

"He's still trying to weasel his way into the promotion I want you to have."

Sarah's stomach clenched. "Should I be worried?"

"That depends."

Jennifer took her elbow again and ushered her back into the sleek-and-gray office. When she closed the door behind her and folded her arms, Sarah's picture of herself at seventeen and in danger of suspension was complete.

"Is it true?" Jennifer said.

Her big hazel eyes would have no playing innocent. Lying was pointless too. As Denise said, she was so bad at it she never even tried.

"Yes," Sarah said.

Jennifer's expression remained impassive. Sarah fumbled.

"Do you think I'll lose the promotion if I decide to have the baby?"

"Technically you can't lose it because it hasn't been offered to you yet." Jennifer leaned against the front of her desk. Sarah still stood before her like an errant schoolgirl. "If you have a baby, will you be able to devote as much time and energy to the job as Thad?"

"Honestly," Sarah said, "I don't know that."

"Look, I've told you, I'm on your side. I want you to have it because every woman in this company needs someone like you on the higher level." Jennifer lifted one side of her mouth. "Someone who won't even lie about being pregnant. But equal rights mean equal responsibility. We're expected to do the same work as the men, whether we've been up all night with a colicky kid or not."

"I understand that." The hair on the back of Sarah's neck was beginning to prickle. "I would never use my child as an excuse for not doing the work."

"You might not even get the chance. If Henry and Nick find out you're pregnant, that promotion will go to Thad so fast we'll both have whiplash." She lowered her chin and looked hard at Sarah. "And I can't let them give it to you without them knowing about this. I've worked too hard to risk losing my credibility. I like you, Sarah, but . . ." She shrugged.

Sarah gazed past her at the perfume ad. Jennifer had won an award and a promotion and this office for that campaign. She could have that, too, with the ConEx account. All she had to do was choose.

Between this and the cherub cheeks.

"I'll be straight with you like I always have," Jennifer said. "If you want this promotion, take care of things by Friday morning."

Sarah jerked back to her. Jennifer's smile was uncertain, as if she'd stepped into territory she normally tried to stay out of.

"You're a young woman, Sarah. There will be plenty of time for a family later, when you're more established."

She stood up and clasped her hands. Prediction made. File closed. Interview over.

Sarah left Jennifer's office and went to Audrey's, but she wasn't there. Panic stirred in her stomach. Had she gone into labor? Was she gone for good?

Okay, stop. Audrey wasn't the person she needed to talk to anyway. She headed straight for the only other person who knew.

Megan was on the phone, obviously with somebody further down on the totem pole. She spoke slow and loud with exaggerated patience.

"They will like the concept if you let them think it was their idea . . . I'm about to *tell* you how . . . Just change it to the font they wanted . . . I know it's hideous, but do it . . . and move everything over to the left . . . Because that will be enough to make them think you changed the whole thing . . . Of course you're going to bill them for the time. That's how we make money. *Comprende?* We good?"

Megan hung up, leaving her hand spread in the air over the phone and rolling her eyes far up into her head.

"Where do we get these people?" she said to Sarah. "Sorry. Sit."

"No."

Megan watched her, eyes cool. "I'm glad you decided to come in. Finally."

"Are you the one who told Jennifer I'm pregnant?"

Megan steepled her fingers under her chin. "Yes."

Sarah gritted her teeth. "Why did you do that?"

"Had to. She called me into her office yesterday and asked me if I had any long-term concerns about your abilities. She was trying to finalize her pitch for you to Nick and Carson."

That didn't make sense.

"And you told her? What were you thinking?"

"Do you seriously want me to get fired? That's exactly what would have happened if they found out later that I knew and didn't tell them. They're all about full disclosure around here."

Sarah sank into the chair in the corner. Megan swiveled to look at her.

"So what did Jennifer say?"

"Take care of it by Friday."

"Which brings us right back to where we've been for over a week now." Megan straightened the already stiff stand-up collar of her white blouse. "How many more people have to tell you to get this over with and get on with your life before you actually do it?"

"I can't just get over Daisy's life!"

Sarah put her hand to her mouth. It was one thing not to lie, but did she have to blurt out everything that was true? And to Megan? Who was looking at her as if she'd grown a third eye?

"Who in the world is Daisy?"

She shifted her gaze to her lap. "The baby. And the six-year-old."

"Whose?"

"Mine."

She looked up to see Megan narrow her eyes into slits. "Did you have another dream?"

"It wasn't like a dream, though. Neither of them was." Sarah tossed her head back. "Why am I even telling you this?"

"Because you know I'll tell you that you're either going psycho on me or you're letting those religious fanatics make you feel guilty. You can't let them do that, Sarah."

Megan's face reddened, and the cool, decisive voice melted down into something so un-Megan Sarah almost didn't recognize it as hers. She'd seen Megan annoyed, irritated, and even ready to cuss someone out in Portuguese. But this voice was thick with guilt of its own.

"Why do I feel like we're not talking about me anymore?" Sarah said.

Megan clearly struggled to get her face under control. "Close the blinds and I'll tell you what I'm talking about. And maybe then you will finally get it."

Sarah went to the wide window that faced the hall and tugged the cord. By the time she returned to the chair, Megan was back in Megan-mode. Except for the rolling of a pen between her palms. Sarah had never seen her do anything remotely nervous before.

"I've been where you are," she said.

"Pregnant?"

"Yep. I was sixteen. A junior in high school and in love." Megan made quotation marks in the air with the pen. "I wanted to have the baby. But I've told you about my mother."

"Um—domineering. Controlling."

"That's her."

And that's you. But Sarah stayed quiet. At the moment Megan's sarcasm was forced and fragile.

"When she's not busy messing up her own life, she's busy messing up mine."

All Sarah could really remember from Megan's tales of her mother was three divorces and several failed attempts at being an entrepreneur.

"Not that I wasn't doing a pretty good job of messing it up myself. I only hated her because she was right."

"About . . ."

"Making me have an abortion."

Sarah felt a surprising pang of pain. It was hard enough trying to make a decision for herself. Having someone make it for her would be excruciating.

"She *was* right," Megan said, though Sarah wasn't sure whether she was trying to convince her or herself. "Do you think I'd be where I am now if I'd had a kid at sixteen? Can you even imagine me with a fourteen-year-old kid?"

Sarah could, actually. That kid would be stunning and trendy and have a smart mouth that would rival Megan's every day of the week. Megan leaned back in her chair and stared at the ceiling and Sarah wondered if she was imagining that kid too. The silence grew uncomfortable.

"What about the father?" Sarah said.

"What about him?"

"Didn't he have an opinion?"

"Not according to my mother."

"Did he even know?"

"Oh yeah. I told him first, and there was this big dramatic scene where we planned to get married, get an apartment. He would get a job and somehow we would all live happily ever after." She dropped the pen on the desk. "And then you know what happened?"

"Your mother."

"And reality. Like a slap in the face. I had the abortion. My mother lived happily ever after, to hear her tell it, and I guess"—she wafted a hand around her office—"so did I."

"What about the father?" Sarah said again.

"The absolute love of my sixteen-year-old life? He delivered a pizza to my mother's house last month." She leaned forward and pointed herself at Sarah. "A pizza. Of course my mother could not *wait* to tell me that. It was *aren't you glad you listened to me* for thirty minutes."

"Listened to her? You didn't have a choice."

"Don't get all indignant for me," Megan said. "She knew what she was doing. Where would I be right now, seriously? Divorced, for sure. I doubt I'd even have finished high school, let alone college. I'd probably be living in some dump of an apartment on welfare. What kind of life would that be for me and my kid?"

Sarah stared, stricken, as Megan's face collapsed. Tears had entered three sentences ago, from someplace they'd obviously been ordered to stay probably about fourteen *years* ago. They eroded Megan's veneer right before Sarah's eyes.

"I never even think about it except for this god-awful time of year." She tried to rally some anger and failed. "I hate Christmas. I refuse to even go to the company party with all the kids and Santa . . ."

Sarah tilted her head. "You went last year."

"And if you'll recall, I said I was sick and left early."

"But you weren't sick."

Megan shook her head. The tears had taken siege, and she was helpless to stop them. "I was fine and then Lisa came with her son. The thirteen-year-old."

Sarah remembered him. Tall and funny-bordering-on-obnoxious and too cute for his own good. The precocious thing had actually tried to hit on her.

"He was the same age as my child would've been, and that just—it just punched me right in the stomach. I went home to my empty apartment and I ripped the wreath off my door. What was I celebrating, you know?"

"Megan, I'm sorry—"

"So here I am: thirty years old, married to my job. I can still hear my mother telling me the day we left the clinic that I would have plenty of time for children when I was ready." A sob broke free from the place it had been stuck, Sarah guessed, since that day. "I don't see that happening."

Sarah gave her a minute to find Kleenex and pull her sorrow back inside. Then she said, "How do I know I'm not going to feel the same way if I have an abortion?"

Megan looked as if something were occurring to her for the first time. It was another expression Sarah had never seen her wear before. Her eyes made an honest channel straight to Sarah.

"I guess you can't know," she said. "My choice was made for me. You need to make your own. Just make sure it's a decision you can live with." Her voice faltered again. "And would you go do that? Because right now, I can't talk about this anymore."

Sarah stood up and with a brush of her fingers on Megan's knee she left her there to put the pieces back where they belonged. She had a feeling they wouldn't fit any more.

She closed Megan's door soundlessly behind her, and as she started toward her office her cell phone went off in her pocket, Matt's ring tone. She couldn't talk to him now, not with Megan's anguish all tangled up with hers. She reached into her pocket to silence it and felt something else in there, like card stock paper.

What had she forgotten now? She pulled it out and stopped cold in her cubicle doorway. It was the Christmas card. Sarah dropped it and clamped both hands over her mouth. She had torn it up this morning. Into small pieces. In her apartment. She hadn't even bothered to sweep them up before she left for work. Yet here were the wise men, two of them looking up at her as if to say, "What more do you want from us? It's all right there in the visions."

It's not all right there! she wanted to scream at them. Where's the part about how I'm supposed to afford to take care of her? Without a good job? Which I can't get if I have her? Where is *that*?

"You dropped something."

Sarah jumped. Thad leaned over and retrieved the card.

"Here you go."

Sarah stared at it.

"Hello?"

"Sorry. Thanks," Sarah said and took it from him.

"Who's it from?" Thad said, for all the world like it was his business. His wheedling voice snapped Sarah back.

"Hey, Thad, personal boundaries?"

He went off muttering about women and their issues. That would be a topic of discussion for his next nine holes with Nick. But he *had* asked the right question. Who *was* it from?

Sarah knew where to start to find out. And maybe the rest of the answers would be there too.

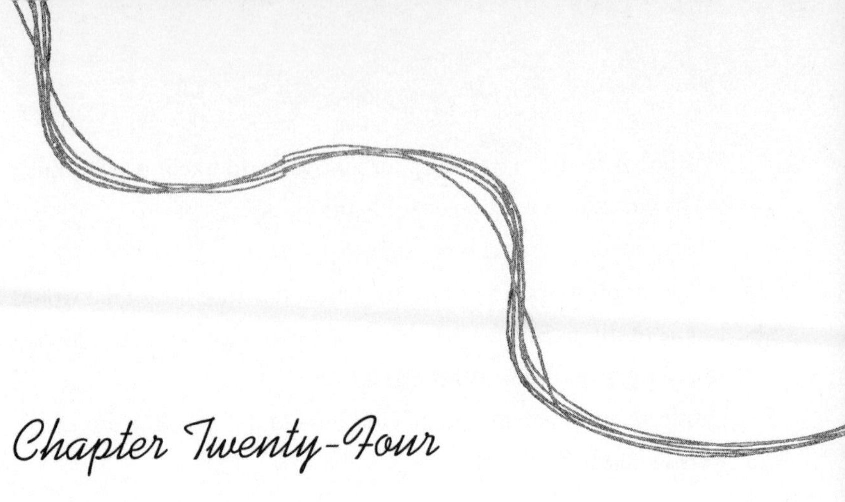

Chapter Twenty-Four

Matt leaned back in his desk chair and tapped his cell phone on his chin as he stared up at the fluorescent light. He was in prime position to see the paper airplane, clearly constructed from United Financial stationery, soar over his cubicle and dive into Cherie's.

She croaked out an unsurprising: "What am I, the tarmac?"

Somebody in the hallway, probably Wes, let out a whispered expletive, followed by a snicker. Followed by an expectant pause.

Matt didn't fill it.

As disappointed footsteps faded down the hall, he studied his phone screen and looked again for a text message, a phone call, an e-mail from Sarah, but all in-boxes were empty, just as they'd been each of the five times he'd checked them in the last fifteen minutes. He'd lost count of how many unanswered messages he'd sent her, and the longer he went without hearing her voice, the harder it was to breathe.

Maybe she was sending him a message with her silence. Matt

squinted at the light. That wasn't her MO. But then, being pregnant wasn't either. Uncle Clay told him women had major mood swings when they were carrying a kid. His Aunt Jerri had dropped all the plates in the cabinet on the floor, one by one, two months before Lucas was born, because Uncle Clay asked her what time dinner was.

Matt couldn't buy that Sarah was having a pregnancy-induced mood thing. It was him. He'd messed this up from the minute she told him, and it looked like his chances of un-messing it were about as good as him winning the lottery.

His father's voice was in his head before he could shut off: *The minute you get real is the minute I'll believe we share DNA.*

He came forward in the chair and held the phone between his knees. How did a guy know when it was time to give up? He'd always been able to pick up on the cues from women before, when he'd stayed around long enough for them to start in the first place. But Sarah wasn't other women. And those women weren't the mother of his child.

Matt tapped her number on his phone. One more time. He wouldn't beg her to talk to him this time. He would just tell her—

"This is Sarah. I'm not available right now—"

Straight to voice mail. She'd probably gotten so sick of him calling that she turned off her phone. His mouth went dry.

The thing beeped and he licked his lips. A full five seconds passed before he could say, "Hey, Sar. I guess you want me to leave you alone, but it's hard to . . . Anyway, just checking in." He closed his eyes. "I love you."

Matt ended the call and slid the phone across his desk. It hit the rubber band ball and sent it tumbling over the side, where it landed at his feet. He kicked it into the corner and watched it take two startled bounces before it rolled against the trash can and stayed like a defeated five-year-old.

That helped, like, not at all. Sarah could totally marry a guy who threw a tantrum when something didn't go like he planned it.

Except—what plan? He turned the chair back to the desk and pulled the Series Sixty-Five manual toward him. Sarah would marry a guy who studied for his exam and got a promotion and gave a rip about his career. Matt flipped the book open and traced a finger along the heading at the top. "Finding Future Values."

Who *did* give a rip about prime rates, seriously? Especially when the rest of his life was falling apart. Did he even have a life without Sarah?

He grabbed the phone from where it had slid into his gripper. What hadn't he tried yet?

Or would it matter what he did at this point?

"I think this was meant for *you*, Evans."

Matt jerked and stared at the figure in the doorway, and with good reason. Cherie was standing there. Cherie, who never came out of her cubicle during the day unless there was a fire drill. He was startled, as he was every time he saw her, by how short she was. Her voice croaking and growling and snarling from the cubicle made her sound like a middle linebacker for the Green Bay Packers. Wearing silver bell earrings.

She carefully patted the comma-shaped portions of impossibly black hair in front of her ears and with burgundy talons shot the paper airplane across the room and onto his desk. It lodged next to the manual.

"The lunatics are taking over the asylum," she said. "Seems their keeper is on sabbatical."

"I'm sorry, Cherie," Matt said.

He steeled himself for the sarcasm or the lecture on what would go down if Clay found out they were using company stationery for aircraft. She had, after all, emerged from her office so it had to be important. Maybe she was there to pass on the rumor that he was being let go. That would chip off the last piece of his life, wouldn't it?

But Cherie merely nodded, bells jingling, and although she continued to nod, her bicycle helmet of hair didn't move. Neither did her eyes from his face.

"I knew it was in there," she said.

Matt cocked his head. "You've lost me, Cherie,"

"What I'm looking at. I knew it was in there."

He glanced at his desk. "What are you looking at?"

"You," she said. "I'm finally looking at you."

She turned to go, like a robot changing direction, but she pivoted back.

"Don't leave her alone, Evans," she said. "Or you'll regret it for the rest of your life."

Matt stared at the doorway long after he heard her settle in at her desk and resume muttering over her time sheets.

I knew it was in there. You.

A *you* so different she had come out of her cell to see it? Matt looked down at his body, still hunched in the chair. What was different? That was the problem, the problem Sarah saw: that he was the same as he'd ever been. Who could trust him to be anything else?

Matt put the phone on the desk again and reached for the manual. With it came the airplane, now flattened down to a mere waste of heavy bond stationery. Something was written on it.

He unfolded it and spread it on the desk. *Texted you twice,* it said in Wes's scrawl. *High noon. North corridor. Dude, it's on.*

Matt read it again and waited for the delicious anticipation of distraction—for the devious ideas to teem in his head—for his thumbs to go automatically to his phone to text something cryptic and clever back to Wes.

None of it came. The only thing he felt was a slow, heavy drag toward the memories of wasted time.

That was what was different.

Matt picked up the paper and wadded it into a ball in his hands. When he tossed it to the trash can, it missed and rested next to the rubber band ball. He crossed the cubicle and dropped them both in.

Audrey still wasn't in the office at two that afternoon. As Sarah signed out for the day a few minutes later, she wondered if she would have told Audrey about the visions. And about what she was about to do. Audrey was the only sane person she knew right now. If she'd told her not to go, to let go of this, she probably would have.

Except that Audrey never had told her what to do or not do. All she did was ask questions.

Sarah was full of questions of her own as she set out for the clinic in Buzz Lightyear. For the first day that week she didn't have to battle snow and ice, and by some miracle Buzz got her to Lincoln Park without having an asthma attack at every intersection.

She avoided the eyes of the knot of people on the sidewalk in front of the clinic building who were apparently setting up for another protest. Good thing Megan wasn't with her, or she'd be calling them Jesus freaks and quoting *Roe v. Wade.*

Actually, Megan would be telling her she needed psychiatric care. But she had to do this, or she really was going to go crazy.

The waiting room was empty except for a twenty-something guy sleeping in a chair in the corner with his feet up on the toy box. Sarah pushed away the scenarios that immediately came to mind—of who he was waiting for and why. She went straight to the window, behind which sat the same round-faced receptionist who had checked her in. She was hanging up the phone.

"If you'll sign in on the computer screen, we'll be right with you," she said into the microphone.

"I don't want to sign in. I just—"

"It's required if you want to see somebody."

"I don't. Look, I'm sorry but I just need to ask a question." Before the girl could tell her she had to sign in for that, too, Sarah rushed on. "I was in here a couple days ago, and there was this older woman that was handing these out." Sarah pressed the card to the glass. "I just wanted to know if you knew anything about her or where I could maybe find her . . ."

She let her voice trail off as the girl leaned forward and studied the card. She moved only her eyes up to Sarah.

"Uh, this is a Christmas card."

"I know."

"We don't hand them out."

Her voice was dismissive, but Sarah kept the card against the window. "You haven't seen anybody hand out anything . . . like this?"

The girl was already shaking her head. "No. Sorry." She went back to the ringing phone.

Sarah pulled the card down and stared at it again. So it was her imagination. If that was what she'd come here to prove, why did she feel so deflated?

She left the card on the ledge and hurried out of the waiting room. She knew why her insides were sagging: because the visions were the only times she liked who she was. The only times when she felt real. If *they* weren't real, then where did that leave her?

She fought back panic all the way down the elevator and out onto the sidewalk where the afternoon sun cut through the cloudless sky and hit her full in the face. She was blinded until she shaded her eyes with her hand. Directly across the street a line of twenty- and thirtyish women held balloons in gloved hands, but their faces didn't reflect the bobbing brightness above them. Some were still and pensive. Some bit their lips as if they were holding back tears. Others let them slide down their cheeks and licked at them when they reached their mouths. Whatever was going on over there, it wasn't a party. But then, she guessed protestors didn't usually get together on the street to celebrate.

"Excuse me," said someone behind her.

Sarah turned to face a substantial woman in a houndstooth-check coat who stood behind a camera on a tripod. Sarah was right in front of it, blocking the woman's shot.

"I'm sorry," Sarah said and stepped aside.

The woman smiled from an open face. Everything about her seemed open, including the unbuttoned coat that flapped in the Chicago wind.

"It's okay," she said. "We're just a couple of minutes away from filming."

She went to the curb and held up five fingers to the group across the street. Sarah wasn't sure why she didn't move on, why she said, "You're filming protestors?"

The woman shook away the thick auburn hair the wind flung across her face. "No. These aren't protestors. These are gals getting ready to send letters to heaven." She turned from the curb to look at Sarah. "It's a post-abortion recovery group, is what it is."

Her eyes invited the next question. Although the *real* next question was, *Why am I still standing here*, Sarah said, "Why the balloons?"

The woman parked her hands comfortably into her pockets. "The balloons give them an opportunity to write a letter to their unborn children, and name them, and then release them into heaven."

Sarah looked up involuntarily at the flawless sky.

"These girls know that God has forgiven them, but they're struggling with forgiving themselves."

Sarah's gaze went back to her. If she'd been in the woman's home, they'd be having coffee and gingerbread by a fire right now. She felt her throat thicken.

"Does it actually work?" she said.

"Yeah." The auburn head nodded. "It does. Anytime in our lives when we make a bad decision, it's great to have a chance to seek forgiveness and move on. And that's exactly what they're doing. It's very powerful. Would you like to stay and watch?"

"I don't want to be in the way."

"You won't be if you stand back here by me."

Still not knowing why, Sarah followed the woman to the camera. Someone across the street whistled, and the woman signaled back. As Sarah watched, fifteen or twenty brilliant orbs floated from upstretched hands and let the wind carry them above the towers and penthouses and satellite dishes and into the vast expanse of blue. Below, the women watched them go. The pensive faces softened. The tear-streaked ones smoothed into wistful smiles. The bitten lips opened and released the cries so long held in.

Sarah had never seen Megan look like any of them.

She felt her own spirit lift at the freedom of it, but a downdraft pushed it back in place. The woman would say it was all God, and maybe it was. But how was she supposed to go back to God now when she'd dissed him for so long?

As the balloons drifted into mere dots in the sky, some of the women slid their arms around each other. A few just wordlessly touched hands.

"They're not alone," Sarah said out loud.

"No, they're not."

Sarah jumped. She didn't mean for her to hear that. It was clearly time to go.

"Can I help you at all?" the woman said.

"No, thank you," Sarah said.

Right now, she could only think of one person who might.

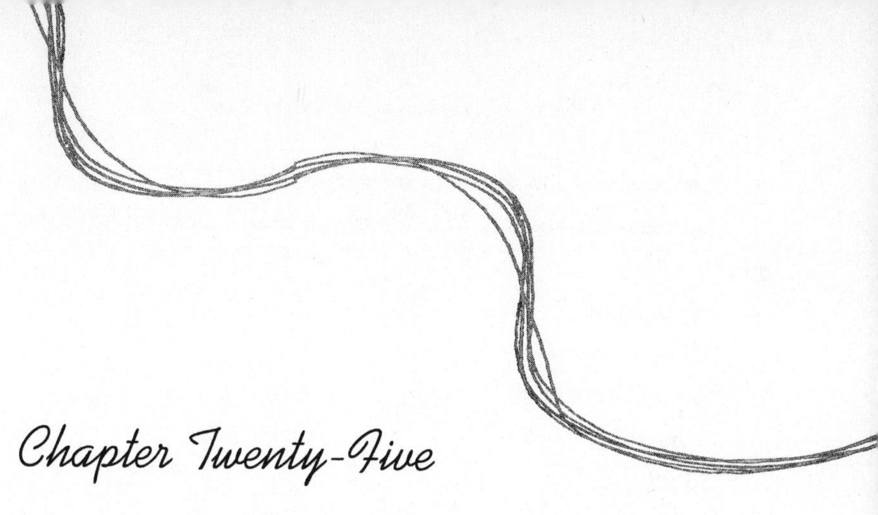

Chapter Twenty-Five

Audrey answered her cell on the first ring.

"If you're in labor, just tell me and I'll hang up," Sarah said instead of hello.

"No such luck," Audrey said. "Why did you think that?"

"Because you left work."

"I went to the doctor to find out the same thing he told me last week: any time now. So what's up? You sound stressed."

"It can wait 'til tomorrow."

"Or not. Where are you now?"

"Lincoln Park."

"What are you doing for dinner?"

"The same thing I always do—not eating."

"Come to my place. The minestrone'll be done by the time you get here."

"What about your husband?"

"He's working extra hours to save up time to be home when the baby's born."

"Are you sure? I mean about me coming over?"

"Let me think about it. Yes. What time shall I pick you up at the train?"

"I'm in my car."

"All right, then."

"What's his name?"

"Whose?"

"Your baby."

Audrey gave a soft giggle. "Alexander John. After my dad and Jack's. Any particular reason you'd ask that right now?"

"I have no idea," Sarah said. "I'll see you in an hour."

Somehow Audrey's house seemed even cozier than it had four days before. Maybe it was because Audrey let her stir the soup and cut the bread and toss another log in the fireplace.

"Thanks," she said when they were settled in with mugs and a loaf of whole-grain. "I'm so tired tonight."

"I can't believe you're working right up to labor."

Audrey looked down into her mug.

"What?" Sarah said.

"I'm actually not. Working, I mean. I was going to, and then I decided not to. Friday was supposed to be my last day."

"Then why are you still there?"

"Because of you."

Sarah let her spoon clatter against the mug.

"After Saturday night I just wanted to be there in case you still wanted to talk."

"Are you—you're serious."

"I am. And don't ask me why because I'm not usually that compassionate."

"That I don't believe."

"It's the truth. It just felt like a God-thing." She waved her spoon. "Not that I'm not enjoying every minute of it because I am. Maybe *enjoying* isn't the right word. Maybe it's more like I'm learning a lot. And like I've told you, you totally crack me up."

"I never thought I was that entertaining. Especially right now."

"Eat first," Audrey said. "Then you can entertain me some more."

The minestrone was by far Audrey's best soup yet, but Sarah only got halfway through her mug and a slice of bread before she put them both aside.

"So you want to talk about why you were so stressed out when you called me?"

"Jennifer knows I'm pregnant. She told me to have—to take care of things or I can forget the promotion."

"Megan told her, didn't she?"

"Yeah. She even admitted it. She said Jennifer asked her and she had to tell her the truth or get fired."

"What? That's ridiculous—" Audrey put a hand up. "Never mind. So you're feeling like the pressure's really on, then."

"Yeah. But if I do that, I just know I'm going to regret it. I'm not sure I can live with it."

Audrey peeled the crust from her bread. "You asked me the other day if I believed in God. Do you mind if I ask you the same thing?"

"Since it's you, no, I don't mind," Sarah said.

She didn't add: *As long as you don't start delivering a homily.* There was no need to. And that was why it was Audrey she'd come to.

"I do believe in God," Sarah said. "I just don't trust God anymore."

"Is that because of your father's death?"

"Not entirely, no. People do die."

"Yeah, but at younger than fifty? That had to be rough."

"It was. But I got that, you know?"

"Uh, no, I don't."

Sarah contemplated the fire. She'd never told anybody this either, not even her mother or Denise. She didn't even like telling it to herself in those middle-of-the-night sessions when it wouldn't leave her alone. But Audrey had asked all the right questions so far . . .

"The evening before my father died . . . I can still see him in his recliner that he always sat in, even before he got sick, but he practically lived in it after that . . . I can see him wearing his red watch cap over his chemo-head. He had a blanket draped over him—you could have mistaken him for a passenger on the deck of a ship crossing the English Channel, if it weren't for the oxygen tube hooked to his nostrils."

"Lung cancer?"

"Yes. And he never smoked. Never spent time in mines or anything like that. It just happened. And I think I've told you he was responding to treatment. There was always the chance that he'd die eventually, but the doctors kept saying he'd probably go into remission and we'd have him for four or five years. I heard them say that myself because now that I was out of grad school and living back at home, I went to his appointments with him so Mom could have a break. She wasn't handling things well."

"It's fallen on you for a long time, then."

"I wanted it to be on me. That night I even talked my mother into going to Bible study, which she hadn't been to in forever. I think the only reason she went was because Reverend Al was coming over. He was our pastor." Sarah crossed her fingers. "He and my father were like this. So they were sitting there and my father was drinking a cup of warm milk I'd just fixed for him. He says to Reverend Al, 'I'd offer you a cup, Al, but I can't say much for the taste.' Reverend Al said something about putting a little Chinese Five-Spice into it, and my father turned green." Sarah smiled ruefully. "I think I know how he felt. It was strange then, because my dad looked at me like he wanted me to leave the room. That was never the case; I was always involved when people came in, but it was so clear to me, so I left. Sort of."

"Did a little eavesdropping, did you?"

"I hadn't done that since Denise and I were kids, but there was this one spot on the steps where you could see what was going on in the living room, but if somebody even looked like they were going to turn around and see you, you could disappear up the steps. We never got caught. That I know of."

"So that's where you went."

"I did, and I had full view of my dad while they were talking. At first I could hear everything. My dad said this wasn't what he expected at this point in his life, and then he said, 'That's what I get for expecting God to follow my plan, right?'"

"Were you okay with that?"

"We haven't gotten to the part where I started being ticked off at God, if that's what you mean."

"Sorry. Go ahead."

"I actually appreciated Reverend Al right then. He said he wasn't convinced cancer was God's doing. He said, 'All I know is that we can expect God to be there, no matter what happens.'" Sarah took a deep breath. "I'll tell you what *I* expected. I expected my father to say he expected God to heal him. That's what I knew God could do." She closed her eyes so she could see. "But my dad just shook his head and I watched the pain lines etch into his face. And that's when I knew my father might actually die. Soon."

Audrey was very still. Sarah didn't move either. She wasn't sure she could. The memory was so fragile she was afraid it would shatter before she finished it.

"They started talking so softly after that, I couldn't hear. Dad hunched over with his head down. Reverend Al got close to him and murmured for a long time. When I realized my father was crying, I couldn't watch any more. I felt like I was intruding on something he didn't want me to know. I went to my room and stayed until Reverend Al left. Then I went downstairs because I couldn't leave my dad alone."

"How did he seem?"

"Exhausted. I asked him if he wanted me to take him to bed, but he would never let anybody but Mom do that. He really did try to keep his dignity."

"That's not all."

"No. I don't even know if I can get through this part. I never even go back and look at it myself. Every time I've tried it's like all this hopelessness pours over me like tar and I can't move, and then I'm just stuck in the pain." Sarah searched Audrey's face. "If I have to stop, you'll understand, right? You won't think it's because I don't trust you. I do."

"I think I know that."

"You're not knitting."

"I can't. It doesn't seem right."

"No," Sarah said. "It doesn't." Once again she closed her eyes. "I didn't want to be alone with him. I mean, I didn't know what to do or say, and that had never happened before and it scared me. So I started dusting the living room—something I never did, partly because my mother did it six times a day. Once I grabbed the feather duster and started going after the picture frames and the Precious Moments figurines, I could relate. It kept me from screaming, *Please! You can't die!*

"I thought my dad had dozed off, and all of a sudden there was this gasp from the recliner. I turned around and there he was standing up. He hadn't stood up without somebody helping him for weeks, but he was upright on his feet. And not steady." Sarah demonstrated. "He was flailing his arms and he had a startled look on his face, as if he was seeing someone he didn't expect to see. If I hadn't run to him and put my arms around his torso, he would have fallen to the floor, and I couldn't have gotten him up."

"You okay?" Audrey whispered.

Sarah didn't risk answering. "He just clung to me, you know, like I was his lifeline. I could feel his bones pressing against me, and I just held on to him and he hung onto me. All I could think was, *No matter how hard we hang on, I can't stop you from dying.* And then . . . it was like all the air went out of him and he said, 'SJ . . . God forgives me.'"

Sarah tried to breathe deep, but her air was gone.

"And that's when I knew, Audrey. It wasn't just that he might die. He *was* going to die. And soon.

"I don't know how I knew, I just knew, and it ripped me apart from the inside out. You remember me telling you it was like I was in a five-car collision?"

Audrey had both hands pressed to her mouth, but she nodded.

"That was really the first car to hit me. Not him actually dying, but knowing it was going to happen. The impact threw me out of that seat where I could believe he'd stay, and I was bruised and broken. I couldn't even imagine how he must feel, because I knew he knew it too. He was the one who had to shift from hanging on to letting go."

Audrey stayed quiet.

"Then it was like he got very small in my arms, and he asked me to help him sit back down. He closed his eyes and he breathed without gasping and he drifted off to sleep. I still don't know if he really was asleep or if he was just pretending, but he stayed that way until Mom came home. All I said to her was, 'I dusted while you were out.' Was that lame or what?"

"No, probably not."

"While she was in the bedroom getting him to bed, I was sobbing on the couch. I couldn't imagine the world without him in it. And not just mine but the world he influenced every day. During his illness people had come to see him that none of us even knew existed except him. People he'd sold insurance to. Guys who met him for coffee in the morning before work. Strangers he'd befriended and listened to, just the way he did to us. Who does that? The world was going to have big holes in it because he wasn't in it bridging gaps for people who had no one else to do it for them."

"I can see you being mad at God."

"That still wasn't it. My mother found me there, and she didn't even ask why I was crying. I didn't know what my father had told her—whether he shared that he knew he would die. Evidently not because she stroked my hair and she said, 'Something happened tonight at Bible study, Sarah, that you need to know. God spoke to me. He told me he was healing your father. Don't worry. God is healing him.'"

"Did you believe her?" Audrey said. There was no hint in her voice whether she would have or not.

"I wanted to," Sarah said. "My mother had a very real relationship with God, I knew that. And even though I felt like mine was deep, surely hers must be deeper. She was the one who read her Bible every day—prayed without ceasing, as they say. You couldn't shake her faith with an earthquake. So why wouldn't I believe that what she was hearing from God was more accurate than what I thought I knew when I was holding onto my father in that very same room? So I went to sleep there on the couch with some hope again." Sarah's breath caught in her throat. "I woke up the next morning to my mother screaming his name. He was dead."

"Car number two."

"It slammed right into me. When they said his heart just stopped beating for no apparent reason, I knew he had just let go. Or was it God pulling him away?" Sarah tried not to let her voice rise. "I was angry and I didn't know who to be angry *with*. Either God had lied to my mother, or she'd heard wrong, or she'd just made it up to comfort me. If she hadn't told me that he was going to be healed, I would have gotten up and I would have gone to my father and I would have told him everything I wanted to tell him because I knew he was going to die. I was cheated out of that—and after a while it occurred to me that maybe none of it was God. It didn't matter. I was through trying to hear God. So I stopped reading the Bible, and I stopped going to church, and I stopped praying. And you know what, Audrey? That's when I stopped living."

Sarah didn't know she was crying until she felt Audrey's arm around her shoulder.

"Go ahead," she said. "That stuff has been in there for way too long."

"What am I supposed to do with it now?" Sarah sobbed. "How can I speak to a God who wouldn't even give me a chance to say good-bye to the person I loved most in the world? I spent the last few precious moments I had with him dusting the teacups. How can I get past that?"

"I only know one thing for sure," Audrey whispered to her. "You're going to find out, because now you're asking the right questions."

Sarah pulled her hands from her face and stared at the goo in her palms. "I have snot everywhere."

"And I have Kleenex everywhere."

Audrey stood up. Sarah heard something liquid hitting the floor.

"Did I spill my water?" she said.

"No," Audrey said, "I just spilled mine."

Sarah blinked at her for a full ten seconds before she realized what she was talking about.

"Is that—"

"Yep, my water just broke."

"Oh, my gosh!" Sarah leapt up and smeared her nose with the back of her hand. "Okay, so what do we do? Do we call somebody?"

"First we stop freaking out," Audrey said. "Jack and I have a plan in place. It's not like this is a surprise."

"Okay, you call him and I'll drive you to the hospital. In your car. I don't trust mine."

"Would you relax? I'm calling Jack, and he'll come home and we'll take it from there. Meanwhile, I'm more worried about you."

"I'm fine," Sarah lied. "This is huge for you. Your baby's coming. I'm not messing that up."

"I'm not even having that many contractions yet."

Sarah felt her eyes bulge. "What do you mean 'that many?'"

"They've been coming all evening, but they're not bad." Audrey poked at her cell and gave Sarah a gentle shove back into the chair. "Hey sweet darlin'," she said into the phone. "I think it's time. And you better bring a mop."

Sarah looked down at the small puddle on the floor.

"I'll wipe it up," she said when Audrey ended the call.

"I want to save that for Jack," Audrey said. "We're in this together."

Sarah managed to grin at her. But she felt unutterably sad.

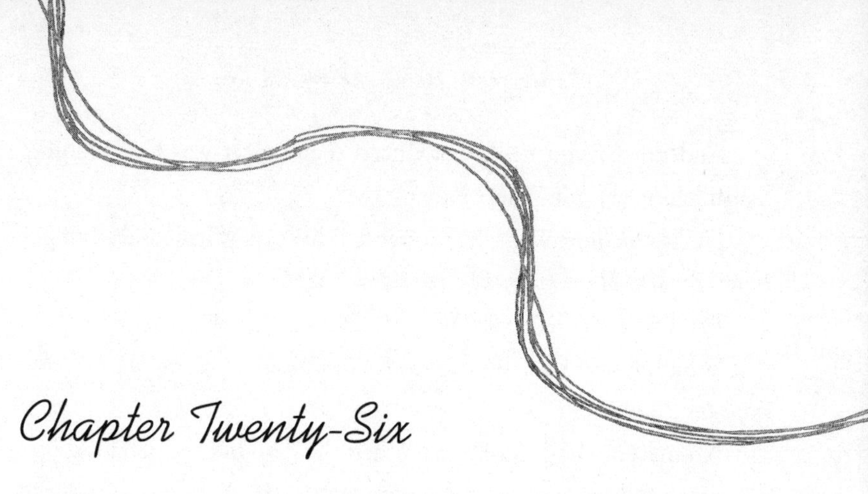

Chapter Twenty-Six

Audrey's Jack assured Sarah he would text her when Baby Alex made his entrance. But tiny beads of sweat had formed on his shaved head, and before they left for the hospital he called her Sally. She was fairly certain he'd forget. Still, Sarah checked her phone every thirty minutes all night. She wasn't sleeping anyway.

It wasn't visions of Audrey in labor that kept her awake. It was the memories she'd allowed out that evening. And not even those, but the questions they raised.

Did she really still believe in God?

Well, yes. Why else would her first reaction at the clinic have been, *I can't have an abortion*?

Then why was this even an issue?

She gnawed on that until 2:00 a.m. when she was nursing a cup of hot milk. The very same way her dad had nursed his the night he died. What was it about that?

Reverend Al telling him to put Chinese Five Spice in it?

No.

And not his not being convinced that cancer was God's doing. Sarah had never gone there either.

No, it was more what the reverend didn't say. What Sarah thought he might say. *Have faith, Bill. You'll be cured.*

He didn't say that. Her mother said that.

What he said was, *We can expect God to be there, no matter what happens.*

No matter what? Like now? When she'd all but written God off?

Sarah got up and put the empty cup in the sink and stared into it. They'd lowered their voices after that, her dad and Reverend Al. If she'd heard what they said when her father was crying, would that have made a difference?

Would it make a difference now?

There was only one way to find out.

Reverend Al's secretary—thankfully not Denise that day—said he could see Sarah at two. That gave her time to try to talk herself out of it. How was she going to get to what she needed to know without outright telling him her situation? He wouldn't have much choice but to tell her not to have an abortion.

She didn't have to tell him she was pregnant and trying to decide what to do. She could ask about visions. She needed to know if they were God anyway. And if they were, maybe she wouldn't have to ask about her father's last hour with Reverend Al.

One thing was clear: the only way she was going to do this without losing it was to outline her approach in her mind. It was there as she slid into a pew in the back of the church beside the reverend. The colored light from the stained glass window behind him danced playfully on his partly bald head. It somehow matched the crinkles at the corners of his eyes that made his full-cheeked face look younger than his years. She'd forgotten the mischievous air he had about him. No wonder Denise saw him as an almost-Dad.

"I know it must seem strange that I called you out of the blue," Sarah said. "I haven't exactly been . . . around."

"You're here now," he said. "Why don't we start with that?"

Sarah let out a little of the breath she was holding. "I have kind of a weird question for you."

His eyes twinkled. "Is it: if God is all-powerful and if he can do anything, can he make a stone so heavy he himself can't lift it?"

"No," Sarah said, almost laughing.

"Good, because I don't have the answer to that one. Anything else, I might be able to help you."

He fell silent, the lines still crinkling.

Sarah pulled out the words she had lined up. "I was wondering if God still speaks to people in dreams and visions like he did in the Bible."

"Challenging question." Reverend Al settled comfortably into the pew, one short leg crossed over the other knee with more ease than Sarah would have expected. "Some people believe God stopped revealing himself through dreams and visions when the Bible was completed. Me? I'm not one to limit our Lord's ability to reveal himself to his children." He regarded Sarah with interested eyes. "Do you know someone who's had a vision?"

"Me. I think." This was where she had to tread cautiously. "I have this important decision to make, and I've had two really vivid dreams that show me what will happen if I decide one way."

He nodded. The other thing she'd forgotten was that he listened like you were the only person left breathing in the world.

"I need to know how I can be sure they're true."

"Because that will help you make your decision."

"Right. I would've just passed them off as dreams if it weren't for this card . . ."

Sarah opened her bag, but the card wasn't there because, of course, she'd left it at the clinic. She rolled her eyes and muttered, "Figures."

The reverend recrossed his legs, never moving his gaze from her. His eyes grew more serious. "The only way to discern the truth of any vision is to measure it against the revealed word of God."

Sarah tried to keep the nettle out of her voice. "I don't have time to read the whole Bible and see how they fit."

"Okay, then let's take a different tack."

The shift didn't seem to bother him at all. In fact, he looked even more intrigued.

"This decision you have to make, and soon, I take it . . ."

"By tomorrow," Sarah said.

"Is the decision morally neutral, where either option would fall within the will of God? Or is it a case where one option definitely falls outside his will?"

"According to the church, it's the second." She tried to keep the sudden bitterness out of her voice, but apparently it was apparently oozing from her pores because Reverend Al leaned forward and said, "Let's put doctrine aside for the moment. I think what's at issue here is where you are with God."

"Nowhere."

"Because of your dad's death."

"Yes."

"You can't be anywhere with God now because he abandoned you then."

Sarah felt her chin drop.

"I saw it at the funeral, Sarah. You were more angry than sad. That's why I haven't reached out to you." He smiled a little as he tilted his head sideways and back. "Prayed for you, yes. And waited for a time when I wasn't going to get my clock cleaned."

Sarah swallowed hard. "I couldn't get past it. And now when I need to, I'm afraid . . ."

"Afraid of what?"

This wasn't part of the plan she'd come in here with. Neither was the whisper. *That's what I get for expecting God to follow my plan.*

"I'm afraid it's too late," Sarah said. "I'm afraid I've turned my back for too long. I don't even know how to find my way to him now."

She wiped the tears from her face with the heels of her hands, but more came. She couldn't seem to stop any of this anymore.

"You don't have to find your way, Sarah," the reverend said. "If you're ready, God will find you. I have no doubt he's been there all along. Maybe even in those visions."

"I think I'm afraid to be ready. I'm afraid I'll just be hurt again."

He folded his hands against his chest, pressing them against his heart. "I know this for sure: God loves you no matter how much you resist. In my opinion, you should be telling *him* all of this."

Sarah paused, her hand on her cheek. "Yell at God?"

"I've been known to do it a time or two myself. I loved your father too." His face worked. "I haven't seen joy in your eyes in a long time. Maybe you need to yell."

Reverend Al folded his hands. He reminded her of Audrey, somehow knowing she wasn't finished.

"I have something else to ask you," she said. "It might be asking you to betray a confidence, so if it is I'll understand, but I have to ask because—"

"Sarah," he said. "Why don't you tell me the question first? Then we'll see."

She nodded. "Do you remember that last night before my dad died, when you were with him?"

"I'll never forget it."

"I have a confession to make: I was listening to your conversation."

"From the stairs." He gave her a soft chuckle. "Your father knew you were there. He asked me to lower my voice so we could talk about something that was troubling him."

"Can you tell me what it was? If you can't—"

Reverend Al put his hand on hers. "I can tell you he was struggling. Something like the way you are now."

"Struggling? My dad?"

"He'd been wrestling with it for years. That night, he was desperate to know if I thought he was forgiven."

First Wife? Sarah wanted to say. It was the only thing it could possibly be.

"He was, wasn't he?" Sarah said. "Forgiven, I mean?"

"Of course he was. That's the nature of this God who loves us." The reverend's shoulders sagged. "Unfortunately, I'm not sure I convinced your father to accept that. I don't like to think that he died with that still weighing on him—"

"He didn't."

"I'm sorry?"

Sarah squeezed his hand. "His last words to me were 'God forgives me, SJ,'" she said.

And then with a murmured thanks she bolted, while she could still see.

She got to the car before that was completely impossible. But she did see one thing. The wise men Christmas card—on the passenger seat as if she'd put it there herself.

This time she picked it up and pressed it against her cheek.

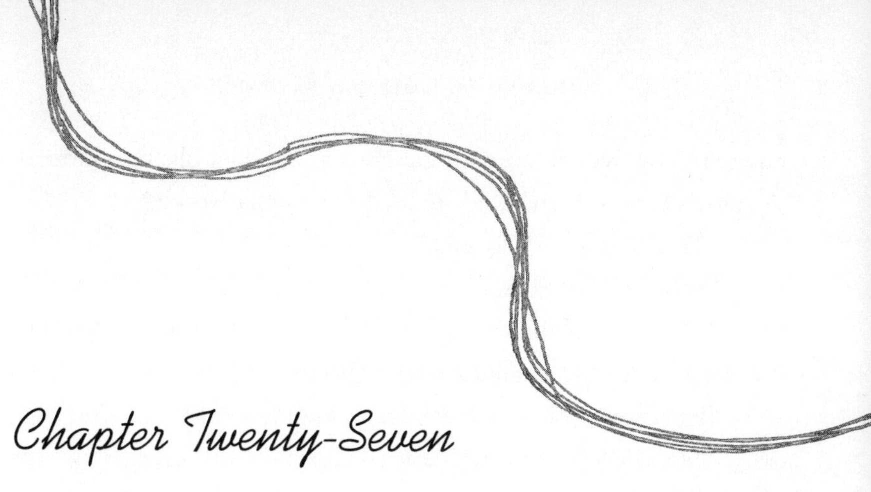

Chapter Twenty-Seven

Outside Matt's office, Wes's voice rose above the din of shouted bets and chairs rolling into place at the other end of the hall.

"You on watch, Cherie?"

"In your dreams," she croaked.

"Gentlemen, start your engines!"

Wes sounded so much like him, Matt wanted to hurl into the trash can. The familiar rattle of chairs wiped out all chance of concentrating, but he turned to his computer screen anyway and scrolled down the list of courses for mechanics. They'd be done out there in about eleven seconds, not counting the time it would take to divide the spoils.

But the expected announcement of the winner was cut off by another familiar sound. As in Uncle Clay barking, "All right, kids. Recess is over."

Matt rolled his own chair back so he could see what was about to go down. The hall was suddenly empty except for Wes, who stood nose to nose with Clay, arms dangling at his sides like the thirteen-year-old he was. Matt could see his Adam's apple working.

"This your gig?" Clay said.

"Well, this time, yeah."

"This time's all I'm concerned about. This happens again and I'm writing you up. And you don't want that."

"How come you never got all over Matt like this?"

Matt winced at the whine in Wes's voice. Make that a twelve-year-old.

"I never caught Matt in the act," Clay said.

He turned on his heel and disappeared from Matt's view. When his footsteps had faded down the hall, Wes rapped his knuckles on Cherie's wall.

"Thanks for the heads-up, Cherie."

"Never said I'd give you one," she said. Her phone rang.

"You always—"

"Good afternoon. United Financial. How can I direct your call?"

Wes put himself in Matt's full view and held out his hands in a clear *What the what?* Matt shrugged.

"Really? *Really?*"

Matt rolled back to the computer. Wes went off, flinging over his shoulder, "Appreciate the support, Matthew."

"Evans."

"Yeah, Cherie," Matt said.

"Your father's on the line. What do you want me to tell him?"

Matt looked at the computer screen, still bright with the website for the Advanced Technology Institute.

"Nothing," Matt said. "Put him through."

"Putting him through."

When Matt's desk phone rang, he wrapped his fingers around

the receiver and let it ring again. Once he heard his father's voice, he'd want to fold. He had to at least start out strong.

"Hey, Dad," he said.

"You decided to talk to me. You must need money."

It didn't take much imagination to see the smirk twist his father's face. He'd have his high-end desk chair tilted back, twirling his Mont Blanc in his fingers. Matt brought his own chair upright and tossed his pencil on his desk.

"Thanks, but I don't need money."

"I wasn't offering any."

Then why the—

"This is about Christmas." The AK-47 was loaded and aimed. "I personally don't see how your being here is going to make life better for your mother, but she seems to think so. Heads don't belong in the sand unless you're an ostrich. She has the feathers to prove it."

"Could we just get to the—"

"Here's what's happening. I've made a plane reservation for you for tomorrow night. That will give your mother Christmas Eve and this party and Christmas Day with you. All of you will be here. That should get her off my back for at least a week."

"Dad—"

"Consider thinking before you open your mouth. What a concept."

Matt stood up.

"This is costing me an arm and a leg," his father went on, "and it's the last time I intend to do it. From now on when it comes to your mother's feelings, you're either going to have to grow up or give up. It's time to choose—"

"Dad, stop." Matt dove through the shocked window of silence. "I'm sorry you went to all that expense, but I'm not coming to Philly for Christmas."

"Don't insult me by telling me you have plans." His father's voice was menacing. "You've never made a plan in your life unless it was to—"

"I have a responsibility here."

Matt should have known the out-and-out guffaw was inevitable, but it still came at him like a barrage of bullets.

"Her name is Sarah," he said. "You met her. She's pregnant with our baby."

The brief silence was devoid of shock this time. "It was only a matter of time. How many times have I said it? Bottom line: you screw it up, you fix it. So you do need money. How much does an abortion cost these days?"

"She's not having an abortion. Not if I can help it. My plan is to marry her and take care of both of them."

"With *what*? Your good looks? That's what got you into this situation, but it's not going to get you out. If you couldn't support it, you shouldn't have chased it."

"I have a job, Dad—" Matt started to say. But he sounded too much like Wes, whining to Clay and not knowing what to do with his arms.

His father swore. "The minute you get real is the minute I'll believe we share DNA."

"Look, tell Mom I'm sorry. No, I'll do that myself."

"You will *not* tell her about this. Not until I—"

"I have to get back to work," Matt said. "Merry Christmas."

His father was still sputtering as Matt hung up the phone. He watched his hand shake.

"How you doing, Evans?"

"You got a barf bag, Cherie?"

"No. I'm putting a call in to Sarah."

"Yeah. Use her landline at her apartment."

"That's where I'm going."

Sarah didn't pick up, of course. She would still be at work. He wanted her to have the message when she got home, when she could think about it.

At the sound of the beep, Matt closed his eyes and pictured her standing over the phone, all that luscious hair curtaining the sides of her face, brown eyes intent, waiting for something she could count on.

"Hey, Sar," he said. "Please listen to me. I have to talk to you. In person. I'm not leaving you alone with this, so if I don't hear back from you by eleven tomorrow morning, I'm coming to you." He drew in more air. "Please don't do anything until we talk. Please. I love you."

Matt returned the phone gently to its cradle. The energy that had powered him through the conversation with his father and his message to Sarah dissolved. The ball was in her court now, and he had no way of knowing if she was even still in the game. He smothered his face with his hand and felt the muscles work against what clawed at his throat.

Only a few minutes passed before he felt a firm hand on his shoulder.

"Thanks, Uncle Clay," he said.

"No problem, my man. No problem."

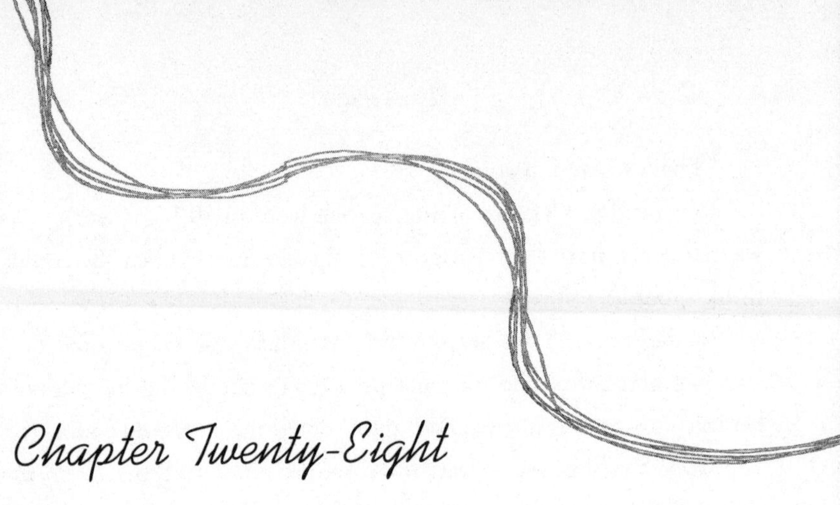

Chapter Twenty-Eight

Sarah had lived alone for two and a half years, and she had spent plenty of nights by herself before that in her New York apartment while her roommate slept at her boyfriend's place. The aloneness was never hard; she actually liked not having someone constantly filling the airwaves because heaven forbid there should be quiet. She'd always liked the freedom to pick her own music and the space to spread out a project. And the silence. The silence was like a cloak she could wrap herself in and magically forget that a boss had made her feel like she wasn't enough or a date had told her she was too much.

But that night it was hard. Part of that was the exhausted but exhilarated voice of Jack on the phone, telling her that Baby Alexander had finally been born, weighing in at nine pounds, two ounces.

"Twenty-four hours of labor," he said, as if he were expounding on the stamina of an NFL quarterback. "But she did great."

"And the baby?"

"He's great too. Got a great set of lungs on him."

"That's awesome," Sarah said. "Please give Audrey my love."

"She said to tell you something. What was it? Sorry—I haven't slept in—"

"It's okay. She can tell me later."

"No, wait. She'll have my head—it was something like, *Keep asking the questions.* Something like that."

"Yeah," Sarah said. "Something like that."

But as they hung up, Sarah sagged. She was tired of asking questions. And she was so lonely she could hardly breathe.

There was always the flashing light on her phone. She knew it would be a message from Matt. Hoped it would be. Was afraid it would be, and that she'd hear the same old thing.

She didn't. There was no hint of a coming punch line or the desperate begging she'd heard in his other messages. The mention of a deadline—eleven tomorrow—was firm. So was the promise to come to her if she didn't get back to him. It made her long for the Matt she'd hoped for.

Yeah, speaking of questions. Was it a Matt who was working out of guilt? Obligation? All the things sure to take them out before they ever got started?

She sank into the desk chair. She would call him back, but not now. Not when she was this lonely and vulnerable. Not when she would have given just about anything to have him in her kitchen burning the toast. She had to make her decision based on real consequences. Right? Didn't she? Even now, after Audrey and Reverend Al and her dad's whisper?

Sarah glanced at the compartments of those real consequences on her desk and then registered a double take. The card perched like a precarious bird atop the plastic container of drawers. The two wise men looked steadily at her, while the third still gazed at the star, as if he hadn't yet seen what he'd come to see.

As if he wasn't going to see it until she did.

"You know what?" Sarah said to him. "Show me what ya got."

She wasn't sure who she was talking to, but she felt a stirring of eagerness as she pulled on sweats and climbed into bed and under the covers she'd thrown aside that morning on the way to the daily upchuck. Real or not, a vision was guaranteed to make her feel happier than she did right now.

I haven't seen joy in your eyes in a long time, Reverend Al said.

Sarah didn't hope for quite that much, but she burrowed in and closed those eyes and waited to see what Daisy would look like at ten or thirteen or seventeen . . .

But as the gold light formed its bright frame, a dark-haired beauty in her twenties placed a puff-cheeked infant into her arms. The little one wore a red sleeper trimmed with white fleece, and a matching cap topped her dark fuzz of hair. If she was three weeks old yet, Sarah would be surprised—yet her eyes were as alert and searching as her mother's had been.

Before Sarah could arrange her thoughts, she whispered, "Oh, Daisy, she's beautiful."

Her eyes went quickly to the young woman, but there was no sign that she'd made a mistake. Daisy squeezed Sarah's shoulders from behind.

"I want you to teach me how to be the mom you were to me," she said.

Sarah swallowed that back and carried her granddaughter to the Christmas tree in the bay window she knew would be there. In a large silver ball she saw the gray in her swept-up hair and the crow's feet around her eyes reflected amid crooked glitter letters that spelled out "Momy." It didn't surprise her that she wore a gold knit sweater and 18-karat earrings, all far more sophisticated than anything she would choose now. Whenever "now" was.

A young man Daisy's age kissed her cheek. "She's already a great mom. Right, little Sarah?"

"When is Dad getting here?" Daisy called from another room.

Sarah felt her arms tighten around the baby. Dad. Did she mean Matt? Why wasn't he there? Had he never lived there?

The gold light blurred at its edges. Sarah turned from the tree, frantic for another sight of Daisy and a chance to ask her those questions. But as she moved across the room, the baby evaporated from her arms and the living room, so sparkling with Christmas promise, gave way to a stark white hallway and the smell of antiseptic that failed to cover the odors of advancing age.

Sarah tried to hug herself close with the gold-knit sleeves, but she was back in her NYU sweatshirt. Her dark hair hung limp on her shoulders.

"Go home, girl. It's Christmas Eve and you are *off* duty."

Sarah turned to a nurse's station decked with bedraggled tinsel garland and an already curling poinsettia. An African-American woman in reindeer print scrubs was talking to a youngish woman with a half-ponytail, half-bun and a backpack slung over her shoulder.

"I'm going," the younger woman said. "I just want to check in on 208 first."

"You talkin' about Sarah?" Reindeer Lady's voice went shrill. "You sure you want to do that? You can't tell from one minute to the next whether she's goin' order you out the room or start in tellin' you what a success she was in the advertisin' business." She tucked her chin. "I don't know about you, but I can't listen to that but about five times 'fore I start noddin' off."

Ponytail Girl shrugged. "I know, but I don't think anybody's coming in to see her tonight. I can at least wish her a merry Christmas."

She started past Sarah, who said, "Excuse me, but could you tell me—"

What? Where I am? From the looks of this place, they would probably declare her senile and put her in a room, and this was not a place she wanted to end up in.

It didn't seem to matter what she asked. The girl looked through Sarah as if she were nonexistent and opened the door to room 208. Sarah waved at Reindeer Lady, who appeared to be staring right at her, but she just shook her head at Ponytail's retreating back and dropped into her chair.

The gold light was gone, and the edges of Sarah's line of sight were foggy. So she wasn't really here. She could just wait until she woke up and she would be back in her apartment, and the sooner the better. She shivered even in the smothering nursing home heat. The emptiness there was better than the emptiness here.

Sarah twisted to search for an elevator, but she was stopped by Ponytail Girl's too-loud voice. She sounded as if she were talking to a preschooler for whom English was a second language.

"I came to wish you a merry Christmas, Ms. Sarah."

Again with the Sarah.

Despite the obvious fact that no one could see her, Sarah looked up and down the hall before she followed Ponytail to the doorway and stood behind her. The patient was blocked from Sarah's view, but she could clearly hear her high pitch.

"You didn't have to do that."

Where had she heard that voice before?

"Well," Ponytail said, "I know you don't have family coming tonight."

"My sister was here this morning. She brought me that tree."

The nurse took a few steps into the room so Sarah could check out the tree too: a potted Norfolk pine no bigger than a houseplant, hung with—

Sarah plastered her hand over her mouth.

"Did her kids make those decorations for you?" Ponytail said.

The old lady gave a thick laugh—or a bronchial cough—Sarah couldn't tell which.

"Her boys are all grown up. No, she and I made them—"

When we were kids ourselves. The cardboard snowman with all of its cotton balls missing. The clothespin reindeer. The crooked stars, stripped of all glitter by the years, now showing only the faint traces of glue. On one, the adhesive trail still read "Daddy."

The nurse began to back out of the room. "You enjoy those memories. If you need anything—"

"I won't. I'm expecting another visitor tonight."

"Are you sure?"

Could this girl be any more patronizing?

"Yes."

Sarah heard the I'm-about-to-order-you-out-of-my-room edge in her voice—that voice she still couldn't place. Maybe it just sounded like a Megan-type as an old woman. Maybe that was it.

But when Nurse Ponytail walked past, if not actually through Sarah, and she was able to venture into the room, the tissue-faced figure in the bed wasn't an aged version of a former executive.

She was the woman from the clinic. The one who gave Sarah the card. The one whose prediction had taken her . . .

Here.

"It's you," Sarah said.

The old lady's smile nearly cracked, as if she hadn't used it in a while. "It is. I was expecting you."

Sarah moved close to the bed and wrapped her fingers around the cold bed railing. It was solid, and when she removed her hands they left the prints of her clammy palms. This was no less real than the visions that had left her bright with hope, even for a moment. The slow-growing fear in her throat was as palpable as the joy when she held her granddaughter.

"Why am I here?" she said.

"To see."

"To see what?"

"The direction your decisions are taking you." The woman raised her white head from the pillows with obvious effort. "You've seen what can be. Now you're seeing what will be if—"

"Did I go through with it?" Sarah gripped the railing again. "Did I have an abortion?"

"No. I did."

Sarah felt an odd stab of disappointment. This visionary old lady *was* just another Megan. And maybe a senile one.

"Not yet," the woman said. She reached her almost transparent white hand under the railing and managed to brush her knuckles against Sarah's belly before she sank back into the pillows. "Your baby's still alive inside you."

"I know that."

Sarah found herself shielding her abdomen with her own hands. This place, so suffocating with its heat a few moments ago, now sent its chill through her sweats and into her bones.

"I don't have long," the woman, this other Sarah, said. "And really, I have no reason to hang on. But you don't want to die alone, do you?" She pointed a knotty finger at the tree. "With only ancient memories to keep you company?" She didn't wait for Sarah to answer. "Trust me, it can be worse than that. You don't want to think every minute that you've done the wrong thing—until you just no longer want to live with it. I was never healed of that."

Sarah hugged her arms around her body. Okay, so this wasn't an old Megan-type. Megan said she rarely thought about her abortion and the child she didn't have except at this time of year. And she, the real Sarah, wasn't Megan: she wasn't even close to being like her any more.

Something pounded in her ears. It took her a minute to realize it was her own heartbeat, driving her to look again, closely, at the old woman with the faded brown eyes and the smile that no longer reached all the way to the laugh lines it had once created in her face. She seemed just as familiar as she had that day in the clinic when she'd pressed the card into Sarah's hands and promised her . . .

"The visions," Sarah said. "I had them, like you said. But how do I know they'll come true that way if I don't . . . if I keep the baby? They didn't tell me how I'm supposed to support her or even if Matt . . . How do I trust them?" She whipped her gaze frantically around the room. "Or this?"

Old Sarah shook her head. Her eyelids, thin as the pages of an old book, closed. "Sarah, you've been given the opportunity to see things from a . . . a divine perspective . . ."

The vision of herself nuzzling Baby Daisy's sweet neck returned in its sunlit frame.

"You have to trust that God will be there . . ."

The frame filled with the purple tassels of Daisy's hat as she leaned into Sarah and squealed into sparkle-filled air.

"And make your choice *regardless* of the consequences."

Sarah was once again in the beauty of midlife, glowing in gold light and beatific Nana-hood.

"Sarah."

Sarah refocused on the old face. Though her voice had faded with weariness, she was at once the new grandmother with her first streaks of silver, the confident woman full of Mommy energy, the young mother budding with a love that outreached first-baby fear. In the light Sarah had grown to love, the vaguely familiar became clear.

"You're me," Sarah said.

"Only if you make the choice I made." The gnarled hands clutched at the bed covers. "God will be there no matter what you choose . . ."

She struggled to sit up. Sarah reached over the bar and supported her back. The weak neck bent until her lips were close to Sarah's ear. "But you will be a far different you if you choose life."

She dissolved in Sarah's arms, but the vision-light stayed, even after Sarah found herself standing in the open doorway of her apartment with the card pressed between her palms. The moon must have beckoned her out there, weaving its silvery beams into the vision-light that still clung like an aura. The night was perfectly still. Not so much as the distant whistle of a train ruffled the quiet. Outside or in.

Sarah uncovered the card in her hands and searched the faces of the Magi. She didn't even blink at the fact that all three of them now looked at her. They had done what they'd come to do: bring her gifts. Now it was clearly up to her to do something with them.

A small wind nudged her, and Sarah backed into her apartment and closed the door. When she turned to head to the warmth of her bed, she caught a glimpse of herself in the mirror. What she saw caught her breath in her throat.

Just a few hours ago—as far as she could tell—that mirror had shown her a young woman bleak with fear and indecision. Now the face that looked back at her was still and pensive except for the biting of the lip, the vain attempt to hold back the tears that coursed down her cheeks anyway. She licked at them when they reached her mouth and she knew: she was every face she'd seen on the women clasping the strings of their balloons, waiting.

She didn't want to look that way anymore.

Matt took the day off Friday, but his mind wouldn't let him sleep in. He hit the gym at 6:00 a.m., pre-coffee, and was pounding the treadmill at six fifteen. Today was the day and he had to be physically ready for it, even if the rest of him was scared spitless.

He tried clearing the mental desk the way Uncle Clay suggested. Item one: go back to the pawnshop when it opened. He'd tried to pick one that wasn't in a seedy part of the city, one that didn't look like armed burglars went in there to sell hot plasma screens and DVD players. None of them actually seemed legit when he went the first time, not with black bars on the windows and guys behind the counters with so many tats you couldn't tell where they stopped and their clothes started. Matt hoped the original deal would still be on the table when he went back.

Item two: try not to go crazy between then and eleven. All hope of Sarah contacting him first had disintegrated at about 2:00 a.m. He could only hope that was because she was as scared as he was.

That was a lot of hoping. None of it was the kind of optimistic thinking that had gotten him into more pyramid schemes and surething sales opportunities than he even wanted to count, now that he'd cleaned out his actual desk and fed six new brochures into the shredder. Without the trumped-up conviction that *this* would be the big one, he was floundering.

Matt tried to focus on the guys on either side of him. One was dressed in shorts and a T-shirt that looked like they'd just come from the dry cleaner. The only thing missing was a matching necktie. He was zoned into CNN and barely breaking a sweat.

The guy to Matt's right, on the other hand, had perspiration marking the sides of his face like sideburns and forming a vest-shaped stain on his T-shirt. Propped on the book stand were some typed pages scattered with red markings. Matt got that sick rush he'd always experienced when the English teacher handed back the essays. The guy murmured a constant monologue ranging from disgusted to flabbergasted, and slowed periodically to add another red mark. The bag on the floor bulged with more of the same, judging from the ones that poked through the opening. No wonder the guy was sweating like a boar.

Given a choice between the two of them, Matt would have traded places with Sweat Vest Guy in a heartbeat.

But the fellow predawn athlete who caught Matt's attention and held it was an older guy who took the indoor track around the clump of treadmills at a pretty good walking pace for somebody sixty-five, seventy. But it wasn't that, or the fact that the dude smiled as if this wasn't an ungodly way to wake your body up, that made Matt stare every time he made another lap. He was sure he'd seen him someplace besides here.

The guy was on his fifth pass before Matt realized he'd seen him at the church, the Sunday he went with Sarah. Yeah, he was the pastor—Jones? Smith? Definitely Smith. The only religious person Sarah didn't sneer at. The guy who made Mary and Joseph's deal seem like it was happening to him.

Which a day later, it was.

Matt wasn't sure how he got from the treadmill to the track or how he wound up walking in stride with the Reverend Smith. It was apparently a normal occurrence for him. His smile pushed his cheeks closer to his eyes and he said, "The good thing about walking here is you don't have to watch the traffic. As involved as I get with my own thoughts, I'd have been run over by now."

"Am I interrupting?" Matt said.

"Not at all. I can talk to myself anytime." He glanced sideways at Matt. "We've met before."

"Yeah, but I don't expect you to remember me. We just shook hands when I was leaving church. I was there with my girlfriend—"

"Sarah."

"Right." Matt raised his eyebrows. "That's impressive."

"Not if you consider the fuss her mother made over you."

Matt had to grin. "Agnes is a trip."

"That she is."

They fell into a walking silence broken only by the squeak of their tennis shoes and the occasional groan from the guy doing crunches in the corner. The quiet didn't make Matt feel like he should say something—anything—but it did invite questions that eventually elbowed their way out.

"You've known Sarah a long time?"

"Since she was a little girl. I'm sure you can imagine what a doll she was. Curly hair. Nonstop motion." The reverend grinned too. "Big white front teeth. She always reminded me of a wise little bunny. But fearless. She didn't back down from anything."

Matt let the shoes squeak some more. There had to be a confidentiality thing for ministers like doctors and lawyers had. He couldn't think of anything else he could ask about Sarah that wouldn't be a violation of that. *Has Agnes told you what's going on with her right now?* was definitely out of the question. He had to give the old guy credit: if he knew, he sure didn't show it.

So . . . if he was that discreet . . .

"Y'know it's weird," Matt said. "But ever since that Sunday—what was it, a week and a half ago?"

"It was."

"Ever since then I've been thinking about what you said in your sermon."

"Wait, let me write this down: someone has thought about one of my sermons." The reverend slowed the pace a little, and an irreverent twinkle took over his eyes. "You're not going to tell me I mispronounced something, are you? I get a flood of e-mails when I preach on the pentecost gospel. Nobody can pronounce all those names of ancient places. I doubt even the people who lived in them could pronounce them." He picked up speed again. "I digress. Please—tell me what you were thinking."

Matt heard a laugh come out of his throat—not a sound he'd made in a while.

"You were talking about Mary and Joseph and the whole thing about nobody believing this vision thing was for real."

The reverend nodded. A light sheen now covered the bald top of his head.

"And you said 'nothing is impossible with God.' Do you really think that's true?"

"I do. I've seen it happen hundreds of times."

Matt let the squeaky silence resume for another half lap before he looked at the side of the reverend's now-rosy face and said, "Can I buy you a cup of coffee?"

"I was hoping you'd ask," he said. "They make it good and strong in the shop downstairs. Sounds like we might need it."

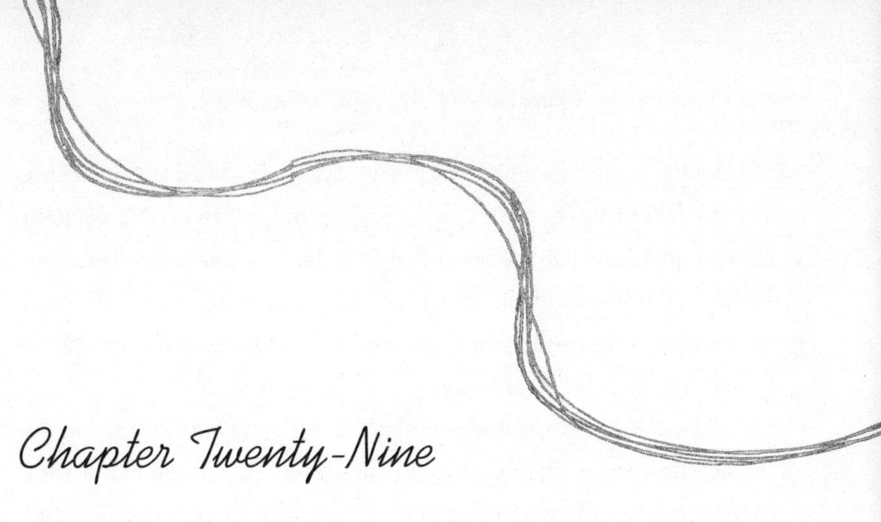

Chapter Twenty-Nine

Sarah's computer calendar wordlessly announced that today was Friday, December 23. Decision Day for Henry Carson.

She had made hers regardless of the consequences, and that was a thing she'd never done before. It had a surreal quality to it. Or maybe it was like Audrey said—it was the real Sarah who'd made it.

Maybe that was what allowed her to leave her cubicle without squaring her shoulders or putting on her game face. About halfway down the hall she turned back . . . and got her Dad-scarf. Megan would have a massive stroke if she saw it wrapped around her cranberry turtleneck, unraveled yarn poking out like hair on a Raggedy Ann. It would help her speak her decision out loud, and that was what she needed to hear herself do. And not just for Henry Carson.

Again she headed down the hall, now strangely empty of all the people who had taken vacation time to start their holidays, and took the elevator up to the executive floor, which housed a hospitality suite and Henry Carson's massive office. Sarah had never been there before.

She'd only listened in rapt attention as Megan described it. Something about a desk made from African mahogany and Italian marble, original artwork purchased at auctions where you had to show your American Express Platinum to get in, and a view of Lake Michigan that was hard to distinguish from the paintings. Megan had gotten a distant gleam in her eyes and said, "Someday, it will belong to *moi*."

Back then Sarah would have settled for the ConEx account. As the elevators doors opened almost soundlessly, as if not to disturb the inner sanctum, she wondered now at how simple Ambitious Sarah's future life had seemed.

She wasn't sure she even knew that person anymore.

The Sarah who emerged from the elevator tightened her scarf and approached Carson's secretary's desk. The woman looked harder up close than she had when Sarah had glimpsed her from afar at company picnics and the rare all-employee staff meetings. Her hair was pushed back severely, and her mouth was small and pursed, like a Barbie doll.

"Can I help you?" she said, as if she sincerely hoped Sarah had made a wrong turn somewhere and could be dispensed with quickly. Her eyes swept over the scarf.

"No," Sarah said. "I'm here to see Mr. Carson."

"You don't have an appointment."

"No, I don't."

"Do you want to make one?"

She obviously couldn't see for the life of her why Mr. Carson would want to talk to this woman who couldn't even pick out decent accessories.

"No," Sarah said. "I need two minutes, and I'm gone."

"Now?"

"Yes. Please."

If eye-rolling had been allowed in the How to be an Executive Secretary Manual, there would have been one. Evidently long-suffering sighs were okay. "You can't go in there now. He's in a meeting."

"I know. With Nick and Jennifer. About the ConEx account promotion. That's why I need to interrupt: I have information that'll make their decision easier."

Sarah turned to the door with the gold plate that read, **Henry Carson, President and CEO.**

"Are you Sarah Collins?"

"I am."

The woman rose from the chair, unfolding a figure that was fairly close to Barbie's too. "If you want this promotion, I strongly advise you not to open that door."

"Thanks," Sarah said, and gave the door in question a polite rap.

"You're going to blow it." The *blow* went up as if she were singing Sarah a warning song. There was a certain solidarity in it which Sarah would have warmed to . . . if she hadn't already blown it.

Her knock was answered with a rather irritated, "Come in," from Mr. Carson. Sarah heard nothing fatherly in it.

She pushed the door open and was momentarily blinded by the light from the window that comprised the entire wall behind Mr. Carson's desk. When her eyes adjusted, she knew Megan hadn't missed a detail. Except to say that the effect was so cold a person wondered why no icicles hung from the track lighting.

Jennifer's stunned face all but shouted, *WHAT are you doing here?* Nick snickered as if he'd expected her all along. Only Henry Carson's reaction surprised her: he looked like an indignant king who had just been walked in on in the royal bathroom. Again, there wasn't a hint of anything paternal in it, which made it easier for Sarah to say what was already rolling off her tongue.

"I'm sorry to interrupt, but there's something I need to tell you before you make your final decision."

"You've got dirt on Thad," Nick said. He all but licked his chops.

"No," Sarah said. "Even if I did, I would keep it to myself."

Jennifer moved her hand from her face long enough to nod at Sarah, and for the first time Sarah hesitated. Jennifer was right. She could bring some integrity to this place. To the snickering Nick who looked openly disappointed that she hadn't come bearing gossip. Even to Henry Carson himself, who had spent more money on one painting than it would cost to . . . support a baby through her first year.

So doing one right thing meant not being able to do another right thing. No, Ambitious Sarah, life is not simple.

"Then what is it, Ms. Collins?" Mr. Carson said.

Sarah lifted her chin. "I think it's only fair to tell you . . . I'm pregnant, and I've chosen to have my baby."

Not even a beat passed before Nick said, "I thought you weren't married."

"Shut up, Nick." Jennifer didn't take her eyes from Sarah, who saw in them the droop of disappointment: not in Sarah but for herself. Sarah made a mental note to apologize to her later.

Henry Carson, in the meantime, seemed to have found his father face. "You did the right thing coming forward with this. You could easily have waited another few months and dropped it on us when you were in the middle of the ConEx campaign. I appreciate your honesty."

Sarah waited for a stab of remorse. It was clear the job would have been hers. But she felt only the quivering of relief, the kind she felt right after she threw up.

Speaking of which—

"I won't keep you any longer," she said. "Thank you for seeing me."

Nick grunted. "Did we have a choice?"

Sarah pushed aside the vision of Nick and Thad at the helm of a sinking ship, waving their golf clubs at the wind, and went back through the still-open doorway.

"I guess Thad's our man, then," Nick said. "At least he won't get pregnant."

"Close the door," Carson ordered.

Before it clicked shut, Sarah heard Jennifer's voice. "Really, Nick? Really?"

Sarah tapped the secretary's desk. "Have a merry Christmas."

Barbie looked over the top of a pair of half-glasses. "Happy holidays. And don't say I didn't warn you."

"Those words will never cross my lips," Sarah said.

And then she literally ran for the elevator. By now she knew the location of every restroom in the building, and there was one right across from the doors when she got back to her floor. She barely made it in time.

Between that and the sheer exhaustion and the vision of Thad gloating up and down the hall when the announcement was made, Sarah decided to take the rest of the day off. There wasn't really anyone around to convince she was sick.

She was almost to the stairs leading to the parking garage when Megan caught up with her. Sarah had considered stopping by her office to tell her, but something drove her to get out of here, to get home. Megan didn't look happy about that or, come to think of it, about anything. Her face appeared to have been in a grimace for so long it had, as Sarah's mother had always warned, gotten stuck that way.

"You told them," Megan said.

"Wow. Word sure travels fast."

"No, I can just read you. You're having the baby."

Sarah nodded. "And I'm keeping her. You told me I had to make my own decision, and I've made it."

"How are you going to do this, Sarah? I just don't see—"

"I don't either," Sarah said. "I just have to do the right thing, regardless of the consequences."

"But the consequences are what make it the right thing . . . or the wrong thing."

"I don't see it that way, Megan." Sarah started to walk away, but she turned back and tried to smile. "I probably won't see you again before Christmas, so have a—"

"Don't say it."

Megan turned on a kitten heel and marched stiffly to her office. Sarah waited until the blinds closed before she went on to her car.

It was done, then. At least that part of it. The rest of it, the part still to come, crashed in on Sarah as she unlocked her apartment and walked into the chaos it had become. She was going to bring Daisy home to this, not the sunny house with the bay windows and the sledding hill. She would change her diapers on the desk, not her mother's dining room table.

She stared at the desk, still piled with the detritus of a life she hadn't paid attention to. She wasn't even going to have this place if she didn't pay Catfish the rent. He hadn't carried through on his threat to involve the landlord yet, but he'd have to soon.

Sarah dropped her bag on the floor and lifted a pile in search of her checkbook. No checkbook there. Just the picture of her and Dad in their choir robes. And Megan's list.

She could only see the bottom half of it, the part she seldom got to because she hadn't been able to check off all the ones before it. Number 10 popped out at her, as if its print were raised and in caps and bold:

> **THE THING YOU RESIST THE MOST IS THE THING YOU NEED TO DO.**

Sarah ran her finger over it. She could hear Megan saying those same words to her that day in her office when she was insisting that Sarah "have the procedure and get it over with."

But even as Megan's voice echoed in her head, Sarah searched for another voice that had used that word. She knew it before her back hit the wall and she slid down to the floor.

God loves you no matter how much you resist. In my opinion, you should be telling him *all of this.*

Above her on the desk, the framed photo lay on its side. Sarah tilted her head to look at it and felt her heart stop beating. Her father's face was turned from the little girl in the picture, straight toward her. His eyes, as bright as they had ever been in life, didn't say, *Sarah, go after your dreams because I never got to go after mine.* They said, *You were my dream.* And they said more than that. They said *I was healed, SJ. Because God forgives.*

Pain flooded over her. Pain that he wasn't there to say it. Pain that she had only a wretched studio apartment to bring her baby home to. Pain that she had ended up here, so alone she was no longer sure she was alive. There was no more holding it back. No more covering the pain with anger and the anger with a plan. There was only the tar-smothering pain, and with it the sobs, and with them the cry to the stained, cracked, sagging ceiling—

"God? Are you here?"

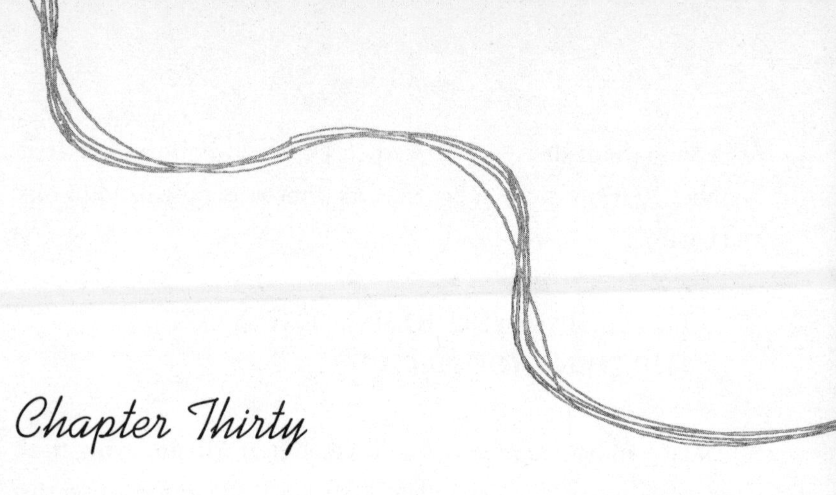

Chapter Thirty

Sarah pulled her knees to her chin and flattened her face against them. No golden frame of light turned her life into a flawless dream. She didn't find herself transformed into a person she could like. The floor was solid beneath her, the wall unyielding behind her, the Dad-smell of the scarf aching in her nose. This was her small, hard, everyday world.

But she clearly wasn't alone in it. And the nearness made her speak to it.

"Are you still listening?" she said. "After all the things I've said about you?" She pressed her forehead harder into her knees. "When I acted like you didn't exist? When I knew you did only because I hated you—"

Sarah gasped. And gasped. And gasped again.

"I'm sorry. I'm so sorry . . . but I just missed my dad—"

Sarah's voice choked out and she rolled to her side, still clinging to her shins. Tears clogged everything except the thoughts crying out in her head.

I had to blame someone. Someone I could shut out.

Sarah listened to her sobs, so like those of an inconsolable child. She wove her next words among them: "And I've been alone ever since."

Another grief-wave washed her breath away. In the stillness, her heart continued its cry. I'm sorry I hurt you, God. I just missed him so much. I *needed* him.

With the first breath she could find, she whispered, "I need him now. I've made the right choice, but I'm still so scared."

Sarah opened her eyes and stared into what was clearer than any Daisy-filled vision: she was terrified because she didn't know how to be a mother.

But her father couldn't have shown her that. Neither could her own mother. Because *she* wasn't Daisy's mother.

Sarah sat up and pulled the hands already grasping for each other against her chest. "I needed *you*," she said. "And you gave me everything. You gave me the visions. You gave me Audrey." A laugh worked its way through the sobs. "You gave me *me*."

She caved to the tears again, but they were soft ones now, wept easily from a deep place. She let them go until they slowed to a trickle. She stayed quiet until the trickle reached her lips. When she ran the back of her hand across her mouth she uttered an "Ugh." She literally had snot everywhere there could be snot.

The Kleenex was in the bathroom. She got unsteadily to her feet and started in that direction, and then stopped. Something faint seeped from her. Something like the first few drops of . . . a period?

Sarah palmed the walls the rest of the way to the bathroom and pulled down her underwear with hands already shaking. Two tiny red stains looked back at her. Small, but there enough to make Sarah cry out, "Daisy . . . no!"

Matt's cell phone read 10:55 when he walked out of the elevator on Sarah's floor at Carson, but he couldn't wait any longer. *I'm-afraid-of-what-she'll-say* had been replaced with *I-have-to-say-this-before-it's-too-late.* He gave the two cups of coffee with Reverend Smith the nod for that shift. More the reverend than the caffeine, actually. Matt had been right as a teenager: Joseph deserved a whole lot more credit than people gave him.

You can do the thing nobody would blame you for, were the pastor's words over their second cup. *Or you can do the best thing.*

Okay, so it was still hard not to cringe in advance at what Sarah might say to his offer of "the best thing." But Matt told that to wait outside as he stuck his head into her cubicle. It was empty, and her desk had that tidy look most people gave it when they left for the weekend. He himself wasn't one of those people, but he knew Sarah. She'd left with a purpose.

Reverend Smith had advised him to pray, and that kicked in before Matt knew he was doing it. *If she's gone to have the abortion—STOP HER!*

He rubbed at the back of his neck and groped for the Plan B he hadn't formulated. He had no idea which clinic she would go to, and even if he did, racing over there and dragging her from the waiting room was out. Okay—okay—um—okay . . .

Matt smacked the side of his head. *Okay* wasn't going to cut it. He scanned the tack board over her desk, but there was no Post-it note for an appointment. Like she would write *8:45 Abortion* and stick it up there, idiot.

He turned to the precisely stacked set of folders on her desk and flipped through them with fingers so clammy he left smudges on the pages. It was all work stuff. No file for a clinic or a doctor or a therapist. Come on, she had to be talking to somebody about this, right?

Actually, no. Matt tried to get the folders back in line and gave up. Sarah was trying to tough it out alone, like she always did. The thought of that brought panic up his throat.

Dude, you can't do that. Think.

All right . . . she wouldn't go have an operation by herself. Somebody had to go with her. Somebody who *would* go with her, which ruled out Agnes and probably Denise. That left only one person.

Constricta.

He would rather crawl into the viper tank at the Brookfield Zoo, but then what was the difference actually?

Matt swung through the doorway and took off down the hall. He'd never had a reason to know where Megan's den was, but Sarah had mentioned it was glass enclosed and sophisticated and all those things she said she wanted that Matt could never believe. He charged toward a bank of clear-walled offices with the intention of sticking his head into one of them and asking, but Megan herself emerged from the one at the end and stood in her doorway like a boa wrapped around a tree. Just the way he remembered her.

He was six feet away when she said, "Sarah isn't here," but he waited until he didn't have to shout before he answered. He was sure his next words were going to be, *Pull your fangs in. I just want to know—*

"Where is she? Do you know?"

The cold blue eyes narrowed in on him. What was he even thinking? The chances of her telling him were nil to none.

"It's not my day to watch her," she said.

Matt chomped down on the inside of his cheek. He wasn't a swearing kind of guy but he was ready to make an exception. But as he watched the eyes go into slits, he realized that was exactly what she wanted him to do: prove he was the loser she had him pegged for. The loser he couldn't go on being.

"Look, I just need to find her," he said. "Did you see her before she left?"

"Yes."

"Did you talk to her?"

"Yes."

"Did she say where she was going?"

Matt heard the desperation in his own voice, and he didn't care. He was just about to take her by her skinny shoulders and shake her when she said, "Oh, for Pete's sake, stop *whining.* She wasn't feeling well so she went home. Okay?"

Matt sucked in air. "Not feeling well as in . . . morning sickness?"

"You're a genius. Yes."

Megan's you-sorry-loser gaze left his face, so Matt was sure she didn't see the hope spring to it.

"Thank you," he said. "Thank you. So. Much."

The kiss he planted on her forehead surprised him probably more than it did her, but he would actually have hugged her if he'd had time. Sarah was still pregnant. There was still a chance. He might even send the Constricta flowers for delivering that news.

Matt's hope revved up even higher when he reached Sarah's apartment building and the Toyota was there. He took the steps two at a time, losing traction near the top where Catfish never did ice-removal. From there he skidded all the way to her door and pounded on it before he even came to a complete stop.

"Sarah! Sar, it's me. Open the door—please?"

"Hey—Sarah's Boyfriend."

Matt recognized Catfish's voice on the stairs, but he ignored it and used his key to unlock the door. Her absence was obvious the minute he stepped in. No Sarah-energy vibrated the air, and she didn't answer when he called her name again. But he still ducked his head into every space, because her scarf hung over the back of the chair. Sarah never went anywhere without that scarf. She was like Linus with his blanket. Fear grabbed at his gut again.

"Hey, while you're here, maybe *you* could write me a check for the rent."

Matt turned to the orange-capped Catfish lurking in the doorway. "Dude, this is not the time."

"Come on, man, you live here half the time anyway." Catfish shrugged his minimal shoulders. "At least you used to—"

"I said it's not the time! I need to find Sarah."

Matt said it more to himself than to Catfish, but the kid said, "They left about ten minutes ago."

Matt turned on him. "They?"

"Yeah. Her and a blonde chick driving a van."

A van . . .

"Did it sound like it needed a valve job?"

"Sounded like it needed something. I tried to mention the rent, but she was bawling—"

"Who was? Sarah?"

"Yeah. The other chick said they were going to the hospital and for me to back off. Which I did . . . even though I'll get canned as manager if the landlord has to evict her—"

"What hospital?"

"I don't know. They didn't stop to give me their full agenda, okay?"

Catfish squirmed and Matt realized he had the guy by the front of his army surplus jacket. He let go.

"Sorry . . . Here . . ."

He yanked his wallet from his pocket and emptied the cash contents.

"Pay what you can out of this," he said, cramming it into Catfish's hand. "I'll give you the rest later."

"Sweet."

"Did you see which way they turned when they pulled out of here?"

Catfish jabbed a thumb to the east. "That way. You can see the tire marks where that blonde chick burned rubber."

The rest was lost as Matt headed for the stairs. He was already calling Uncle Clay to find out the closest hospital east of there.

"Why would they keep an ER so blasted cold?" Denise pulled the blanket up to Sarah's chin. "You're shaking."

"It's not from the cold," Sarah said. "I'm scared."

Denise put her impossibly warm hand to Sarah's forehead. "Two tiny drops doesn't mean you're losing the baby. I had that with one of mine. I don't even remember which one: that's how meaningless it probably is."

Sarah wished she could believe her, but even the voice that could soothe small boys and panicking mothers and probably your average savage beast didn't stop the shaking she hadn't been able to control since she first saw she was bleeding. Only the words in her head kept her from flying off the table to pace: *Please, God . . . don't take my Daisy.*

The door opened and a tenor voice entered before its body did.

"Hi—you're Sarah Collins?"

Sarah nodded.

"I'm Dr. Painter."

The resonance seemed to vibrate from the doctor's high forehead, but nothing else about him registered except the bright blue eyes that scanned her chart like an intelligent bird.

"So you've had some first trimester bleeding."

Sarah nodded for the second time. She was afraid if she spoke or moved or breathed it would start again.

"It's not necessarily anything to worry about. The hormones are still settling in."

"That's what I told her," Denise said.

"And you are . . ."

"Her sister."

He gave Sarah a smile that revealed two slightly crossed front teeth. "You mind if your sister stays while we take a look and see what's going on?"

"Don't even think about leaving, Denise," Sarah said.

The crooked toothed smile broadened. "She's pretty clear on that. Let me get a nurse."

While he stuck his upper body out into the hall, Sarah grabbed for Denise's hand. "You know what's scaring me about this?"

"Everything?"

"If this had happened a week ago, I would have actually been relieved. Now that I've fallen in love with this baby, do you think God is punishing—"

"Okay, just stop. God does *not* work that way." Denise put her face close to Sarah's. "There are only about five things I know for absolute certain, and that's one of them, so don't even start there with me."

The rich voice preceded Dr. Painter through the doorway again. "All right then, Sarah, let's have you slide all the way to the end of the table."

Sarah grabbed onto Denise's hand and didn't let go of it as she followed the rest of his instructions. She was sure her sister's fingers must be turning purple.

The nurse, who Sarah had barely looked at, stood at the end of the table next to the doctor. She had freckles that folded as she smiled—as if this wasn't a matter of life and death.

The silence that fell then was louder than the sound of her heart banging in her ears. Why was it taking so long? Why didn't he say something—

"Good news so far. No active bleeding. No dilation. Let's have you sit up."

"So I'm not having a miscarriage?"

Denise pulled Sarah to a sitting position and adjusted the hospital gown that slid off of her shoulder.

"Not as far as I can tell." The doctor peeled off his gloves and glanced at the chart. "You're—what—almost nine weeks?"

"Yes."

"If you want we can do an early ultrasound just to make sure. You want to do that?"

For the first time Sarah focused on his face. His mouth was ripe for humor, and his long eyebrows said more than that mouth allowed.

"Let me think about it," Sarah said. "Yes."

"I like a woman who knows her mind." He turned to the freckled nurse. "Let's get her down to Imaging." He patted Sarah's leg. "It should just be a few minutes."

He and Freckles left, and Denise put her arms around Sarah.

"It sounds like it's going to be all right."

"He's going to look to see if my baby is still alive. That's what's happening, right?"

Denise let her go and tilted her head, swinging the ponytail she'd obviously pushed her hair into as she flew out her front door, probably calling out warnings over her shoulder to a hapless babysitter.

"Leave it to you to get it right down to the core. Let's think of it as he's going to validate what he's already seen: your baby is still in there making you want to lose your lunch." Her eyes danced. "You look a little green. You okay?"

"I'm trying to be."

"Who tries to be okay? Who does that?" Denise put up a finger. "Wait, we're talking about you."

"You know what I told you in the car, about what happened right before I saw I was bleeding."

Denise nodded.

"I was starting to feel like God was really there . . . and then this happened . . . but I still want to believe he's, you know, in this with me."

Denise's arms folded her in again. "Sarah, I promise you—"

"Please don't tell me God won't let her die because we prayed."

Slowly Denise pulled back, mouth shaping an a-ha moment. "*That's* when you turned away: when Mom said Dad wouldn't die . . . and he did." She rubbed Sarah's cheek with her thumb. "The only thing I can promise you is that if you cling to God through this, you'll get through it no matter what." Her eyes misted. "That's how I survived Dad's death."

Sarah covered the hand still on her cheek. "Denise, I'm sorry. I was so—"

"That's for another time." Denise stood up, ponytail swinging like a pendulum. "Listen, *a few minutes* in hospital time equals at least a half hour. I'm going to go grab a drink and call Mom. I need to make sure the boys haven't tied her up or something. You be okay alone?"

"I'm not alone, right?"

Another hug and Denise was gone. Sarah lay back on the table and closed her eyes. The self-assurance that she could handle everything, that there was a logical way to fix anything, that if she kept her emotions under control she would see her way clear—none of the things she would normally do at a time like this even showed up.

And she thanked God for that.

The door swished opened, and the anxiety pricked at her again. "You're going with me to the ultrasound, right?" she said.

"Just try going without me."

She bolted up, losing her gown down her shoulder again. Matt got to it before she could and inched it back into place. She was sure he could see her pulse throbbing in her neck. All *she* could see were his brown eyes, wide with the concern he was clearly trying to hide.

"How did you find me?" she said.

Matt fiddled with the ties on the back of the gown. "Your buddy Catfish. He gave you up like chocolate for Lent when I bribed him." He kissed her hair. "Denise filled me in. How you doing, Sar?"

Possible answers shuffled in her mind, a blur of everything from *I'm terrified out of my skull* to *Fine, now that you're here . . .* to *If you're doing this out of duty, you can forget about it.*

She couldn't choose any of them, and she didn't have a chance. The door opened yet again and Nurse Freckles pushed a wheelchair in.

"I can walk," Sarah said.

"Hospital policy." Freckles looked at Matt. "Are you staying here with her stuff?"

"Uh, no," Matt said. "I'm going with."

Sarah searched his face. "You don't have to do this, Matt."

"Yes, I do." His smile wobbled, but the brown eyes looked straight into hers. "I'm the daddy."

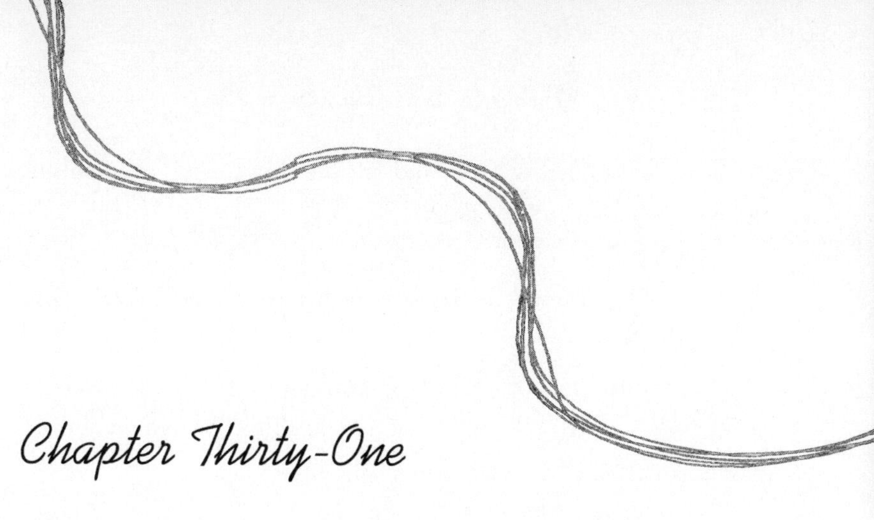

Chapter Thirty-One

Nothing on the screen looked like anything human to Matt, even though the technician was pointing out tiny features in a hushed, excited voice. Sort of like Jane Goodall describing the behaviors of baby gorillas from behind a bush. Matt squeezed Sarah's icy hand, as much to keep himself from saying, *So our child is an alien?* as to reassure her.

"Now if I can catch the little bugger being still for a second . . ."

There was more clicking and zooming, none of which made any sense to Matt. He focused on Sarah, whose eyes were riveted to the screen. One thing was clear. She wanted this baby.

As much as he did.

The technician made a sound like she'd been poked. "Gotcha, little one. And there it is, Mom and Dad."

"What am I looking at?" Matt said.

Sarah raised her head. "Is that her heartbeat?"

"Yep. Pumpin' strong."

Matt leaned across Sarah and felt his chin drop. "That pulsing thing there—that's a little heart?"

"Uh-huh."

Sarah's hand went all the way up his arm. "She's okay. Daisy, you're okay!"

The cry in her voice went straight through him. "She is, Sar. Look at that. She's a little athlete. What do you think? Marathon runner? Basketball player? No, wait: prima ballerina."

Sarah wrapped his sleeve in her fingers. "Can I finish gestating the child first?"

The technician looked up from her clicking. "You know, we won't be able to tell the gender until about eighteen weeks."

"She's a girl," Sarah said.

Matt kissed the back of her other hand. "How do you know, Sar?"

"I just know," she said.

She didn't let go of his sleeve. It was okay again. More than okay. It was, very possibly, the great stuff.

Matt told her to go straight to the bed and lie down while he made her some tea. Sarah, of course, didn't. Who could rest in the middle of an apartment that looked like it had been ransacked?

She made the bed, opened the blinds to the first of the stars, and gathered all the dirty clothes into the laundry basket. No wonder she could never find anything to wear. She was headed toward the kitchenette with it when she saw the piece of paper halfway under the door.

"That's not lying down," Matt called to her, sounding like he had his head in the refrigerator. "That's scampering, is what that is, which is the total opposite of lying down."

Sarah felt less dread than usual as she stooped to pick up Catfish's latest rent-due creation. Knowing she was going to be here for a while longer would make it easier to write the check. She didn't need to be pregnant *and* homeless.

"You know what you sound like?" Matt said, head still buried in some large household appliance. "You sound like a squirrel, building a nest."

Sarah unfolded the paper and stared at it.

"Not that I've ever watched a squirrel build a nest, come to think of it. I did have a hamster named Princess Leia once that made a nest out of newspapers in her cage."

NOVEMBER, PAID IN FULL

DECEMBER, BALANCE DUE . . . $150

JANUARY, DUE DECEMBER 31

"I was thirteen before it occurred to me to ask how Princess Leia had babies when there was no Han Solo."

Matt appeared in the kitchen doorway, cup and saucer in hand. Steam curled from it, hot as the butter that melted on the triangles of toast on the saucer.

"What's wrong?" he said.

"Nothing's wrong. It's just weird. Actually, I think it *is* wrong."

"You're making zero sense, Sar. Didn't I say you should be horizontal?"

"This says my rent for November's paid and most of December. Catfish is flakier than I thought."

Matt balanced the tea setup on one palm and took the receipt from her with the other. He glanced at it and stuck it in his pocket.

"Matt, I need that."

"It's taken care of. Sit, willya? This thing's burning a hole in my hand."

Sarah felt her eyes pop. "You paid my rent?"

"It was the only way I could get Catfish to tell me where you went yesterday." Matt nudged her toward the bed with his knee. "Okay, that's a lie, but it makes a better story, right?"

"But how did you—"

"Sit. Eat. Drink. Daisy's gotta be tugging on the umbilical cord by now. 'Mommy, send down some Daddy toast.' "

Sarah gave up and sank to the bed. Matt nestled the cup and saucer into her hands and sat next to her. His hands looked trembly, and he was suddenly very still.

She turned to the toast. "Wow, Matt. You didn't burn it."

"I've been practicing. I ate the ones that didn't work out."

Sarah froze with a warm triangle halfway to her mouth.

"You okay?"

She returned the toast to the saucer, but it sat cockeyed. When she tried to adjust it, she saw the reason. A diamond winked up at her from its tiny throne on a gold band.

It was suddenly impossible to swallow.

Matt picked up the ring and pressed it into her palm. "Don't say anything yet, okay? I've messed up a lot of things lately, and I don't want this to be another one, so just listen."

Sarah opened her mouth, but Matt put his finger to her lips. His eyes were deep—too deep for someone who was about to try to merely cheer her up—but this . . .

"Matt, please don't do this just because I'm having a baby."

"*We* are having a baby. That little tadpole we saw swimming around in there is *ours*." He pulled Sarah's hands together around the ring and held them under his chin. "I'll be responsible for her and take care of her whether you marry me or not, but she needs both of us . . . all the time."

"But that can't be the whole reason—"

"It's not. I need you. And I want a life with you." She watched his face struggle. "If things hadn't turned out the way they did, if she hadn't made it, I'd be doing this anyway."

Sarah didn't want to pull away, and she didn't. But the memory of endless, pointless conversations about his dreams and schemes stiffened her hands. Matt held them tighter.

"Sar, you've been trying to get me to grow up for way too long. Now I'm doing it—me. I mean financially, with solid plans for the future." He shook his head before Sarah could protest. "I said solid, Sar."

Sarah pulled her head back to look at him, full in the eyes. The shine in them wasn't the reflection of impossible riches and a short way to get them. It was the sheen of tears.

"Look, however I support us, what you need is for me to be the man I am. I'm not perfect. But I will do my very best to become the best that I can." His hands tightened. "I can't promise you I won't make mistakes. I can't promise you I won't be human. But what I can promise you is that I will never leave you."

It was hard to swallow again. Maybe that was how a person felt when she was about to let go of her last wisp of control.

"I'm going to say one more thing, and that's this," he said. "You're taking a chance on being a mother. Won't you take a chance on being my wife too?"

He let go of her hands, but Sarah grabbed one back and held it to her cheek.

"I didn't make my choice by myself," she said. "And you need to know this: I went to God."

Matt's mouth twitched into a smile. "Who'd a thought, Sar? So did I."

"You're not just saying that."

It was a statement, not a question. The sense of someone else there filled what spaces were left in the tiny studio. And it didn't feel crowded with four.

"Yes," Sarah said.

The grin raised the bar on all grins forever after. So did the kiss.

"Are you going to put this on my finger or what?" Sarah said finally.

Matt pulled it from the nest of her hand and slid it onto the fourth finger.

It fit.

From the chair where he'd sat all night, Matt watched Sarah wake up, hair all tousled, eyes blinking, face soft and mushy as a three-year-old's. She squinted at him as if she were looking through fog and smiled. Then she held up her left hand and gazed at it.

"So it really wasn't a dream," she said.

"If it was, I was in it with you. Especially the part where you kissed me. That was a really good part."

He leaned over to kiss her again, but she drew back.

"I don't want you to have a complete personality transplant. You can go ahead and say it."

"Say what?"

"That the price you paid for this ring was no dream."

Matt dropped next to her. "Actually, this one didn't cost as much as the first one I bought you."

"I'm sorry?"

"You want full disclosure?"

"Ya think?"

He waggled his head back and forth. "Okay, so I went out and bought you one with a big diamond. And then I realized that was probably not responsible, so I pawned it so I'd have money for whatever you needed. And then I bought it back and returned it for this one so I'd have both a ring and some cash for us—"

"And that's how you paid my rent."

"Yeah. When do I ever have that much cash on me? Freaky-weird, huh?"

"Nothing seems freaky-weird to me anymore." Sarah put her arms around him. "Thank you. I'll pay you back."

"What? No. It's *us* now. You got that?"

She wrinkled her nose at him. "Yeah, I got that."

Man, he loved this woman.

Matt stood up. "Okay, so you're gonna veg here today while I pamper you with French toast and—"

Sarah put her hand over her mouth and shook her head.

"I forgot. Do you need to go do that morning sickness thing?"

"Not yet." She moved her hand. "And as much as I would love to have you wait on me all day, I have a couple of things I need to do. It *is* Christmas Eve."

"Then I'll go with you."

She got to her feet and wrapped her arms around his neck. "I'll meet up with you at lunchtime and we'll go shopping, okay? But I need to do this part by myself."

Matt pulled her closer. "You sure? I'm here for you."

"You know what? I believe you." She licked her lips. "*Now* I need to . . ."

Matt let her go and cringed as the bathroom closed and the coughing started. How did she handle this? He'd be crying like a little girl.

Okay, so if she was headed out, he could finish the tidying job they'd started last night. He straightened the covers on her bed and pulled the chair back to the desk. That was the one thing they hadn't tackled: the piles. Matt grinned and opened the drawer. She was right, it *was* Christmas Eve. They could always deal with reality later.

And . . . where was that in the promises he made to her last night? I'll be the man you need *after* the holidays?

He took a seat in the chair and picked up the first stack.

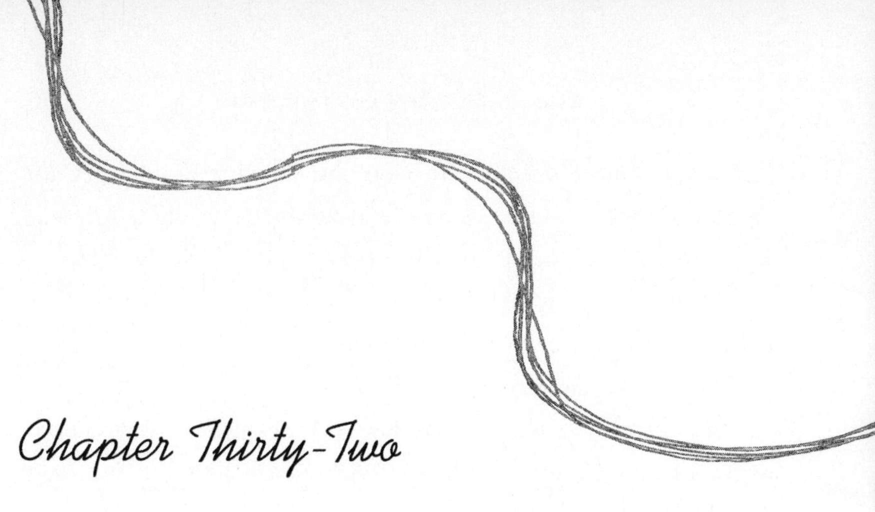

Chapter Thirty-Two

Her mother's house didn't have its Christmas Eve feel when Sarah slipped into the front hallway. The stair rail was wrapped in a fresh-greens garland, and a clump of mistletoe hung by a ribbon from the ceiling, but the joy was missing. The sadness that replaced it clung to her as if she'd walked through its cobweb on the way in. The only sound was a utensil clanking the sides of a bowl.

"Mom?" Sarah said.

The clanking stopped and metal clanged to the floor. Agnes appeared in the hallway, and even in the windowless light Sarah could see her eyes were red and swollen. Even her nose bore the raw signs of serious crying. Sarah couldn't see her mouth. It was covered with her hands.

"Hi," Sarah said. "Merry Christmas."

Agnes didn't move, and for a cold moment Sarah was afraid she was about to be ordered from the house. It was, after all, Denise she called when she was in trouble, not her mother. And she hadn't talked to her personally when she and Matt left the hospital. There were probably ten more reasons why Mom just stared at her through the crimson slits her eyes had become, and Sarah was searching for them when Agnes took a stumbling step forward and held out her arms.

The figure Sarah folded into hers felt frail, as if her bones might crumble the way her spirit obviously had.

"Mom, are you okay?" she said.

"Of course I'm okay. You're here." Agnes pulled away enough to hold Sarah's face in her hands. "And you're all right? No more bleeding?"

"Nope. Still pregnant."

Agnes put her hands on her own face and smiled through the next round of tears, the happy ones. Amazing how the same salt water could come out of the same tiny ducts and mean entirely different things. While her mother dug in her apron pocket for the tissue that was sure to be there, Sarah looked around the darkish hallway again. The last time the two of them had stood here together, Sarah had brought on a different kind of tears. That seemed like another lifetime. Actually, it was.

When Agnes had tucked the Kleenex back into her pocket, Sarah said, "Denise told you—"

"Yes. She said you didn't lose the baby. Nothing could make me happier."

"I don't know about that. I think this will."

Her mother's brow puckered.

"I came to tell you that I've come back to God."

For someone who had been so vocal about wanting to hear that news, Agnes's response was underwhelming. Sarah watched as every possible reaction passed through her mother's eyes and creases and nervous lips—everything from pure disbelief to childlike joy. She seemed to land on cautious hope.

"Does that mean . . . what does that mean, Sarah?" she said.

"It means I won't be making any more decisions without God." Sarah spread her hands across her belly. "Going to God is how I made this one."

Agnes clutched the stair rail and lowered herself to a step. Sarah crouched in front of her.

"Mom, what? What's going on?"

"Then you're keeping the baby?"

Sarah felt her eyes widen. "Yes, I'm keeping the baby. Denise didn't tell you?"

"No. She just said you had a scare and the baby was fine and you would tell me everything yourself." Her mother's voice was fragile, chipped at the edges like a china teacup. "Oh, Sarah . . . this is a good choice."

"I know." Sarah covered both her hands. "I can *see* you with her, Mom. I totally can."

"You're going to be a wonderful mother."

Sarah rocked back on her heels and watched Agnes give in to that childlike joy she hadn't dared to moments before. Something struck her, and she almost spoke it.

Would you still have loved me if I'd had the abortion?

It would have shattered the moment and everything in it. Because even before she shoved the question away, she knew the answer. Mother's love lasted through everything.

"Maybe I will be a wonderful mother, Mom," she said. "If I get a lot of help."

"You know you will! And most of that is going to come from God, you know that."

"I do."

Agnes kissed her cheek and stood up, shooing Sarah toward the kitchen.

"Now, I know there's a Bible study group for young mothers at the church," she said as she headed for the stove. "Denise can tell you about that."

The rest was covered by the rush of water going into the teakettle. Sarah felt herself stiffen. *Oh, Agnes, why do you always have to push?*

When her mother turned to set the kettle on the burner, Sarah put a hand on her arm. "Mom, the way you practice your faith and the way I'll practice mine are going to look a whole lot different. That's something we'll have to talk about if we want to still be speaking to each other a week from now."

"I won't pressure you—"

"Mom. Really? Let's just start with church tonight. Matt and I want to go with all of you. We have a lot of thanking God to do."

"Matt?"

"Didn't I mention that?"

Sarah pulled off her left glove way more slowly than she should have, but she couldn't help herself. When her mother saw the ring, her squeal deadened any trace of the sadness Sarah had had to push through to get in the door.

"Have you set a date? We have so many plans to make—"

"Mom. Let's do Christmas first, okay?"

"I know. This is just so exciting. All right, I'm making tea, so why don't you sit down and I'll cut you a piece of—"

"I can't, Mom. I have another stop to make, and then Matt and I are going Christmas shopping. It kind of sneaked up behind me this year."

"I can understand that. Now, don't worry about a gift for me. This is enough. This is *more* than enough."

Agnes was still delivering instructions when Sarah kissed her now very warm cheek and made her way to the front door. And then she stopped.

"There's one more thing I want to say to you, Mom."

Her mother looked immediately on guard.

"This is a good thing," Sarah said. "You know how you told me the night Dad died that God was healing him?"

"I don't know what that was about—"

"I do. And you heard right. Before Dad died, God did heal him." Sarah pressed her hand to her chest. "Right here."

Slowly, Agnes folded her hands under her chin.

"You get that, don't you?" Sarah said.

"Yes," Agnes said. "I do."

"And, Mom, that's why I believe. That's how I decided."

She left her mother to softly weep.

Sarah had been to Megan's apartment only once, but it wasn't hard to spot. Hers was the only one on the hall without so much as a sprig of holly on the door.

Just after she rang the bell, Sarah glanced at her watch. It was only 10:30. Megan wasn't going to be happy if she woke her up. Of course, Megan probably wasn't going to be happy anyway.

But the door opened and Megan stood there looking as if she hadn't been to bed at all. Not judging from the dark half-moons under her eyes.

"I guess I should have called first," Sarah said. "I'm sorry—"

Megan shrugged. "I probably wouldn't have picked up. Come on in."

This wasn't getting off to a good start.

"You're that mad at me?" Sarah said when the door clicked shut behind her.

"I'm not mad at you at all. I'm just in a foul mood and I didn't want to talk to anybody. But as long as you can handle that, sit down."

Megan gestured toward the sleek black leather couch that didn't look much different from her office furniture. Sarah didn't remember the place seeming this stark when she was here before. Of course, at that point she'd been imaging her*self* living in such digs. Again, in another lifetime.

Megan picked up a mug from the glass coffee table. "Do you want coffee?"

"No thanks."

"Still puking?"

"It's not so bad now. I think finally making a decision helped."

"Did you make the decision, or did Matt?"

Sarah realized Megan's blue eyes were riveted to her ring. Her disapproval was obvious.

"I decided to keep the baby. Then Matt proposed. And I said yes."

It was hard not to sound defensive with Megan shaking her head as if Sarah was wearing an outfit that was clearly all wrong.

"You're actually going to marry a guy whose idea of financial security is still having checks in his checkbook."

Sarah didn't answer. She and Matt had stayed up late the night before talking about what he really wanted to do with his life. It was the first time she'd ever seen him show any real passion for anything besides her, or heard a plan come out of his mouth that showed not only good sense but integrity. But she wasn't telling Megan any of that. She would start in on how becoming a mechanic and saving for his own shop sounded about as much like financial security as betting on the horses. When she heard that Matt wanted to use at-risk kids as apprentices, she'd probably spit coffee all over that glass-topped table.

"He's not perfect," Sarah said. "But we're good together, and we're going to work at it. I love him."

"Love. Now *that'll* pay the . . ." Megan put her hand up. "You know what, forget it. I'm not going to change your mind at this point, right?"

Sarah shook her head.

"Since you're marrying him, does this mean you're quitting work?"

"No. We'll need two salaries for a while."

"Until the baby's born."

"We haven't worked out all the timing. I'm not going to give up my career entirely—"

"They didn't announce who got the promotion yesterday. Jennifer said they're waiting until Tuesday."

She lifted her eyebrows at Sarah. When Sarah didn't say anything, she set her mug on the glass and got up, arms folded. As she turned her back, Sarah realized she really was still wearing the clothes she'd had on yesterday.

"I'll tell you what's happening here," Megan said, still turned away. "Seeing you so happy is just making me more aware of my own misery. And like I told you, this time of year is the worst, so you should probably just leave me to it."

Sarah leaned forward. "I didn't just come to tell you about my decision. And I sure didn't come to throw it in your face."

"Oh, I know that." Megan looked over her shoulder. "You're better than that. Always have been."

"I wanted to invite you to spend Christmas Eve with me and my family."

Megan turned to face her.

"And I'm not doing it because I feel sorry for you. I don't."

"You should. I'm pathetic." Megan sank into the chair across from Sarah's. "I just think I'd put a damper on the Christmas mood."

"Then just come to church with us. You don't have to be anything for anybody there."

"Church. Yeah, I haven't faced God since I was sixteen."

Sarah didn't see that one coming. Megan actually *had* faced God at one time? Although, how would she know that? They had never talked about anything besides work and clothes and how clothes would help you at work. Her pregnancy had taken them into deeper waters than Sarah even knew existed.

"So while we're on the subject of God . . ."

"Okay," Sarah said.

"I have a confession to make."

"Okay," Sarah said again.

"I lied to you when I said I told Jennifer you were pregnant because I was afraid they'd fire me. They wouldn't fire me for that."

Sarah nodded.

"And she didn't come to me. I went to her and I told her because I knew she'd tell you to have the abortion if you wanted the promotion, and then if you did it, it would be on her, not me."

"It would have been on *me*—no one else."

Megan's eyes turned to the skylight. "See, that wasn't my experience. I didn't have a choice. And now, seeing you make your own decision just makes me even more bitter."

Sarah wasn't seeing bitter in the eyes that fought so hard against tears. She was seeing grief.

"I haven't stopped thinking about it ever since we found out you were pregnant," Megan said. "We would have been all right, my kid and me. I know myself. I wouldn't have let anything stop me from having a career *and* raising him. I was too young, but Jeremy's parents would have helped us. They were great."

So the father had a name and a family. And Megan had regrets she was even now clinging to with the fists knotted in her lap.

"You can still make good decisions about that," Sarah said.

Megan gave her a look that should have frozen her from the room. It didn't.

"There's at least one you can make. If you decide you want to, call me." Sarah stood up. "The invitation for tonight still stands."

Megan nodded without looking at her.

"But if you decide to stay here . . . you might want to order a pizza."

When she closed the door behind her, Sarah could hear Megan crying against it.

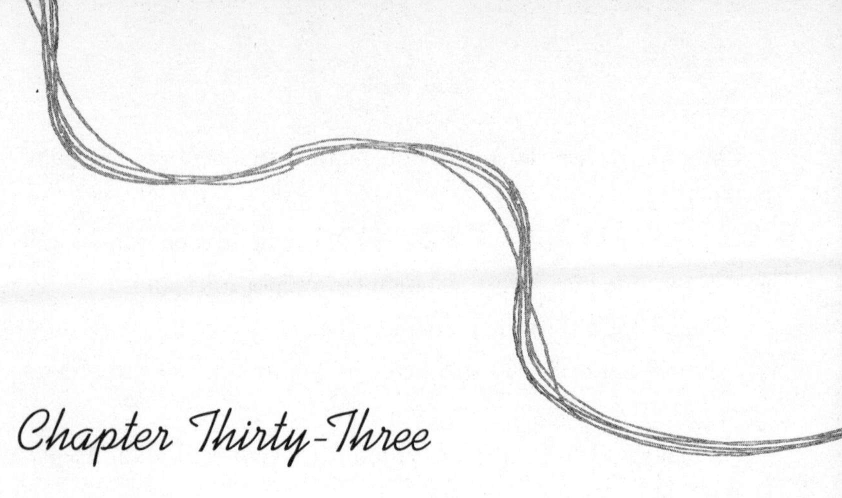

Chapter Thirty-Three

It was squeezing room only at the church that night, and even that was debatable at times. Sarah was wedged so tightly between Matt and her mother, she was practically breathless.

Although maybe it was due to more than lack of space. When she made eye contact with Reverend Al during "O, Come, All Ye Faithful," his face became a wreath of smile-lines. He tapped the corner of his eye and pointed to her. She nodded. *Yes, it's back. The joy is back.*

Sean and Tim were both angels in the reenactment of the Nativity, roles Justin whispered were cast against type. Tim mostly stood with his finger in his nose, but Sean flapped the oversized wings Denise said she'd spent most of the night gluing cotton balls to and jumped from the chancel steps with his arms spread out. When the Sunday school teacher finally whispered what was obviously, "Enough," in his ear, he said, loud enough for the Presbyterians across the street to hear: "I'm flying. Angels are supposed to fly."

Matt stuck most of his fist in his mouth, but his laughter practically snorted out of his ears. Sarah looped her arm through his and let it bubble through her too. Agnes smiled as if her grandsons weren't stealing the entire show from Mary and Joseph. Her father would have been yukking it up right along with Matt.

Maybe he was. She was definitely feeling his presence, so palpably that she whispered, "I went to God, Daddy."

When the bath-robed shepherds had finally returned to their fields and the angels were relieved of their wings (with audible protests voiced by Sean all the way back to the choir room), Reverend Al came halfway down the aisle to make announcements. Sarah couldn't resist exchanging eye rolls with Denise as he delivered the spiel he'd done as far back as they could remember—the whole thing about welcoming the Christmas and Easter people and letting them know that the church was open the rest of the year too. Fortunately she'd focused back on him before he said: "And congratulations are in order for one of our members." Dramatic beaming pause. "Our Sarah Collins is going to be married. Blessings on you and Matt, Sarah."

Sarah felt her smile spread beyond the sides of her face, but it was Matt the reverend was grinning at. The way you grin at an old fraternity buddy. Sarah looked up at Matt in time to see him give Reverend Al a thumbs-up, which the reverend returned.

"What was that about?" Sarah whispered as "Joy to the World" rose from the trumpets.

Matt kissed the top of her head. "Reverend Smith and I go way back."

"How far back?"

"To yesterday."

Sarah stared at him, but Matt just grinned. Yeah, nobody grinned like him.

Christmas morning was, of course, chaotic. Sean was still playing the role of super-angel, jumping off the arm of the chair, the back of the couch, and the banister in the front hallway. Justin put a stop to it when he climbed onto the dining room table.

"See what you have to look forward to?" he said as he carried Sean upside down past Sarah and Matt.

"Can't wait," Matt said.

"Not gonna happen," Sarah whispered to him. "Daisy will never behave like that."

"Bummer," Matt said.

It was the first happy Christmas Sarah had spent since her father died, but she was ready for the quiet of the apartment when she and Matt begged off and returned there in the late afternoon. Her mother only let them go when Matt told her Sarah and the baby needed a nap.

"*You* needed a nap," Sarah said when he flopped down on the bed.

"Y'know, come to think of it, I haven't slept for two straight nights. Okay, maybe three."

He treated her to a cavernous yawn, complete with the roar of an about-to-hibernate bear. But Sarah was somber as she curled up beside him.

"I'm sorry, Matt," she said.

"For what, Sar?"

"For shutting you out when I was trying to decide what to do. I think it bordered on cruel. Didn't it?"

"Nah. It's cool, Sar. Baby needs a nap . . ."

His breathing evened out, and Sarah came up on one elbow. He was already snoozing.

She kissed his nose and got up.

Now that he was out, there was something she needed to do, that she could only do when nobody was around to tell her she was nuts.

And maybe she was, because the wise men card was missing. At least so far. She hadn't seen it since late Thursday night. In an apartment the size of Jennifer Nolte's walk-in closet, how hard could it be to locate?

She tried the desk. Matt had tidied that up Christmas Eve morning, but she knew he wouldn't throw anything of hers away. Matter of fact, any Christmas cards he'd found in the mail pile he'd tacked around the doorframe to the kitchenette. Adorable—but no wise men looking straight into her eyes as if to say, "You're getting this, right?"

Sarah scoped out the closet, under the bed, and behind the refrigerator. She even looked in the oven. After combing through the trash can, she gave up and sat on the floor, leaning against the bed where Matt was snoring like a peaceful puppy.

She could hear Audrey telling her to ask the right questions.

So had the card just disappeared—like the old lady who gave it to her?

Or had it been a figment of her confused imagination all along?

Sarah shook her head at no one. If she'd imagined the card, she'd imagined the visions. Did that really matter, as long as she'd come to where she now was? Still scared but finally real.

As real as the hunger pang that surprised its way into her stomach. Some hot chocolate would go good right now. Or some Audrey soup.

Huh. Imagine that. Something edible actually sounded good.

As she headed for the kitchen, Sarah heard her phone buzz in her bag. Who was texting her on Christmas afternoon?

Megan, actually.

Call me tomorrow?

"No, I will not call you tomorrow," Sarah said to the phone. "I'm calling you right now."

The day after Christmas dawned cold and so bright Sarah had to put on her sunglasses when she went down to the parking lot to meet Megan. Even the Chicago smog seemed to be celebrating the season by going into hiding so the blue of the city's skies could shine, just this once. It was like the day she and Daisy went sledding.

Sarah shrugged that off as she climbed into Megan's BMW. No more questions about the visions. It just didn't matter. "It's a perfect day for this," she said to Megan.

"Yeah," Megan said. "Why am I so nervous?"

"Because this is a big deal, maybe?"

"I got the stuff you told me to get. I didn't write the note yet, though. I'm not sure what to say."

"It'll come to you," Sarah said.

They rode in silence for a while. The streets were all but deserted this early, and most offices were closed until tomorrow. A slight breeze swayed the wreaths attached to the streetlight poles. Sarah realized she hadn't noticed any of the holiday decorations until now.

"I got the sausage and pepperoni," Megan said.

"Yeah? How was it?"

"Not bad. I think the guy that took my order was a little weirded out when I asked for a specific delivery person." Megan shrugged. "But then I guess he figured it was Christmas and I was probably drunk."

"How *was* the delivery?"

"Surreal."

"Was he embarrassed? You in that apartment and him—"

"Not at all." Megan started the BMW up the hill and let the corners of her mouth curve ever so slightly. "Delivering pizzas is a side job."

"Yeah?"

"He's working his way through law school."

Sarah threw her head back. "I. Love. That."

"Don't get excited. Like I said, it was surreal."

"Or maybe it was the real you," Sarah said.

Megan pulled the car to a stop and stared through the windshield. "We'll see."

Sarah didn't press her. Megan's face was suddenly pensive. It was time to focus.

Sarah pulled the balloon out of the garbage bag in the back of Megan's car. It was yellow, and it bobbed in her hand like a child bouncing in the backseat with the playground in sight.

"I got yellow because that works for a girl or a boy," Megan said. "Can you believe it took me twenty minutes to decide?"

She pulled a note card out of her coat pocket. Even in gloves Sarah could see that her hands were shaking.

"Then I spent another thirty picking out the notepaper. This from the woman who makes hundred-thousand-dollar decisions every day."

"I get that," Sarah said.

Megan leaned against the trunk, card in one hand, a pen in the other. A green gel pen.

"What do I write?"

"Whatever you want him to know."

Megan squinted. "Him?"

"You always talk about him like he's a boy."

"Then I should've gotten the blue."

"So tell him that."

Megan chewed at her lip. That was only the second nervous thing Sarah had ever seen her do.

"He's your son," Sarah said. "You'll know what to say."

Then she left Megan perched on the tailgate and wandered a few feet off. When she looked back, Megan was writing.

Whenever we make a bad decision, it's always good to know we're forgiven, the open-faced woman in the houndstooth-check coat had told her. Sarah looked up at the balloon, still bobbing to get loose. That really was all it took. Just letting go.

"I think I'm ready."

Megan stood just a few feet away. Her face was pale. And pretty.

Together they tied the note to the string of the balloon. Sarah folded Megan's fingers around it and stepped away again. She watched as Megan climbed to the top of the hill and stretched her arm up and held it there. And then she opened her hand, and the balloon and its message broke free and let the breeze carry them.

Up to heaven, the woman had said. Seeing Megan watch it go, her blonde hair hanging wistfully behind her, Sarah was inclined to think she was right.

When the balloon had shrunk to no more than a yellow dot in the sky, Megan turned to Sarah, and Sarah ran to her. Megan was sobbing so hard when Sarah reached her she couldn't quite stand up. Sarah held her and let her weep. She knew the sound well.

And she knew it would go on until the grief gave way to freedom, so she just waited and looked over the top of Megan's head. As she gazed someone crested the hill, someone a little stiff, and maybe a little old to be out for a hike in the cold.

As the figure strode closer, Sarah held her breath. The woman's gait was strong and as she drew even nearer, Sarah could see a peace in the lines of her face that was never there before, not as long as she'd known her. She held something loosely in her surprisingly sturdy fingers. Something white that fluttered up like Megan's balloon when she let it go.

And then before she turned to hike back over the crest of the hill, she gave Sarah a smile exactly like her own. Because it mattered.

"We made a good choice," Sarah whispered to her. "We chose God."

Reflection Questions and Resources for Sarah's Choice

Although we want girls and women who are in Sarah's situation to find hope in her story, we don't think you have to have been there personally to relate to her and find a way to make whatever choice *you're* faced with. As you consider our suggestions for pondering, just apply them to your own decisions and see what happens. As always, we've got your back in prayer.

Blessings,
Rebecca and Nancy

Questions to ponder:

1. Just to get focused on you, what about Sarah and/or her story made you go, "Oh, I hear *that*!"
2. Sarah got herself into the situation she was in, no doubt, but do you feel any compassion and empathy for her? Why is that?
3. For reasons not entirely of her doing, Sarah's priorities are sort of confused. What do you see when you look at your own priorities right now?

4. Sarah's unresolved grief over the death of her father continued to impact her decisions. Do you have any unprocessed pain in your life? Is that affecting you and your choice-making?
5. Both Megan and Audrey mentored Sarah, but obviously in entirely different ways. Was there any merit to Megan's advice or help? Did Audrey actually ever GIVE her any advice? Do you have a mentor? Is she the right one? Do you need one—and what qualities will you look for?
6. Ah, Sarah and Matt. Did you think they were going to make it as the story progressed? They definitely had some foundational issues. If you're in a relationship, can you learn anything from theirs?
7. Now, about those visions. Were they plausible for you? Do you think God actually speaks to us that way? Or did you see them as metaphorical somehow? Do you long for that kind of certainty?
8. What about Sarah's taking on so much financial responsibility for her mother? She did it largely out of guilt . . . do you think that was admirable? Can you take a look at the responsibilities you've assumed? Are they actually yours?
9. Sarah's relationship with God will be different from her mother's. How so? What path do you think Sarah will take in further deepening that? What about you?
10. Both Sarah and Megan found healing and forgiveness in God's love for them. In your current situation, are you aware that that's true? How can you embrace that?
11. Do you know someone in a situation like Sarah's? Could you be an "Audrey" to her? After all, Audrey just asked the right questions . . .

If you have questions for *us*, feel free to contact Nancy at nnrue@att.net. Blessings on all your choices.

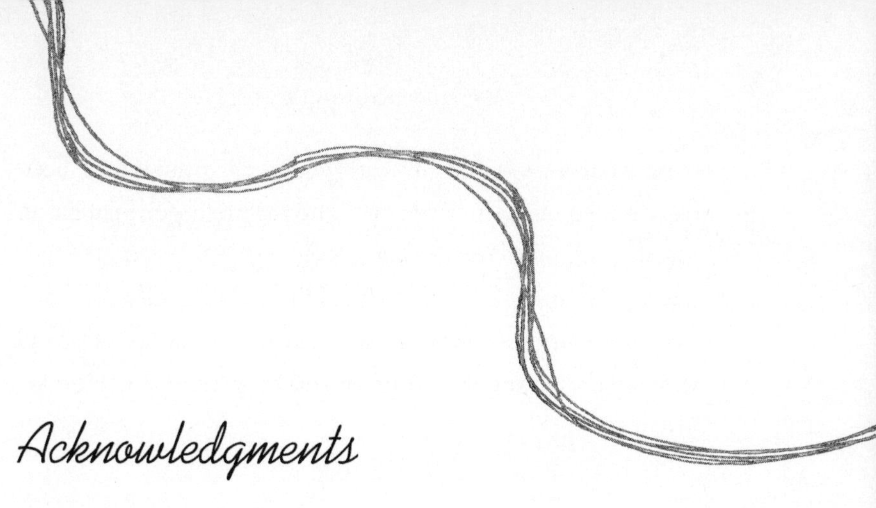

Acknowledgments

Even though two of us created Sarah's story, we weren't the only ones involved in bringing it to life. If you're one of those readers who likes to know that kind of thing, here's our list:

Rebecca would like to thank:

- **Nancy Rue**, for being such a treasured partner in this work and for consistently being such a joy!
- **Chad Capper, David White, Sean Paul Murphy, Tim Ratajczak**, and the Pureflix team for an incredible experience on the set of *Sarah's Choice*. Thank you for believing in this story and making it come to life on the big screen!
- **Andrea Heinecke** for being my friend, cooking club buddy . . . and amazing agent.
- My dad, **David Smallbone**, for being a wonderful father and for championing this project as both novel and movie.
- **Amanda Bostic** and our Thomas Nelson team for your incredible support of Nancy and me.
- **My husband**, my sweet love, my treasured best friend . . . My

Cub, what a joy to do life with you! And to now have been blessed with our own "little one" and the privilege of parenting together . . . bliss. You are my forever love!

- **Jesus** . . . thank you for the gifts of life and love. Use this book to honor yourself, to protect the unborn and their mothers, and to show the power of your grace and forgiveness . . . How we love you!

Nancy would like to thank:

- **Marijean Rue**, who shared her emergency room miscarriage scare with me. As in, I was there.
- **Amanda Bostic**, who, in addition to being our editor and my awesome brainstorming partner, told us more than we really wanted to know about pregnancy tests.
- **Jamie Chavez**, our copy editor, who as always found things which escaped us entirely. Wonderful eyes, that lady.
- **Lee Hough**, my literary agent, who brought this opportunity to work with Rebecca to my door, and to my new agent **Joel Kneedler** who has seen it through so beautifully since Lee passed away.
- **Paula Hough**, who demonstrated for me how God heals, truly heals.
- **William Naylor**, my beloved father, who years after his death still showed me Sarah's father's wisdom in how to live and how to die.
- And of course to my kindred spirit **Rebecca St. James**, whose love for God and young women was the mustard seed for our work together, and whose commitment to it is nothing short of awesome.

AN EXCERPT FROM

The Merciful Scar

REBECCA ST. JAMES AND NANCY RUE

Part ONE

He . . . went a day's journey into the wilderness, and came and sat down under a solitary broom tree. He asked that he might die.

1 Kings 19:4

Chapter ONE

It was the only real fight Wes and I had ever had. Actually it was the only fight I'd ever had with anyone. That's probably why I wasn't very good at it.

Now *discussions* . . . we'd had those, and that's how it started out that night. Another conversation about Wes moving in with me.

I should have known that was where we were headed when he tugged at the back of my shirt and pulled me against his lean self and said, "You know what I love about your couch?"

"That you never have to get off of it from the minute you walk in the door?" I said.

He let his blue eyes droop at the corners until they teased at his cheekbones. That was Wes pretending to be hurt. "Are you saying I'm a couch potato?"

"I'm saying I wait on you like you're the couch prince." I leaned forward and picked up the all-but-licked-clean plate from my IKEA coffee table. "More quesadillas, your highness?"

Wes scooped me into him, plate and all. "It wouldn't be that way if I wasn't a guest, Kirsty."

Yeah, there it was. Again.

"First of all," I said, "you know I hate it when you call me that. It makes me feel like I'm on a Jenny Craig commercial."

"Huh?"

"Kirstie Alley. She was their poster girl before Valerie Bertinelli—"

"You're getting off topic."

"What topic?"

Wes scooted himself sideways so he could face me without letting go. He knew as well as I did that I was about to wriggle away and go do . . . something. Anything to not have this discussion for the ninety-sixth time.

"Come on, babe, you know what I'm talking about. It doesn't make any sense for me to get an apartment for the summer when you've got room here."

"I have one bedroom." Which, may I just add, was incredibly difficult to say with his long-fingered hands holding my face and his nose headed for mine for that irresistible pre-kiss thing he did. "And I need my other room for my studio—"

"I know."

"And you also know where I am on this."

"I do. You've been there for three years, six months, two weeks, four days, and . . ." He glanced at his watch. "Twenty-seven minutes."

He let his lips bounce off my nose and onto my mouth but I talked right through the kiss.

"It's going to be another however long," I said, "so get over it."

This was the part where he was supposed to say, *You're killin' me, Kirsten. Killin' me.* And then I would let him kiss me one time and then I'd get up and make another batch of quesadillas. That was how this déjà vu conversation was supposed to go.

But Wes stiffened all six foot two of himself and took me by both shoulders and set me away from him like he was stacking a folding chair. I watched him step over the coffee table and shove his hands into the pockets of his cargo shorts and pace to the back window where he stopped, rod-necked and tight-lipped, his blondness standing stiff on his head. It wasn't a pose I'd ever seen him take. That's when my skin started to burn.

"What does 'however long' mean, Kirsten?" he said.

Until we're married. That was the answer, stuck in my throat where it had been for three years, six months, two weeks, four days, and twenty-seven minutes. I just closed my eyes and crossed my arms so I could rub both shoulders. The burning kept on.

Wes faced me now, muscles working in his square jaw. "Do you know how hard it is to love you and not be able to . . . love you?"

I attempted a wry look. "Uh, yeah, I do."

"Then what the—" He crossed to the coffee table and sat on it. "Look, I think I've been way more patient than any other guy would be."

"Good thing I don't want any other guy," I said.

"Stop it, okay? Just stop it."

"Stop wh—"

"The cute remarks and the little dance you always do. I want to talk about this. Now."

I pressed myself into the couch. "We've talked about it a thousand times, Wes. We've worn it out."

"So you just want to keep on dating forever?"

I swallowed, hard. "Way back when we first started dating, we both agreed that neither one of us wanted to have sex outside of marriage."

Wes let his mouth soften and took both my hands. "How old were we then, babe? Eighteen? Nineteen? I think we were pretty naïve."

We'd never gotten this far into the discussion. If we had, I might have come up with a retort to get us out of it. Something along the lines of *No, naïve is when you think you can lose ten pounds before Christmas.* But here we were, and my determination that I wasn't going to be the first one to say it seethed under my skin.

"I thought we were being true to the faith that, if you'll recall, *you* introduced me to," I said.

"I'm not buying it," Wes said. "We haven't been to Faith House since you started grad school. What's that, nine months? When was the last time we went to church, either one of us?"

"That doesn't mean I don't still believe—"

"Nuh-uh." Wes let go of my hands and waved his palm like he was erasing my words. "That's not what this is about. You want me to marry you, don't you?"

My throat closed in on itself. At least once a day during those three years and twenty-seven minutes or whatever it was, I had imagined Wes broaching the subject of marriage. The images went from Wes on one knee amid glimmering candlelight to a proposal tucked into a Big Mac. But none of them had included an accusation in those blue eyes or all my anxiety mobilizing under my flesh.

"That's it, isn't it?" he said. "Why didn't you just come out and say it?"

"Because I wanted you to say it first!"

The words sliced their way out of me before I could stop them, and they seemed to want to keep on slicing all on their own.

"I don't want us to be like everybody else—just having sex and living together and then someday deciding we might as well get married. Look at Caleb and Tess. They're like a pair of reclining chairs. I'm not doing that, Wes. I'm not."

He was staring at me as if I was a stranger suddenly intruding on the conversation that had long since stopped *being* a conversation.

"Y'know," he said, "I've been practically begging you for, like, forever to open up with me and tell me what's on your mind."

"I wanted it to be on yours." My words had lost their edge. Others spun in my head. *Clever, Kirsten, very clever. You picked a fine time to, I don't know,* grow a backbone.

Wes sagged onto the couch beside me. "Look, babe, I'm not in a good place for this. I didn't graduate—I have to make up the class this summer—I don't know what I'm gonna do after that."

"I know all that—"

"But you—you're set. You always are. That's why you're my rock. I just need you to be here for me just a little while longer. Can you do that?"

What does that even mean*?* I wanted to scream. But I'd done all the slicing I could do for one night. It was more slicing than I'd done my whole life. At least, that kind.

"Okay, look, I'm gonna go," Wes said.

"Now?"

Nice touch. Pathetic is always good.

"Now." Wes gave me half of his usual who-loves-ya-baby smile. "Before I get you drunk and take advantage of you."

My reply was automatic. "Like either one of *those* things is gonna happen."

Again, that was his cue to say, *You're killin' me, babe.* But what he said was, "Yeah." Just yeah.

He pulled me up from the couch and walked ahead of me to the door. Hand on the knob, he turned only slightly toward me. "A bunch of people from my class are hiking the M tomorrow."

I groaned silently. Hiking the M was a Montana State graduation tradition that entailed making one's way up a steep trail and a long ridgeline in the brutal Montana sun to get to a huge M made from white rocks, and then partying and turning around and coming back in the now even more brutal Montana sun to party some more. I'd skipped that when I graduated the year before; I would actually rather poke a fork in my eye than have that kind of fun. Since Wes had missed graduating by one class, he hadn't gotten to have that kind of fun either.

"I'm sorry," I said.

"No, they want me to go with. What's three credits? To them I'm there. I just didn't have to sit through a bunch of speeches in a bathrobe with a board on my head."

"I don't even know what to do with that," I said. "So what time?"

"We're leaving Caleb and Tess's at seven." Wes lifted a sandy eyebrow. "If I can get them out of their reclining chairs."

Ouch. Bet that gotcha right in the heart.

"You want me to pack a picnic?" I said.

Wes's gaze shifted away and he ran a hand over his flattened blond spikes.

"Or we can grab something at the store in the morning," I said.

"Here's the deal . . . I think I just need to go single. Most of these people I'll never see again, which is weirder for me because I'm staying here. I don't know, it's just a thing."

Right in the heart fell far short. I was stung to the bone. I didn't want to go. I just wanted him to want me to go.

Beyond pathetic. We've moved into pitiful. I mean, way *in.*

"Okay, so . . . okay," I said.

"I knew you'd get it." Wes kissed my neck. "You always do."

The Nudnik voice didn't wait until Wes was out the door before she started in. I always thought of it as the Nudnik, which was what my kindergarten teacher used to call us kids when we pestered her to the brink. *Nicely done,* the Nudnik said now. *Ya made everything all right when it* clearly *isn't. Another layer of unadulterated bad stuff, right under your skin.*

Forget it. I'm not doing it. I haven't done it for—I don't know—a long time.

Not since Valentine's Day when yet again our sweet Wesley didn't come through with a ring. Or was it Easter? Yeah, you did it on Easter. But then, who's keeping track?

You are! I wanted to say out loud. But I always stopped short of audibly answering the Nudnik. If I did that, I really would have to admit I was crazy.

But she was right. I'd been holding back for six weeks, since the beginning of April. I promised myself that was the last time, because I was so sure Wes would propose when he graduated. And then he didn't. He'd spent last Saturday hiding out here playing Scrabble with me instead of walking with his class to receive his diploma. It wasn't a good time for a proposal. Clearly there never was a good time.

The story continues in *The Merciful Scar* by
Rebecca St. James and Nancy Rue

About the Authors

Author photo by Allister Ann

Rebecca St. James is both a Grammy and multiple Dove Award recipient as well as a best-selling author whose books include *Wait for Me* and *What Is He Thinking??* Her leading role in the pro-life film *Sarah's Choice* won critical acclaim. A passionate spokesperson for Compassion International, Rebecca has provided sponsorship to more than 30,000 children through her worldwide concerts.

Author photo by Hatcher and Fell Photography

Nancy Rue is the best-selling author of more than 100 books for teens, tweens, and adults, two of which have won Christy Awards. Nancy is also a popular speaker and radio guest due to her expertise in tween and teen issues. She and her husband, Jim, have raised a daughter of their own and now share their Tennessee lake home with two yellow labs.